The Self-Conscious Novel

Artifice in Fiction from Joyce to Pynchon

The Self-Conscious Novel

Artifice in Fiction from Joyce to Pynchon

BRIAN STONEHILL

upp

University of Pennsylvania Press / PHILADELPHIA

PENN STUDIES IN CONTEMPORARY AMERICAN FICTION

A Series Edited by Emory Elliott, Princeton University

Alan Wilde, *Middle Grounds*

Brian Stonehill, *The Self-Conscious Novel: Artifice in Fiction from Joyce to Pynchon*

Library of Congress Cataloging-in-Publication Data

Stonehill, Brian.
  The self-conscious novel : artifice in fiction from Joyce to
Pynchon / Brian Stonehill.
    p. cm.—(Penn studies in contemporary American fiction)
  Bibliography: p.
  Includes index.
  ISBN 0-8122-8098-9
    1. American fiction—20th century—History and criticism. 2. Self-
consciousness in literature. 3. Illusion in literature.
4. Fiction—Technique. 5. English fiction—20th century—History
and criticism. 6. Joyce, James, 1882–1941—Criticism and
interpretation. 7. Pynchon, Thomas—Criticism and interpretation.
I. Title. II. Series.
PS369.S7681988   87-30784
813'.54'09—dc19   CIP

Consciously for Brenda

Contents

Preface and Acknowledgments

The Self-Conscious Novel asks why so much modern and contemporary fiction talks about itself. By exposing itself as a mere fiction, doesn't a book turn its back on real life? Why are writers putting mirrors in the house of fiction where windows used to be?

Although accused of narcissism and self-indulgence, texts that contain their own context stand at the very heart of the debate over the proper relationship between fiction and Truth. Should the novel concern itself with the outside world? Or should it refuse to serve as reality's scribe, and seek its justification elsewhere? I contend, in the pages that follow, that by balancing mimetic and anti-mimetic effects—by acknowledging imitations's limitations—the best self-conscious fiction may "render the highest kind of justice to the visible universe" *and* at the same time "not mean but be." The self-conscious novel, that is, may be both esthetically neat and ethically right.

To test these claims, I examine in "The Repertoire of Reflexivity" the array of distinctive devices and themes shared by self-conscious novels, and then briefly survey the genre's distinguished heritage. I offer close readings of five exemplars of fiction's self-depiction: Joyce's *Ulysses,* Nabokov's self-conscious novels, William Gaddis's *The Recognitions,* Thomas Pynchon's *Gravity's Rainbow,* and John Barth's *LETTERS.* Though these fictions employ a common repertoire of devices, the results of their reflexivity are considerably diverse. More recently, writers seem to be moving away from a preoccupation with self-consciousness, towards an accommodation with it. But both modern and contemporary texts confirm that the self-conscious novel is an essentially playful genre that retains its claim to ethical responsibility.

Some excellent work has already been done on literary self-consciousness; I try to keep track of my debts and divergences in the footnotes. More personally, I would like to thank Ray Frazer and my friends and colleagues at Pomona College for aiding and abetting in the final stages of revision. I am also grateful to those who read and commented helpfully upon earlier versions of various chapters: John Barth, the late Richard Ellmann, Robert Ferguson, Bruce Morrissette, the late Sheldon Sacks, James Schiffer, Richard Stern, and William Veeder. Martha Andresen, Dick Barnes, Edward Copeland, Robert Dawidoff, Sir Ernst Gombrich, Clay Jenkinson, Mitchell Marks, Robert Mezey, Cristanne Miller, Thomas Pinney, Arden Reed, and Steven Young helped to shape my thoughts on this subject.

I owe a great intellectual debt to my two doctoral advisers at The University of Chicago, Wayne C. Booth and Saul Bellow. While I have benefitted by their attentive and generous expertise, the results are still in no way to be blamed upon the editor of *The Knowledge Most Worth Having* or the author of *Seize the Day*.

Finally, my sister and my parents have been unself-consciously supportive throughout. At times, even at a distance, the sight of someone writing about writers who write about writers writing must have been trying indeed.

Chapter I

Imitation's Limitations; or, Why Writers Write About Writers Writing

ARISTOTLE, in the *Poetics,* made the point quite firmly: "The poet should speak as little as possible in his own person, for it is not this that makes him an imitator."[1] Since antiquity it has been agreed that the task of literature and of art in general "was and is," as Hamlet put it, "to hold, as 'twere, the mirror up to nature."[2] The more convincing the illusion, that is, the better the art. What we value in art is the artist's inobtrusiveness, just as Ovid found it praiseworthy in Pygmalion's work:

> He made it lovelier than any woman born, and fell in love with his own creation. The statue had all the appearance of a real girl, so that it seemed to be alive, to want to move, did not modesty forbid. So cleverly did his art conceal its art.[3]

Art concealing art—this has indeed marked the character of much of the best literature, and fiction in particular, for centuries. The novelist's goal, as Ford Madox Ford wrote of Joseph Conrad, "is to keep the reader entirely oblivious of the fact that the author exists—even of the fact that he is holding a book."[4] Mimesis—the creation of a convincing and uninterrupted illusion of life—has seemed so central to the novelist's art that it has been possible to portray the whole of Western literature as an expression of the mimetic impulse. As Stephen Dedalus puts it in *A Portrait of the Artist as a Young Man,* "The artist, like the God of creation, remains within or behind or beyond or above his handiwork, invisible, refined out of existence, indifferent, paring his fingernails."[5] And the

1. The *Poetics* 24.7; trans S. H. Butcher (New York: Hill and Wang, 1961), p. 109.
2. *Hamlet,* III, ii, 20–21.
3. *Metamorphoses* 10.249–52; trans. Mary M. Innes, (Harmondsworth: Penguin Books, 1955), p. 231.
4. Quoted in Miriam Allott, *Novelists on the Novel* (New York: Columbia University Press, 1959), p. 273; cited in Louis D. Rubin, Jr., *The Teller in the Tale* (Seattle: University of Washington Press, 1967), p. 4.
5. James Joyce, *A Portrait of the Artist as a Young Man* (New York: B. W. Huebsch, 1916; New York: The Viking Press, 1964), p. 215.

novelist who neglects to conceal his own hand in the composition of his work commits, in Henry James's words, "a betrayal of a sacred office" and "a terrible crime." [1]

These things being so, what is one to make of a passage such as the following, from Sterne's *Tristram Shandy?*

> ———How could you, Madam, be so inattentive in reading the last chapter? I told you in it, That my mother was not a papist. —Papist? [. . .] I declare, I know nothing at all about the matter.—That, Madam, is the very fault I lay to your charge; and as a punishment for it, I do insist upon it, that you immediately turn back, that is, as soon as you get to the next full stop, and read the whole chapter over again. [2]

Sterne seems to have thrown Aristotle's advice out the window, as Tristram would say. Far from trying to "speak as little as possible in his own person," Sterne's narrator appears to do as *much* as is possible to draw attention to himself as the author of his story. The reader is not, as Conrad would have it, encouraged to forget that he is reading a book. On the contrary, he is reminded of it again and again. What it going on here? Why has Sterne elected to betray so emphatically the Jamesian novelist's "sacred trust"?

Novels that perversely *display* their own art rather than conceal it are not limited to Sterne's eighteenth-century comic masterpiece. What are we to make, for instance, of lines such as these from that monument of modernism, Joyce's *Ulysses:*

> By heaven, Theodore Purefoy, thou hast done a doughty deed and no botch! Thou art, I vow, the remarkablest progenitor barring none in this chaffering allincluding most farraginous chronicle. [3]

How do we reconcile this reference *in* the text *to* the text with Dedalus's depiction of the "invisible" author "refined out of existence"? What happens, in short, when novelists assert the artifice of their own creations?

These questions are raised, perhaps more compellingly than ever, by fictions in our own day. In the works of Vladimir Nabokov, William

---

1. Henry James, "The Art of Fiction," in *The Future of the Novel,* ed. Leon Edel (New York: Vintage, 1956), p. 6; cited in Rubin, *The Teller in the Tale,* p. 5.

2. Laurence Sterne, *The Life and Opinions of Tristram Shandy, Gentleman* (London, 1759–67; New York: Modern Library, n.d.), Book I, Ch. 20. In all quotations, I have bracketed my ellipses to distinguish them from those in the original.

3. James Joyce, *Ulysses* (Paris: Shakespeare and Co., 1922; New York: Random House, 1986), p. 345. All references are to the latter edition, the "Corrected Text."

Gaddis, Thomas Pynchon, John Barth, and to varying degrees in those of many others as well, the fictional illusion of reality is repeatedly destroyed so as to remind the reader that the fiction is in fact an illusion. It was, in part, as an effort to understand the motives and implications of this procedure that I undertook a study of the self-depiction of modern fiction. On another level, though, my aims may be stated more simply. I found, while reading them, that self-conscious novels intrigued me. I wanted to know why.

I would like to examine, then, a class or genre of literary creations which I shall call the *self-conscious novel,* which may be defined as an extended prose narrative that draws attention to its status as a fiction. To distinguish clearly between self-conscious novels and novels that are *not* self-conscious, I should like to borrow for a moment the simplifying, "metacritical" analysis of R. S. Crane, in which the myriad possible ways of approaching any literary text are resolved into four basic approaches:[1]

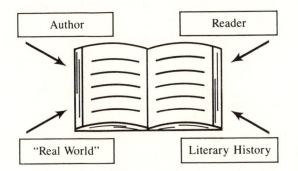

To ask to what degree does Stephen Dedalus depict the unfledged James Joyce is to approach *Ulysses* from the direction of the Author ("biographical" criticism); to determine whether *Lolita* requires us to condemn Humbert Humbert's sexual perversion, or rather lulls us into a state of "esthetic bliss," is to approach Nabokov's novel from the direction of the Reader ("rhetorical" criticism); to assess William Gaddis's debt to Dante in the composition of *The Recognitions* is to practice "lit-

1. R.S. Crane, *The Languages of Criticism and the Structure of Poetry* (Toronto: University of Toronto Press, 1953). I am indebted to Wayne C. Booth for the diagram, although I take liberties with it below.

erary-historical" criticism; and to seek verification of the corporate conspiracies uncovered in *Gravity's Rainbow* is to approach Pynchon's novel under the aspect of the "Real World" ("thematic" criticism). Each of these approaches implies, of course, a different assumption about what a work of literature essentially *is:* whether it is a revealing expression of its author's subconscious; a verbal machine constructed so as to create a specific effect upon its reader; an artifact which is, at least partially, determined by and determining a tradition; or, a representation of a political, social, sexual, racial, or economic reality.

A fifth approach, that of "intrinsic" criticism—a more useful and less dated term for the invention of the "New Critics"—ideally excludes all reference to these four external grounds, and thus may be visualized schematically as an arrow meeting our diagrammatic text perpendicularly, from outside the plane of the page. Pluralism apart, my generation of readers was taught that, both because it encourages close reading and because it regards the literary text *as* a text and not as a mode of discourse, a disguised confession, or any other thing, intrinsic criticism accords the greatest intellectual respect to the object of study.

But when focused upon the self-conscious novel, the lens of intrinsic criticism discerns something very striking. We find that in a self-conscious novel, the four grounds that we had defined as external—author, reader, literary history, and "real world"—are all included as characters or features *inside* the novel itself:

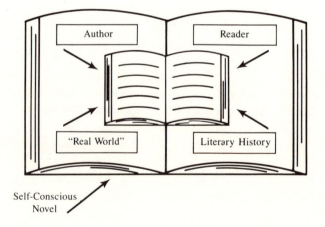

The self-conscious text dramatizes and encapsulates its own context; and even when we approach it through intrinsic criticism, it obliges us to practice biographical, rhetorical, literary-historical, and thematic criticism as well.

Let us look at how this can be so. In Vladimir Nabokov's novel *King, Queen, Knave*, we come across the following description:

> The foreign girl in the blue dress danced with a remarkably handsome man in an old-fashioned dinner jacket. Franz had long since noticed this couple; they had appeared to him in fleeting glimpses, like a recurrent dream image or a subtle leitmotiv—now at the beach, now in a cafe, now on the promenade. Sometimes the man carried a butterfly net. The girl had a delicately painted mouth and tender blue-gray eyes, and her fiancé or husband, slender, elegantly balding, contemptuous of everything on earth but her, was looking at her with pride; and Franz felt envious of that unusual pair, so envious that his oppression, one is sorry to say, grew even more bitter, and the music stopped. They walked past him. They were speaking loudly. They were speaking a totally incomprehensible language.[1]

The couple is speaking Russian, of course, and the man carrying a butterfly net is an image of the author, Vladimir Nabokov himself. In John Barth's recent novel *LETTERS,* one of the characters signs his letters "The Author," and the other characters address him as "Mr. John Barth."[2] In both of these examples, and in Molly Bloom's plea to her author near the end of *Ulysses*—"O Jamesy let me up out of this"[3]—we find the author dramatizing himself within his fiction. We can hear a musical parallel to this procedure in some of J. S. Bach's compositions in *The Art of Fugue*—in Contrapunctus II, for example, where one of the fugue subjects is based upon the notes *B–A–C–H*. Authors who mingle among their characters—much as Alfred Hitchcock's face or distinctive profile momentarily appears in some of his films—have sometimes been accused of narcissism or self-indulgence. Christopher Lasch, in his recent study *The Culture of Narcissism,* takes such a view, and Philip Roth a quarter-century ago called self-conscious novels "not so much an attempt to understand the self, as to assert it."[4] These accusations of narcissism and self-indulgence are serious, and we must return to them.

1. Vladimir Nabokov, *King, Queen, Knave* (New York: McGraw-Hill, 1968), p. 254.
2. John Barth, *LETTERS* (New York: G.P. Putnam's Sons, 1979).
3. Joyce, *Ulysses*, p. 633.
4. Christopher Lasch, *The Culture of Narcissism: American Life in an Age of Diminishing Expectations* (New York: W.W. Norton, 1979), esp. Chap. IV, "The Banality of Pseudo-Self-

Much as the dramatizations of the author serve to remind us of the process of *writing* that has produced the text, so dramatizations of the reader remind us that we are *reading,* as in this excerpt from John Barth's collection of self-depicting fictions, *Lost in the Funhouse:*

> The reader! You, dogged, uninsultable, print-oriented bastard, it's you I'm addressing, who else, from inside this monstrous fiction. You've read me this far, then? Even this far? For what discreditable motive? How is it you don't go to a movie, watch TV, stare at a wall, play tennis with a friend, make amorous advances to the person who comes to mind when I speak of amorous advances? Can nothing surfeit, saturate you, turn you off? Where's your shame? [1]

On one level, such direct assaults on the reader tend to alienate us from the fiction—they prevent us from believing in the fictional illusion, by reminding us that it has been invented by the author for his or her readers. Self-conscious novels attain something very like what Bertolt Brecht pursued in epic drama under the name of *Verfremdungseffekt.* Brecht's intentions in distancing his audience from the actions onstage were politically propagandistic, but certain of his techniques for breaking the illusion of "realism" bear analogies to those of the self-conscious novel. To quote Brecht:

> There is a point in showing the lighting apparatus openly, as it is one of the means of preventing an unwanted element of illusion. [. . .] Displaying the actual lights is meant to be a counter to the old-fashioned theatre's efforts to hide them. [2]

Brecht seeks to remind his spectators that they are watching a play so as to prevent them from empathizing with the characters onstage. The audience is thus freed to heed the political message which the drama conveys. The self-conscious novel, however, is not usually an instrument of political education. While it may display its own artifice so as to remind its readers that they are in fact reading a novel, its motives in doing

---

Awareness." Philip Roth, "Writing American Fiction," *Commentary,* 31 (March 1961), 225. According to James Schiffer (personal communication, 1978), Roth has also said, "It doesn't take much imagination to write about writing." But see below, Chap. X, for a discussion of Roth's own *Zuckerman Unbound.*

1. John Barth, "Life-Story," in *Lost in the Funhouse* (New York: Doubleday and Co., 1968; Bantam pbk. ed., 1969), p. 123.

2. Bertolt Brecht, "Short Description of a New Technique of Acting which Produces an Alienation Effect," in *Brecht on Theatre,* ed. and trans. John Willet (New York: Hill and Wang, 1964), p. 141.

so lie elsewhere. By dramatizing within its pages a version of its own reader, the self-conscious novel welds a bond of intimacy with its actual readers that is beyond the means of naturalistic, non-self-conscious novels. By acknowledging what they are, self-conscious novels show an honesty and a respect for the reader's intelligence which novels that pretend to be life itself do not. There is thus an alienation of the reader from the novel's action at one level—these are, the reader sees, characters and actions invented by the novelist solely for purposes of his or her own—while at another level the reader, by being made conscious of his or her role as a listener confronted by a storyteller, is drawn into a stronger bond of intimacy. What the novel apparently renounces at one level of its engagement with the reader, it effectively reclaims at another.

We may also attempt to characterize the *kind* of reader that the self-conscious novel seems to address, as a further means of distinguishing it from other novels. There is a strong tinge of élitism to the self-conscious novel, a sense that those who do not share a certain body of knowledge are excluded from the implied audience. The generous use of Greek and Latin in *Tristram Shandy* and in William Gaddis's *The Recognitions* suggests that these self-conscious novels are aimed at the happy few. With respect to the frequently obscure allusiveness of Joyce's novels, Saul Bellow has observed that "these are works for initiates."[1] Even when foreign languages are not used, self-conscious novels often begin with what Frye has called, in another context, "the opening dismissal of catechumens."[2] The first sentence of Nabokov's *Ada* offers a typical example:

> "All happy families are more or less dissimilar; all unhappy ones are more or less alike," says a great Russian writer in the beginning of a famous novel (*Anna Arkadievitch Karenina*, transfigured into English by R. G. Stonelower, Mount Tabor, Ltd., 1880).[3]

Readers who don't get the jokes nonetheless sense that they've missed something; they are thus excluded from the implied audience of the novel. Given certain preconceptions, then, it is possible to find fault with the self-conscious novel on the basis of its élitist cast. Gore Vidal, for instance, in an essay entitled "The Hacks of Academe," has complained, "I suspect that the works of Professor Barth are written not so much to

1. Comments in a seminar on *Ulysses*, The University of Chicago, Winter 1977.
2. Northrop Frye, *Anatomy of Criticism: Four Essays*. (Princeton: Princeton University Press, 1957; New York: Atheneum, 1967), p . 202.
3. Vladimir Nabokov, *Ada* (New York: McGraw-Hill, 1969), p. 3.

be read as to be taught."[1] Nabokov has freely if somewhat disingenuously confessed, "I write mainly for artists, fellow-artists and follow-artists."[2] Like the charge of narcissistic self-indulgence, the accusation of élitist obscurantism is one to which we must return.

The particular intimacy which the self-conscious novel achieves with those readers who are capable of sorting out its obscurities is further abetted by what may be called a *conspiratorial mystique*. In part, this derives from the novel's implied élitism: excluding so many of "them," brings "us" closer together. The mystique is enhanced, however, by the self-conscious novel's conspicuous rejection of many of the conventions of the "traditional" novel. There is something palpably subversive about a self-conscious novel, despite the distinguished tradition which it itself enjoys. Even when, as today, self-depicting fictions are fashionable, they still strike a pose of bold defiance of literary norms. The title of Philip Stevick's collection of short self-conscious fiction, *Anti-Story,* and Sartre's discussion of *"anti-romans"* indicate the pervasiveness of this subversive aura.[3] By dramatizing its own subversiveness, self-depicting fiction enters a conspiracy with the willing reader.

In order to strike this pose of bold defiance, the self-conscious novel includes within its pages a representation of the historically dominant regime of realistic fiction against which the novel itself is to be seen as staging a courageous and heroic revolt. In André Gide's *Les Faux-monnayeurs,* for example, the novelist–character Edouard is working on a novel to be called *Les Faux-monnayeurs* which itself will have as its central character a novelist at work upon a self-conscious novel. Edouard attempts to justify the sort of novel he is writing by explaining to his friends that throughout literary history the novel has suffered from the tyrannical obligation of having a subject. Edouard proposes to liberate the novel from that tyranny by giving to his own novel no other subject than itself. He will absolve the novel of its responsibility to mirror reality by turning the novel's mirror upon itself, producing an endless regression of barbershop self-portraits. Gide called this procedure of the novel-within-the-novel a *mise-en-abyme,* taking the term from the practice in

1. Gore Vidal, "The Hacks of Academe," in *Matters of Fact and of Fiction: Essays 1973–1976* (New York: Random House, 1977), p. 97.

2. Vladimir Nabokov, *Strong Opinions* (New York: McGraw-Hill, 1973), p. 41.

3. Philip Stevick, ed., *Anti-Story: An Anthology of Experimental Fiction* (New York: The Free Press, 1971). Jean-Paul Sartre, "Préface" (1947) to *Portrait d'un inconnu,* by Nathalie Sarraute (Paris: Gallimard, 1956), pp. 5–14.

heraldry where one quadrant of a coat of arms reduplicates in miniature the structure of the entire coat of arms in which it appears:

mise-en-abyme

The play-within-the-play of *Hamlet* is a self-conscious *mise-en-abyme,* and so is, in certain Flemish paintings, the convex mirror seen on the back wall which reflects in miniature the composition as a whole. In more contemporary media, the video feedback that results when a TV camera is turned upon its own monitor offers an infinite *mise-en-abyme,* one which John Barth was able to reproduce in language by publishing a Moebius strip that reads, "Once upon a time, There was a story that began, Once upon a time, There was a story that," and so on.[1] When Gide's Edouard explains his literary theories and intentions to his companions, however, they respond with a significant warning: *"Mon pauvre ami, vous ferez mourir d'ennui vos lecteurs."*[2]

This notion of criticism *of* the text *within* the text offers a second guise in which literary history appears inside the self-conscious novel. In *Don Quixote,* to go all the way back to the beginning of the novel form itself, we find the Knight in the second volume reading of his own exploits in the first, and finding them woefully misrepresented. From this point on, Cervantes's narrative is itself self-depicting. The burning of Don Quixote's library of chivalrous romances dramatizes that repudiation of the dominant modes of literary history referred to earlier. In *Tristram Shandy,* Tristram engages in frequent and lively debate with critics of the early volumes of his novel, and even invites the critics to lend a hand at diffi-

1. John Barth, "Frame-Tale," *Lost in the Funhouse,* pp. 1–2.
2. "My poor friend, you'll bore your readers to death." André Gide, *Les Faux-monnayeurs* [*The Counterfeiters*] (Paris: Gallimard, 1925), p. 233.

cult points in his narrative. James Joyce, as we shall see, encapsulated the whole of literary history in the 'Oxen of the Sun' episode of *Ulysses* by parodying the evolution of styles from the ornate complexity of its Latinate origins to the mindless clichés of modern slang. And in Flann O'Brien's novel *At Swim-Two-Birds,* the narrator and his friends subject the novel that the narrator is writing to intense critical scrutiny, obliging the narrator to formulate his theory of what a novel ought to be:

> In reply to an inquiry, it was explained that a satisfactory novel should be a self-evident sham to which the reader could regulate at will the degree of his credulity.[1]

The inclusion of self-directed literary criticism in these novels reminds the reader that he or she is reading a novel, but it does much more besides. By means of such criticism, the self-conscious novel challenges the assumptions upon which it itself is based. This rejection of complacency, this skeptical examination of its own validity dramatizes the question of what it is to be a novel into a central theme of the novel itself. The self-conscious novel characteristically contains in explicit form the esthetic criteria by which it seeks to be judged. In the self-conscious film, such as Woody Allen's *Stardust Memories,* we find the self-directed filmic criticism serving essentially the same purpose of probing the work's own first principles.

The relations between a novel, its author, and its readers, together determine the relations between the novel and the "real" world in which its author and readers live and die. The self-conscious novel keeps itself and that world clearly distinct. The novel may sporadically encourage the reader to believe in the world it has constructed, but it misses no opportunity to remind him or her that this "world elsewhere" is not one that he or she lives in. We may take as its emblem in this regard the "NOTICE" which Mark Twain addressed to readers of *The* [non-self-conscious] *Adventures of Huckleberry Finn* (1884):

> Persons attempting to find a motive in this narrative will be prosecuted; persons attempting to find a moral in it will be banished; persons attempting to find a plot in it will be shot.
>
> BY ORDER OF THE AUTHOR
> Per G.G., Chief of Ordnance

1. Flann O'Brien [Brian Nolan], *At Swim-Two-Birds* (New York: Pantheon, 1939; Plume, 1976), p. 33.

The self-conscious novel denies that its obligation is "to hold the mirror up to nature." It asserts instead that art has virtues of its own to admire, and that if there is any mirroring to be done, the novel should mirror itself. By spurning the goal of imitation—as Robbe-Grillet puts it, *"Je ne transcris pas, je construis"*[1]—the self-conscious novelist also rejects the mimetic *premise* of Aristotle's injunction to "speak as little as possible in his own voice," This is, ultimately, how the self-conscious novelist is able to "get away" with violating Aristotle's admonition.

Oscar Wilde is perhaps the most colorful opponent of mimesis. In an essay entitled "The Decay of Lying," he dismisses its stodgy defenders with characteristic panache:

> They will call upon Shakespeare—they always do—and will quote that hackneyed passage about Art holding the mirror up to Life, forgetting that this unfortunate aphorism is deliberately said by Hamlet in order to convince the bystanders of his absolute insanity in all art-matters. [. . .] Art finds her own perfection within, and not outside of, herself. She is not to be judged by any external standard of resemblance.[2]

The conception of art as a self-contained and self-justified activity is hardly new, of course. When Kierkegaard wrote that "The beautiful is that which has its teleology in itself," he was giving new and concise voice to an ancient concept.[3] Wilde's non-mimetic esthetic thus embraces beauty while it spurns truth and goodness. Such a view of "Art for Art's Sake" may even lead to a denial that truth exists at all. Whereas for Keats, the two goals are one—

> "Beauty is truth, truth beauty,"—that is all
> Ye know on earth, and all ye need to know[4]

—for the self-conscious novelist the case is better put by Pursewarden, the writer, in Lawrence Durrell's novel *Clea:*

> Art's Truth's Nonentity made quite explicit.
> If it ain't this then what the devil is it?[5]

---

1. "I don't transcribe, I construct." Alain Robbe-Grillet, *"Du Réalisme à la réalité"* (1963), in *Pour un nouveau roman* (Paris: Les Editions de Minuit, 1963), p. 139.
2. Oscar Wilde, "The Decay of Lying" (1891), in *The Artist as Critic: Critical Writings of Oscar Wilde,* ed. Richard Ellmann (New York: Random House, 1969), p. 306.
3. Søren Kierkegaard, *Either/Or* (1843), trans. Walter Lowrie (Princeton: Princeton University Press, 1944), II, 277.
4. John Keats, "Ode on a Grecian Urn" (1819).
5. Lawrence Durrell, *Clea* (New York: E.P. Dutton and Co., 1960), p. 130.

The temptation to generalize from fiction to Art, or to assume that what is true of Art is also true of fiction, is a dangerous one, especially on this issue. The freedom of fiction wholly to reject the demands of mimesis so as to embrace some abstract ideal of beauty is obviously limited by the nature of the medium itself. Here, as an example of what an abstract style can look like, is the opening of Chapter A from Walter Abish's 1974 novel entitled *Alphabetical Africa:*

> Ages ago, Alex, Allen, and Alva arrived at Antibes, and Alva allowing all, allowing anyone, against Alex's admonition, against Allen's angry assertion: another African amusement . . . anyhow, as all argued, an awesome African army assembled and arduously advanced against an African anthill, assiduously annihilating ant after ant, and afterward, Alex astonishingly accuses Albert as also accepting Africa's antipodal ant annexation. Albert argumentatively answers at another apartment. Answers: ants are Ameisen. Ants are Ameisen?[1]

As this citation suggests, the hypertrophy of style induces an atrophy of story. Language is essentially referential, or so it would seem, and efforts to insist that the words of a fiction refer to nothing beyond those words will always be problematical in some sense. It is clear, however, that by dramatizing within its pages fictional versions of its author, its reader, and its literary context, and by reminding its readers in these and other ways that the text has been *written* and is being *read,* the self-conscious novel manages both to create and to destroy a convincing and meaningful illusion of reality; it seems, that is, to be both about the world and about itself. Life is both the subject *of* and subject *to* its language. In its esthetic and epistemological implications, therefore, self-depicting fiction stands at the very heart of the debate over whether fiction can or should embody Truth.

*   *   *

Any novelist who hopes to abandon mimesis, immediately faces a very tough question. If I deny that the task of my novel is to reproduce nature, how can I avoid utter randomness and chaos? How can I organize my fiction in a way that is not mimetic, but which will still engage my reader's interest and reward it with a sense of satisfaction? There is, fortunately, an answer to this question, and it is to be found in the *ludic* theory of art—the conception of art as a game or form of play.

1. Walter Abish, *Alphabetical Africa* (New York: New Directions, 1974), p. 1.

The term comes from J. Huizinga's 1938 study, *Homo Ludens,* or man as the game-playing animal,[1] but the ludic theory of art may be traced as far back as Plato, who rather cheerfully uses this premise to dismiss art from the realm of serious concerns. To quote from the *Republic:*

> We seem, then, so far to be pretty well agreed that the artist knows nothing worth mentioning about the subjects he represents, and that art is a form of play, not to be taken seriously.[2]

We have to wait until Immanuel Kant before art as a ludic activity is treated with intellectual respect, and for Schiller's formulation of *Spieltrieb* out of Kantian ideas.[3] In the ludic view which thus emerges, literature, like the other arts, is to be seen as a game in which the goal is "esthetic satisfaction," and in which "truth to life" is irrelevant. A novel, for example, proceeds according to stringent rules which have no necessary application outside the game.

Clearly, the self-conscious novel is an essentially ludic art form. The great humor manifest in many of the self-conscious passages I have quoted emphasizes how playful the self-conscious genre can be. It has been frequently remarked, and it has even been frequently remarked that it has been frequently remarked, that Vladimir Nabokov's novels are much concerned with game-playing. Card games inform the structure as well as the title of *King, Queen, Knave,* just as chess games do those of *The Defense.* Alain Robbe-Grillet's novels have been identified as elaborate games,[4] and, more recently, Italo Calvino has used the tarot deck to generate the narrative of *The Castle of Crossed Destinies.*

An important consequence of the ludic theory of art is an at least partial or tacit acknowledgment by the self-conscious novel of Plato's estimation that art is "not to be taken seriously." The announcement in the novel's final lines that *Tristram Shandy* is nothing but a "story about a Cock and a Bull" is a case in point. The last two-hundred pages of Julio Cortázar's *Hopscotch*—another self-conscious novel whose title proclaims its ludism—appear under the heading of "Expendable Chapters." From its ludic diminution of seriousness comes also the self-conscious novel's

---

1. J. Huizinga, *Homo Ludens: A Study of the Play-Element in Culture* (1938; Boston: Beacon Press, 1955).

2. Plato, The *Republic,* X, 601; trans. Francis MacDonald Cornford (New York: Oxford University Press, 1945), p. 333.

3. Friedrich von Schiller, *Letters on the Aesthetic Education of Man* (1795).

4. Bruce Morrissette, "Games and Game Structures in Robbe-Grillet," *Yale French Studies,* 41 (1968), 159–67.

habit of self-parody, as in the image of the "chicken-scratched scrap" on the "midden-heap" by which *Finnegans Wake* refers to itself. The self-conscious novel overtly acknowledges that, as Ortega y Gasset put it, "Art is a thing of no consequence."[1]

And yet—paradoxically—the esthetic of the self-conscious novel owes a great deal to the school of Art for Art's Sake, which deems artistic values to be *more* important than any other. As Oscar Wilde put it, "The first duty in life is to be as artificial as possible. What the second is no one has yet discovered."[2] It was, after all, Gustave Flaubert, that dedicated esthete, who first dared to hope that a consummately pure style might enable him to write "a book about nothing."

The self-conscious novel's embodiment of these two paradoxical views—that art is both a thing of no consequence, and the supreme source of value in our lives—is intimately linked to the paradox we noted a few moments ago, that the self-conscious novel seems both to create and to destroy a meaningful and convincing illusion of life; that it seems to be both about the world and about itself. For, the astounding and intriguing thing about the best self-conscious fiction (and I'm sneaking a value judgment in here) is that even as it exposes its own artifice, and professes itself to be an invention, it is still able to fire our imaginations and move our emotions as do events in real life. Nabokov offers perhaps the best example of this paradoxical combination; for, in such masterpieces of self-depicting fiction as *Lolita* and *Ada,* even as the author reveals the strings that bind his characters to the puppeteer's hand, his stories succeed in tugging at our own heartstrings as well. Grieving at the loss of his beloved nymphet, Humbert Humbert cries out, "Oh, my Lolita, I have only words to play with!"

Humbert Humbert's grief touches us; and yet his statement is literally true—true not only of his effort to bring back to life his "dolorous and hazy darling" Dolores Haze by recording her story on paper, but true also of Nabokov's novel as a whole: Humbert Humbert is himself a play on words. Nabokov's texts are not, of course, the first to acknowledge their own textuality while not renouncing their power to reach us with

1. José Ortega y Gasset, "The Dehumanization of Art," in *The Dehumanization of Art and Other Essays on Art, Culture, and Literature* (1925), trans. Helene Weyl (Princeton: Princeton University Press, 1948), p. 49.
2. Wilde, "Phrases and Philosophies for the Use of the Young," in *The Artist as Critic,* p. 433.

their meaning. When Polonius asks the hero of another play made of words, "What are you reading, my lord?," Hamlet answers, playfully, "Words, words, words." Which is just where we must look for the source of all our paradoxes.

For in the word, the unit of language itself, we find in elementary form that same duality of creation and disruption of illusion which the self-conscious novel enacts on a macrocosmic scale. A written word is an arbitrary sign; a spoken word is an arbitrary sound. We have merely *agreed* to let these arbitrary sounds and signs "stand in for" or "repre-sent" the objects around us and the thoughts and feelings within. "If ants were called elephants and elephants ants, I'd be able to squash an ele-phant," as Danny Kaye once sang. When we speak, write, listen, or read, we tend to forget that there is no necessary connection between, for example, the word *apple* and the crisp, sweet fruit into which we sink our teeth. We experience, that is, in every contact we have with language, that same phenomenon which Coleridge described as occurring when we read supernatural poetry or, as it is more clearly seen, what we attend a play in a theatre. We know that we are watching actors on a stage, and yet we respond, quite often, as if we were watching real life. We partici-pate in Coleridge's "willing suspension of disbelief," *every* time we use language—until we start punning, puzzling over crosswords, or other-wise sporting with our words' playful bodies. All *fictions* similarly require us to suspend our disbelief. The realistic novel does so covertly, as it endeavors to pass itself off as real life. But *self-depicting* fictions, by ac-knowledging the limitations of their own imitations, invite us to suspend our disbelief not only willingly but wittingly.

This discussion of the basic duality at the very root of language sug-gests that by implying a clear demarcation between self-conscious and non-self-conscious novels as I did at the outset, I oversimplified. Since all language and all fictions contain the potential paradoxes which authors may explore or leave hidden as they see fit, it would be more accurate to conceive of a *spectrum* of fictional modes, composed of varying *degrees* of self-consciousness. Realistic novels, and most popular fiction, as well, focus on the values of versimilitude, and pay little overt attention to the medium of language itself. When I began my study, I assumed that the more self-consciousness the better; that the more reflexive or opaque a text became, the more interesting it got. I soon found this not to be the case; that works like Abish's *Alphabetical Africa*, or Robbe-Grillett's later novels, or the production of a French group called OULIPO,[1] while *theoretically* interesting, make for pretty dull reading. It seems that it is possible to sacrifice too much of the traditional narrative values, after which one loses something essential for which we read fiction in the first place. The most engaging and rewarding self-conscious fictions, I suggest, are those which manage to combine a story that we care about with reminders that it *is* a story; and the best of these will be those in which the appeal of the art and the reminders of artifice are both developed to their fullest possible extent. By this standard, *Tristram Shandy*, *Ulysses*, several of Nabokov's novels, *The Recognitions*, *Gravity's Rainbow*, and *LETTERS* stand out as the major achievements of fiction's self-depiction.

The self-conscious novel also stands at the heart of the debate over literature's duty and capacity to express Truth. Joseph Conrad is perhaps the most eloquent spokesman for those who believe that fiction has a moral responsibility to address our most serious concerns. Conrad wrote:

> A work that aspires, however humbly, to the condition of art should carry its justification in every line. And art itself may be defined as a single-minded attempt to render the highest kind of justice to the visible universe, by bringing to light the truth, manifold and one, underlying its every aspect.[2]

In his Nobel Lecture, Saul Bellow quoted with approval these observations of Conrad, concluding, "What Conrad said was true, art attempts to find in the universe, in matter as well as in the facts of life, what is fundamental, enduring, essential."[3]

On the other side of the issue, William H. Gass has warned readers, "The appeal to literature as a source of truth is pernicious. Truth suffers, but more than that, literature suffers."[4] And Archibald MacLeish, in his poem "Ars Poetica," wrote,

> A poem should be equal to:
> Not true.
> [. . .]

1. OULIPO, *la littérature potentielle* (Paris: Gallimard, 1973).

2. Joseph Conrad, Preface to *The Nigger of the 'Narcissus'* (1897), rpt. in *The Theory of the Novel*, ed. Philip Stevick (New York: Free Press, 1967), p. 399.

3. Saul Bellow, *Nobel Lecture* (Stockholm: The Nobel Foundation, 1976), p. 13.

4. "William H. Gass," (an interview by Carole Spearim McCauley), in *The New Fiction: Interviews with Innovative American Writers*, ed. Joe David Bellamy (Urbana: University of Illinois Press, 1974), p. 34.

A poem should not mean
But be.

I submit that by virtue of its dual nature, its mingling of illusion and disillusion, imitation and limitation, text and context, the self-conscious novel may do *both*—"render the highest kind of justice to the visible universe" and at the same time "not mean but be." At its best, a self-conscious novel may be both ethically effective *and* esthetically reflexive. In *The Recognitions,* for example, William Gaddis offers a Dantesque portrait of the myriad ways in which we all counterfeit and forge what little we have of value, for the sake of financial or social gain. At the center of the novel appears a writer named Willie, at work on a novel called *The Recognitions.* "Willie" Gaddis thus places his own novel at the nexus of the "imitations" and "forgeries" that *The Recognitions* itself derides—and he does so without blunting the edge of his novel's cutting satire.

A self-depicting fiction, surprisingly enough, can thus tell us, in Joseph Conrad's phrase, "how to be." Not only do the ethical values of such novels survive the novel's self-conscious disclaimers—they would actually be incomplete without the necessary qualifications and contextual limits which the self-conscious frame provides. In fact we are likely to find, in our discussion of *Ulysses, Ada, The Recognitions, Gravity's Rainbow, LETTERS,* and the rest, that what interests us most in these novels are the ways in which each of them makes distinct ethical assertions both despite *and* by means of its very self-depiction. Joyce, Nabokov, Gaddis, Pynchon, and Barth, for all the esthetic reflexivity of their novels, are, as I hope to show, by no means morally irresponsible in their art.

The argument being made here, and in more detail in the chapters that follow, does not base approval of self-conscious novels on their resemblance to old-fashioned, naturalistic, "moral" fictions. Not at all. The attributes of the self-conscious novel are a sophisticated awareness of the inherent limitations of both language and thought, a philosophic thorough-goingness as to its own presuppositions, and an intimate kind of honesty with its reader, all of which the naturalistic novel fundamentally lacks. Aristotle argued in the *Rhetoric* that what is ultimately objectionable in literary self-consciousness is that it is unconvincing, that it fails to persuade:

Thus we see the necessity of disguising the means we employ, so that we may seem to be speaking, not with artifice, but naturally. Naturalness is persuasive, artifice just the reverse. People grow suspicious of an artificial speaker, and think he has designs upon them—as if some one were mixing drinks for them.[1]

I wish to contend, *pace* Aristotle, that by virtue of its greater honesty, its manifest awareness of its own limitations, and its peculiarly sophisticated humility before life itself, self-depicting fiction can in fact be *more* persuasive than purely naturalistic fiction. Further, in the matter of making assertions of ethical value, I would even suggest that modern fiction can *only* proceed so as "by indirection [to] find direction out," if it is to avoid seeming offensively naive and presumptuous. While, as we have seen, such novels lay themselves open to charges of élitism and self-indulgence, it is clear that their motives in doing so are not narrowly narcissistic but part of a broad esthetic strategy. Far from being decadent, gratuitous, or morally irresponsible, self-depicting fiction may, at its best, remain playful while retaining serious literary claims to ethical responsibility. It may in fact be one of the most convincing and compelling forms available to our writers for the expression of what is truly important today.

1. Aristotle, The *Rhetoric,* 3.2 1405a; trans. Lane Cooper (Englewood Cliffs, N.J.: Prentice-Hall, 1960), p. 186.

Chapter II

The Repertoire of Reflexivity

WHAT *makes* a novel self-conscious? Can *any* story, long or short, funny or sad, betray its own artifice with equal success? Or is there a set of narrative resources that is peculiarly appropriate to self-depicting fictions? How can we distinguish between sophisticated self-consciousness and mere clumsy writing? Clearly, it would be useful to have a catalog of those procedures of narration, style, structure, characterization, and theme that regularly recur in self-conscious novels, and so comprise a "Repertoire of Reflexivity."

*   *   *

Since self-depicting fictions typically dramatize the process of their own composition, dramatized narrators and self-conscious novels go together. A dramatized narrator does not, however, a self-conscious novel make. That is, it is not enough for a character in the story to be the story's teller; he must also be its author. Pip may be the narrator of *Great Expectations* at the same time that he is that novel's protagonist, but we never suspect Pip of having "made up" his story. If we do, Dickens' novel has in some sense failed. In a self-conscious novel, however, the narrator is visibly engaged in the *invention* of his narrative. Fielding's use of "Fielding" as the narrator of *Tom Jones* offers an early example of this procedure. The "authorial intrusions" in *Tom Jones* serve to remind the reader of that pleasant and learned gentleman who is distinctly in control of the story he is telling. These reminders are essential to the novel's success, for much that happens to Tom would make for painful reading were it not for our confidence that "Fielding" is sure to give his story a happy ending. As Wayne Booth has shown, Laurence Sterne put Fielding's lesson to good use in Sterne's creation of the self-conscious narrator of *Tristram Shandy*.[1]

---

1. Wayne C. Booth, *"Tristram Shandy* and its Precursors: The Self-Conscious Narrator" (unpublished Ph.D. dissertation, The University of Chicago, 1950); "Did Sterne Complete

In both *Tom Jones* and *Tristram Shandy,* it is the narrator who is shown to be engaged in the act of composition. More recent self-conscious novels have complicated this effect by distinguishing more clearly than Fielding or Sterne did between dramatized narrator and implied author. The multiplicity of narrators within many modern self-conscious novels—*Ulysses* is a prime example—provides the clue to this distinction. The narrator, in the more modern arrangement, is not necessarily shown as engaged in the act of composition, but is used to draw attention to the author implied *behind* the narrator. The first section of John Barth's *Chimera,* for example, is narrated by Dunyazade, Scheherazade's sister. But the "Dunyazadiad" contains such events as this:

> "As soon as she spoke these last words a genie appeared from nowhere right there in our library-stacks. He didn't resemble anything in Sherry's bedtime stories: for one thing, he wasn't frightening, though he was strange-looking enough: a light-skinned fellow of forty or so, smooth-shaven and bald as a roc's egg. His clothes were simple but outlandish; he was tall and healthy and pleasant enough in appearance, except for queer lenses that he wore in a frame over his eyes."[1]

The "genie" is of course a dramatized version of Barth himself, whose implied presence behind the narratives of Dunyazade, Perseus, and Bellerophon must constantly be felt if *Chimera* is to succeed as a self-depicting fiction. In like manner, Vladimir Nabokov offers a glimpse of the implied author in the last line of *The Real Life of Sebastian Knight:* "I am Sebastian, or Sebastian is I, or perhaps we both are someone whom neither of us knows."[2]

Narrators visibly engaged in the act of composition, and reminders of the author in control behind a succession of narrators, thus clearly belong in our Repertoire of Reflexivity. It is important to remember, however, that these features, along with the others to be added to the list, are not criteria that a novel must meet in order to be deemed self-conscious, but are rather resources at the disposal of the self-conscious novelist, to be adopted or discarded as the novelist sees fit. *Gravity's Rainbow,* for

---

Tristram Shandy?," *Modern Philology,* 48 (1951), 172–83; *The Rhetoric of Fiction* (Chicago: University of Chicago Press, 1961), esp. Ch. 8, "Telling as Showing," pp. 211–40.

1. John Barth, *Chimera* (New York: Random House, 1972), p. 8.
2. Vladimir Nabokov, *The Real Life of Sebastian Knight* (Norwalk, Conn.: New Directions, 1941), p. 205.

instance, as we shall observe in greater detail below, has only one narrator and a relatively undramatized one at that; but by *other* narrative means—including directly addressing the reader *as* reader, and by the narrator's referring to himself as, for instance, a "sentimental surrealist"—Pynchon nonetheless succeeds in reminding us that we are, in fact, reading a fiction. The Repertoire of Reflexivity must therefore take into account these and other similarly self-conscious narrative devices.

While there is no single *style* of self-consciousness, all self-conscious novels are stylistically ostentatious. In the eighteenth century, Buffon had declared that *"le style est l'homme même."*[1] Self-conscious novelists give the maxim a more literal interpretation than Buffon intended by using *le style* to turn a spotlight on *l'homme lui-même.* If literary styles may be said to vary between the pole of *naturalness*—say, the language spoken daily by the common man or woman—and the pole of *artificiality*—language which no one can speak extemporaneously—then the styles of the self-conscious novel are consistently artificial. The model of extremest artificiality in English prose style is of course Euphuism:

> There dwelt in *Athens* a young gentleman of great patrimony, and of so comelye a personage, that it was doubted whether he were more bound to Nature for the liniaments of his person, or to Fortune for the increase of possessions. But Nature impatient of comparisons, and as it were disdaining a companion or copartner in hir working, added to this comelynesse of his bodye such a sharpe capacity of minde, that not onely she proved Fortune counterfaite, but was halfe of that opinion that she hir self was onely currant. This young gallaunt of more witte than wealth, and yet of more wealth then wisedome, seeing himselfe inferiour to none in pleasant conceits, though himselfe superiour to all in honest conditions, insomuch that he thought himselfe so apt to all thinges that he gave himselfe almost to nothing but practising of those thinges commonly which are incident to these sharpe wittes, fine phrases, smooth quippes, merry tauntes, using jesting without meane, and abusing mirth without measure.[2]

A comparison of this opening of John Lyly's *Euphues: The Anatomy of Wit* (1579) with that of John Barth's *The Sot-Weed Factor* (1960) suggests

1. Georges-Louis LeClerc, comte de Buffon, "Discours [. . .] prononcé à l'Académie française par M. de Buffon le jour de sa réception [. . .] le samedi 25 août 1753," in *Œuvres complètes de Buffon* (Paris: Delangle Frères, 1874), 1:13.
2. John Lyly, *Euphues: The Anatomy of Wit* (London, 1579; London: Constable, 1904), p. 33.

the extent to which modern self-conscious novelists have relied on Euphuistic styles to achieve self-conscious effects. Here is Barth's first sentence:

> In the last years of the Seventeenth Century there was to be found among the fops and fools of the London coffee-houses one rangy, gangling flitch called Ebenezer Cooke, more ambitious than talented, and yet more talented than prudent, who, like his friends-in-folly, all of whom were supposed to be educating at Oxford or Cambridge, had found the sound of Mother English more fun to game with than her sense to labor over, and so rather than applying himself to the pains of scholarship, had learned the knack of versifying, and ground out quires of couplets after the fashion of the day, afroth with *Joves* and *Jupiters,* aclang with jarring rhymes, and string-taut with similes stretched to the snapping-point.[1]

Euphues is not itself a self-conscious novel, because it neither reminds the reader that he or she is reading nor suggests that its story is invented. Euphuism is more properly considered the literary expression of the Baroque spirit in England, corresponding to Marinism in Italy and Gongorism in Spain.[2] Euphuism's utility to the self-conscious novel lies in its extreme artificiality, as Edmund Gosse's observation suggests:

> Euphuism did not attempt to render the simplicity of nature. On the contrary, in order to secure refinement, it sought to be as affected, as artificial, as high-pitched as possible.[3]

The artificiality which Lyly sought in the baroque style of *Euphues* did not strive to make the matter of the story more vivid or more convincing to the reader. Rather, Euphuism pursued its own particular virtues of elaboration, antithesis, alliteration, and classical or natural example for their own sake independently, if not altogether at the expense, of the story values. Artificiality becomes a virtue in itself, irrespective of the "sense" it is meant to convey. The ensuing conception of the writer as a *virtuoso,* as one whose writings are better designed to display his or her own skill rather than to express any particular idea or story, will directly confront us when we consider *Ulysses,* in Chapter IV.

The appropriateness of stylistic artificiality to the self-conscious novel is suggested by an observation of Wittgenstein:

1. John Barth, *The Sot-Weed Factor,* 2nd ed. (New York: Doubleday, 1967), p. 3.
2. William Rose Benét, ed., *The Reader's Encyclopedia,* 2nd ed. (New York: Thomas Y. Crowell, 1965), S.V. "baroque."
3. *Encyclopedia Britannica,* 11th ed. S.V. "Euphuism."

> The language-game of reporting can be given such a turn that a report is not meant to inform the hearer about its subject matter but about the person making the report.[1]

If, as we have postulated, the self-conscious novel disrupts its illusion of reality so as to assert the mediating spirit of the novelist, then the appropriateness of stylistic artificiality to this novel becomes clear. Styles which are not "natural," which eschew the clearest and most direct way of saying something in favor of elaborately convoluted sentences and the most *recherché* of diction, specifically imply that what is said matters less than the impressive performance of the speaker; *le signifiant* matters more than *le signifié*. Compared to a natural style, an artificial style is essentially less referential.

From this viewpoint, artificiality of style may be considered chiefly a matter of linguistic opacity. In a naturalistic painting, to trespass briefly upon the visual arts, the picture plane functions as a transparent window-pane *through* which one may view some depicted scene. Every element of such a painting is disposed so as to enhance the verisimilitude of the illusion which apparently lies beyond the canvas. In non-naturalistic painting, in abstract expressionism, for example, the picture plane becomes as if opaque, arresting the viewer's eye *at* the plane of the canvas, focussing attention on the daubs of paint *as* daubs of paint and not as elements of a depicted reality. Paintings which combine both transparent and opaque elements, such as Magritte's and Escher's surrealist pranks, make the viewer conscious of the visual Gestalt upon which the perception of such works depends.

Within limits, linguistic opacity functions in much the same way. Transparent language creates the illusion of a depicted reality behind the words, and the reader's attention is transmitted to this depicted reality without being snagged at the level of the language itself.

> The bell rang furiously and, when Miss Parker went to the tube, a furious voice called out in a piercing North of Ireland accent:
> —Send Farrington here!
> Miss Parker returned to her machine, saying to a man who was writing at a desk:
> —Mr Alleyne wants you upstairs.

1. Ludwig Wittgenstein, *Philosophical Investigations,* 3rd ed., trans. G.E.M. Anscombe (New York: Macmillan, 1958), IIx, p. 190e.

The man muttered *Blast him!* under his breath and pushed back his chair to stand up.[1]

Opaque language, meanwhile, arrests the reader's attention at the level of the language itself, and only dimly suggests the existence of some "prior" reality behind the words employed.

The fall (bababadalgharaghtakamminarronnkonnbronntonnerro nntuonnthunntrovarrhounawnskawntoohoohoordenenthur nuk!) of a once wallstrait oldparr is related early in bed and later on life down through all christian minstrelsy.[2]

Abish's *Alphabetical Africa,* from which I quoted earlier, offers perhaps the purest example of an opaque style that draws attention to the novelist's particular word choices at the expense of the importance of "story." Self-depicting fiction more commonly contains admixtures of both transparent and opaque language; an excellent example is the opening of the 'Oxen of the Sun' episode in Joyce's *Ulysses,* discussed later. In *Tristram Shandy,* Sterne pursued stylistic opacity beyond the bounds of language itself, confronting his reader with completely black or blank or marbled pages. Such extravagances, beyond being funny, may be seen as part of the self-conscious novelist's endeavor to arrest the reader's attention at the "canvas plane" of the book, to remind us that we are holding a self-conscious artifice and not an unmediated transcription of reality.

Flaubert, whom Pater called a martyr to literary style,[3] pursued a consummately "pure" style until it led him, as we have noted, directly to the conception of a novel "about nothing," a literature without subject-matter:

Ce qui me semble beau, ce que je voudrais faire, c'est un livre sur rien, un livre sans attache extérieure, qui se tiendrait de lui même par la force interne de son style, comme la terre sans être soutenue se tient en l'air, un livre qui n'aurait presque pas de sujet ou du moins où le sujet serait presque invisible, si cela se peut. [. . .]

C'est pour cela qu'il n'y a ni beaux ni vilains sujets et qu'on pourrait presque établir comme axiome, en se posant au point de vue de l'Art pur, qu'il n'y en a aucun, le style étant à lui tout seul une manière absolue de voir les choses.

Il me faudrait tout un livre pour développer ce que je veux dire. J'écrirai sur

1. James Joyce, "Counterparts," in *Dubliners* (1916; New York: The Viking Press, 1961), p. 86.

2. James Joyce, *Finnegans Wake* (New York: The Viking Press, 1939), p. 3.

3. Walter Pater, "Style," from *Appreciations* (1888), in *Selected Writings of Walter Pater,* ed. Harold Bloom (New York: Signet, 1974), p. 115.

tout cela dans ma vieillesse, quand je n'aurai rien de mieux à barbouiller. En attendant, je travaille à mon roman [*Madame Bovary*] avec coeur.[1]

Flaubert's theories may be patently impracticable, as his deferment of such a project to his old age suggests, but they lie at the heart of the self-conscious novel's attitudes towards style and theory. The styles of self-conscious novels vary so widely as to produce effects of humor or pathos, and to arouse derision or awe. But they are always fundamentally artificial and at least partially opaque in a way that diminishes the importance of story while asserting the teller's performance.

*   *   *

We cannot distinguish the *structure* of self-conscious fiction from that of non-self-conscious fiction on the basis of an opposition between non-mimetic and mimetic, or artificial and natural procedures, as we have done in the instance of *style,* for the structure of all fiction is of an inherently different order from that of the life which it may purport to describe. Yet there are certain *kinds* of structures, and certain ways in which they inform the fiction's texture, that are particular to self-conscious novels.

In general, the structural principles which govern the composition of a self-conscious novel are emphatically conspicuous. Like style, structure may draw attention to itself. In *Tristram Shandy,* for example, Sterne goes so far as to supply the reader with fanciful line graphs to document the seeming lawlessness of his novel's structure:

> I am now beginning to get fairly into my work; and by the help of a vegetable diet, with a few of the cold seeds, I make no doubt but I shall be able to go on with my uncle Toby's story and my own in a tolerable straight line. Now,

1. What seems beautiful to me, what I would like to do, is a book about nothing, a book without connections to the outside, which would maintain itself by the internal force of its style, as the earth hangs without support in the air; a book that would barely have a subject or at least whose subject was invisible, if that were possible. [. . .]
That's why there are neither handsome nor ugly subjects, and why it's practically axiomatic that, from the perspective of pure Art, there are no subjects at all, style alone being an absolute manner of seeing things.
It would take me a whole book to work out what I mean. I shall write about all this in my old age, when I'll have nothing better to scribble. In the mean time, I'm working wholeheartedly on my novel [*Madame Bovary*]. Gustave Flaubert, letter of 16 janvier 1852 to Louise Colet (No. 398), *Œuvres complètes* (Paris: Club de l'Honnête Homme, 1974), XIII, 157–60.

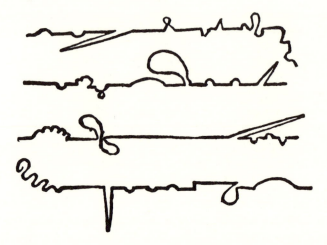

These were the four lines I moved in through my first, second, third, and fourth volumes.—In the fifth volume I have been very good,—the precise line I have described in it being this:

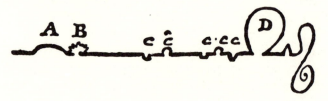

By which it appears, that except at the curve, marked A, where I took a trip to Navarre,—and the indented curve B, which is the short airing when I was there with the Lady Baussiere and her page,—I have not taken the least frisk of a digression, till John de la Cass's devils led me the round you see marked D.—as for *c c c c c* they are nothing but parentheses, and the common ins and outs incident to the lives of the greatest ministers of state; and when compared with what men have done,—or with my own transgressions at the letters A B D—they vanish into nothing.   (Bk. VI, Ch. 40)

Self-conscious novels which, unlike the seemingly chaotic *Tristram Shandy,* are composed upon readily apparent principles of organization need not rely upon illustrative graphics in order to draw attention to their structure. *Alphabetical Africa,* for example, requires no diagrams to alert its reader to what is manifest on every page, that the novel's structure is governed by alphabetic principles wholly unrelated to the novel's material action. In *Ulysses,* the Homeric architecture announced in the novel's title remains unsuspected by the characters who inhabit that edifice, while the symmetries and juxtapositions yielded by its contrived structure succeed in reminding the reader of the artificer who has thus crafted his narrative with such cunning and skill. Similarly, the overt circularity of *Finnegans Wake* or the figure-eight configuration of Robbe-Grillet's *Les gommes* enforce by their incongruous symmetry the artificiality of those novels. All fictional structures are, as we have noted, inherently artificial, but no story is "naturally" annular or lemniscate. Structures of such conspicuous symmetry achieve virtuoso effects, inviting the reader to admire the novelist's skill.

The Gidean *mise-en-abyme,* which we have already noted as an essentially self-conscious device, belongs in our Repertoire; a neat example is offered in the following litany, recited by the Daughters of Erin in the 'Circe' episode of *Ulysses:*

> Kidney of Bloom, pray for us.
> Flower of the Bath, pray for us.
> Mentor of Menton, pray for us.
> Canvasser for the Freeman, pray for us.
> Charitable Mason, pray for us.
> Wandering Soap, pray for us.
> Sweets of Sin, pray for us.
> Music without Words, pray for us.
> Reprover of the Citizen, pray for us.
> Friend of all Frillies, pray for us.
> Potato Preservative against Plague and Pestilence,
>   pray for us.   (p. 488)

The first line of this passage designates the 'Calypso' episode; the second is an emblem of 'Lotus-eaters;' and so on, through 'Hades,' 'Aeolus,' 'Lestrygonians,' 'Scylla and Charybdis,' 'Wandering Rocks,' 'Sirens,' 'Cyclops,' 'Nausicaa,' 'Oxen of the Sun,' and 'Circe' itself. In Robbe-Grillet's *Dans le labyrinthe,* the painting on the wall which initiates that novel's action additionally provides a *mise-en-abyme* of the novel's structure. *Mises-en-abyme* function like Sterne's line-graphs in *Tristram Shandy:* by drawing our attention to the novel's overall structure, they remind us that that structure has been consciously, artificially contrived. By representing metonymically the work's own principles of organization, the *mise-en-abyme* reinforces the self-conscious novel's dramatization of its own process of composition. It offers yet another means by which the novel refers to itself.

* * *

Characters in self-conscious novels tend to be less convincing than other novelistic characters, and are clearly meant to be so. "All the puppets in this book whinge sooner or later, except Murphy, who is not a puppet," the narrator of Samuel Beckett's *Murphy* tells us.[1] Characters must obviously be plausible and sympathetic enough to engage and sustain the reader's interest, but self-conscious novels at times wilfully deprive their characters of these qualities. In *Gravity's Rainbow,* for instance, the apparent protagonist Tyrone Slothrop simply disintegrates as a character well before the novel's conclusion. Such an anomaly makes one wonder, at the least, what the novelist is up to. As Sharon Spencer has noted, "[. . .]character is likely altogether to disappear in a composition that is preoccupied with itself *as a composition.*"[2]

The use of grotesque or comical names for characters is a related device by which the self-conscious novel dehumanizes its characters. Recktall Brown and Agnes Deigh, in *The Recognitions,* or the Russian thief Nicolai Ripov in *Gravity's Rainbow,* for example, automatically lose a great deal of their believability as characters in direct consequence of the names their authors have given them. The frequent use of doppelgangers is yet another aspect of characterization by means of which the self-conscious novel draws attention to its own fictionality.[3] In much the same manner that the *mise-en-abyme* shrinks the whole novel's structure into an episode within the novel, the doppelganger procedure permits the novelist to parody, or to render conspicuously symmetrical, the actions of the characters within the book. Hermann and Felix in Nabokov's *Despair* and Oliveira and Traveler in Cortázar's *Hopscotch* are typical.

Characters in self-conscious fictions tend also to be aware of their fictional status as characters, and are given to speaking back to their authors, often in a critical tone. Pirandello's *Six Characters in Search of an Author* familiarized theatre audiences with the dramatic equivalent of this

---

1. Samuel Beckett, *Murphy* (1938; New York: Grove Press, 1957), p. 122. "Whinge" is not a typo.
2. Sharon Spencer, *Space, Time and Structure in the Modern Novel* (New York: New York University Press, 1971), p. 6.
3. This has been previously noted by Robert Alter in his *Partial Magic: The Novel as a Self-Conscious Genre* (Berkeley: University of California Press, 1975).

reflexive device. Molly Bloom's plea to "Jamesy" not only echoes Don Quixote's criticisms of Cid Hamete Benegali, but also prefigures the opening of John Updike's *Bech: A Book,* in which the fictional protagonist addresses a letter to Updike himself:

Dear John,
    Well, if you must commit the artistic indecency of writing about a writer, better I suppose about me than about you.[1]

As we examine individual self-conscious novels more closely, several intellectual and imagistic *themes* become prominent by dint of their recurrence. Foremost among these is the element of self-parody—the self-conscious novel challenging its own presuppositions by ridiculing its own procedures. Often this self-parody is accompanied by a thematic skepticism concerning the efficacy of language itself, as is seen most clearly in Beckett's nihilistic fictions or in Oliveira's rather didactic insistence, in Cortázar's *Hopscotch,* upon "man's rape by the word."[2] Language would pose no threat, of course, were we not in danger of confusing our words with the things we mean by them; and for this and other reasons, the ancient interplay between "reality" and "illusion" enjoys salience among typically self-conscious themes. By truthfully acknowledging its mimetic falsity, the self-depicting fiction opens the door to a host of paradoxes—making of paradox itself another essential theme in the Repertoire. Mirrors, incest, and masturbation recur uncannily in these novels—as physical, psycho-social, and sexual images, respectively, of reflexivity itself. Finally, Death—the great breaker of Life's illusion, as self-consciousness breaks the illusion of fiction—performs a crucial function in these novels, not only as the ineluctable end to all our stories, but also as the standard against which all human endeavor may seem but a brief and inconsequential pretense. As Robert Alter has observed, "it is the tension between artifice and that which annihilates artifice that gives the finest self-conscious novels their sense of urgency in the midst of play."[3]

None of these techniques, of course, is the exclusive property of the self-conscious novel, but they constitute what Wittgenstein would term the "family characteristics" of fictions that depict themselves. Although

1. John Updike, *Bech: A Book* (New York: Knopf, 1970), p. v.
2. Julio Cortázar, *Hopscotch* (1963); trans. from the Spanish by Gregory Rabassa (New York: Random House, 1966; New York: Avon, 1975), Chap. 19, p. 90.
3. Alter, *Partial Magic,* p. 235.

still finer discriminations may be required for the close reading of individual texts, the following outline summarizes and adds a few features to those already discussed:

THE REPERTOIRE OF REFLEXIVITY

Narration:
1. Narrators visibly engaged in the act of composition.
2. Reminders of the author in control behind a succession of narrators.
3. Direct address to the reader, *as* reader.
4. Textual self-reference; that is, other reminders that the book is a book.
5. Overt and eccentric moralization.
6. *Verfremdungseffekt;* the intentionally unconvincing rendering of character and action.
7. Description that de-visualizes.
8. Ostentatious manipulation of point-of-view.
9. Abrupt transitions between scenes.
10. Contradictions and "false" scenes.
11. "Unaccountable" disruptions of chronological sequence.

Style:
12. Conspicuously artificial styles, especially Euphuism.
13. Manifest incongruities of style and sense.
14. Linguistic opacity.
15. "Parabasis;" "a sudden revelation of the discontinuity between two rhetorical codes."[1]
16. "Foregrounding;"[2] the hypertrophy of style at the expense of story.
17. Use of non-referential language, including incantations.
18. Use of polysemous language, including puns, anagrams, and palindromes.

Structure:
19. Conspicuous subordination of the plot to artificial generative principles.
20. "Spatial form;"[3] narrative structures that are perceived spatially, as if in a single moment of time, by means of "reflexive reference."
21. "Architectonic" or "closed" structures, which "may claim near-total freedom from the laws of reality."[4]
22. *Mises-en-abyme.*

1. Paul de Man, "The Purloined Ribbon," *Glyph,* 1 (1977), 48 n.
2. Tony Tanner, *City of Words: American Fiction 1950–1970* (London: Jonathan Cape, 1971), pp. 20–27.
3. The term comes from Joseph Frank, "Spatial Form in Modern Literature" (1945), in his *The Widening Gyre: Crisis and Mastery in Modern Literature* (New Brunswick, N.J.: Rutgers University Press, 1963), pp. 3–62.
4. The term and its definition come from Sharon Spencer, *Space, Time and Structure in the Modern Novel,* p. 27.

23. Infinite regresses of structure; endo- and exo-narratives.[1]

Characterization:

24. Dehumanization of character.
25. Characters aware of their fictional status; addressing their author, etc.
26. Doppelgangers of parodic or symmetric intent.
27. Grotesque or comical names.

Themes:

28. Thematic concern with the relations between fiction and reality.
29. Deliberate and overt resistance to the traditions and conventions of literary naturalism.
30. Inclusion in the text of literary criticism of the text.
31. Self-parody.
32. Paradox.
33. Thematic images of reflexivity, both in physical setting (facing mirrors, concentric rings, etc.) and in reflexive behavior by the characters (incest, masturbation, repetition of one's past; etc.).
34. Death, rendered both as destroyer of illusions and as creator of the need for fictions.
35. Intimations of fiction as a self-contained game.
36. Celebration of the imagination's freedom to transcend the stubborn facts of reality.

To answer our question at the start of this chapter, we now see that *not* any story is suitable for the mode of self-consciousness. This list makes it clear that only those narratives that are in some sense about *themselves* as well as about their ostensible subjects will be endowed appropriately by the features we have identified. Fictions that tell their stories without directly confronting their own ontology will not draw extensively from this repertoire.

The self-conscious novel bears a particular set of relations to writer, reader, and real world that distinguishes it from other novels. The intellectual, emotional, and esthetic effect of the self-conscious novel's insistence upon its own artifice is fundamentally and demonstrably different from that of a novel which preserves its illusion of life inviolate. It is in fact a distinct and legitimate genre. Its repertoire of narrational, stylistic, structural, characterizational, and thematic techniques is broad yet capable of definition. Additionally, the self-conscious novel is, as a genre, the inheritor and result of a specific literary tradition. Its historical development will be explored in the chapters that follow.

1. The term "endo-narratives" is used by Robert Martin Adams, *Afterjoyce: Studies in Fiction After* Ulysses (New York: Oxford University Press, 1977), p. 51.

Chapter III

The Self-Conscious Tradition

T HE history of the novel begins and ends in self-consciousness. As Robert Alter has shown, *Don Quixote* first poked fun at other books, and then went on to talk about itself. "The novel begins out of an erosion of belief in the authority of the written word, and it begins with Cervantes."[1] Whether or not *Don Quixote* was in fact the first novel, Alter's demonstration of the work's essential self-consciousness is perceptive and convincing. Scenes such as those in which Don Quixote is shown reading the book in which his own activities are described, and challenging the author's veracity, emphasize the extent to which Cervantes's novel is concerned with the problem of distinguishing its own fiction from the reality it purports to describe. The book's deliberate multiplication of narrators behind narrators keeps the reader aware of the essential fictitiousness of the represented action. And the novel's events, while delightfully satisfying in themselves, serve also as metaphors of the ontological problems of the novel itself.

But starting with Cervantes is perhaps not going back far enough. In *The World and the Book* (1971), Gabriel Josipovici suggests that literature's rejection of verisimilitude in order to confront its own fictionality may be seen at work in the medieval allegories of Langland and Dante. Indeed, self-conscious literature was composed in classical times, as Aristotle's strictures against it confirm. The term *parabasis,* in fact, originally referred to that section of the Greek comedies where the chorus directly addressed the audience in the poet's name, often without reference to the action of the drama. We cannot, therefore, locate the beginning of the self-conscious tradition more precisely than to say that self-consciousness existed in literature long before the novel itself developed into the form in which we know it. Rabelais's *Gargantua and Pantagruel* (1532–34), for example, is not yet a novel but, as Josipovici has shown,[2] it is clearly self-conscious.

1. Robert Alter, *Partial Magic: The Novel as a Self-Conscious Genre* (Berkeley: University of California Press, 1975), p. 3.
2. Gabriel Josipovici, *The World and the Book: A Study of Modern Fiction* (London: Macmillan, 1971).

The great originators of the self-conscious novel in English were Fielding and Sterne. We have already mentioned the crucial importance of "Fielding" as the highly visible narrator of *Tom Jones* (1749) to the success of that novel. By dramatizing within the novel its own implied author, Fielding discovered a means of reminding his readers of his story's essential inventedness, at the same time that he allowed them to thrill to that story's unfolding. The intrusive narrator's implicit assurances that the story will end happily allowed Fielding to betray the illusoriness of his fiction in a way that guaranteed the illusion's success. It is only in the best of self-conscious novels that this tension is so skillfully maintained and exploited.

A fine follower of Fielding, Laurence Sterne has been called "the great *jusqu'auboutiste* of the self-conscious novel."[1] We can best see Sterne's artful display of his own art in *Tristram Shandy* (1759–67) if we distinguish three discrete "levels" of action going on simultaneously in the novel. The incidents of Tristram's conception, birth, and breeching and uncle Toby's acquisition of modesty may be said to constitute the *first* level of action. Tristram's laughable but ultimately successful efforts to tell the story of these events constitute a *second,* perhaps "higher" level. On a *third* level is the "story" of our own responses to our reading of *Tristram Shandy,* to which our attention is drawn by the novel's dramatization within its pages of a variety of implied readers.

> What these perplexities of my uncle Toby were,—'tis impossible for you to guess;—If you could,—I should blush; not as a relation,—not as a man,—nor even as a woman,—but I should blush as an author; inasmuch as I set no small store by myself upon this very account, that my reader has never yet been able to guess at any thing.   (Bk. I, sec. 25)

Sterne's narrative, by dramatizing the reader's ignorance (and, elsewhere, the reader's own sexual hobby-horse), makes our experience of the novel a part of the novel itself. As we have seen, self-conscious novels characteristically employ this device to achieve a particularly close relation between reader and text.

Curiously, the novel's first-level events—that is, the doings of Tristram's father and mother, of his uncle Toby, and of Tristram himself as an infant—are consistently deprived of their logical consequences. During Tristram's entry into the world, for example, his nose, we are told, is

---

1. Alter, *Partial Magic,* p. 31.

"crushed [. . .] as flat as a pancake to his face" (Bk. III, Ch. 27). Despite Slawkenbergius's claim that a problematic proboscis rarely escapes notice, however, mention is never made of Tristram's supposed deformity in the narrative of his later life and travels. Instead, Sterne uses the episode as a pretext for dramatizing his characters' hobby-horses:

> Did ever man, brother Toby, cried my father, raising himself upon his elbow, and turning himself round to the opposite side of the bed, where my uncle Toby was sitting in his old fringed chair, with his chin resting upon his crutch—did ever a poor unfortunate man, brother Toby, cried my father, receive so many lashes?—The most I ever saw given, quoth my uncle Toby (ringing the bell at the bed's head for Trim) was to a grenadier, I think in Mackay's regiment.   (Bk. IV, Ch. 3)

Similarly, when Tristram is accidentally circumcised, the extent of the damage done is obscured rather than indicated; the violence done to the boy's feelings is barely mentioned; and the effect of the accident upon his later life is never alluded to. The event is deprived of any objective value of its own, and used instead to illuminate the characters' peculiar responses to it:

> —Nothing is left, cried Susannah,—nothing is left—for me, but to run my country.   (Bk. V, Ch. 17)

> —I would be picquetted to death, cried the corporal, as he concluded Susannah's story before I would suffer the woman to come to any harm,—'twas my fault, an' please your honour,—not hers.
> Corporal Trim, replied my uncle Toby, putting on his hat which lay upon the table,—if any thing can be said to be a fault, when the service absolutely requires it should be done,—'tis I certainly who deserve the blame,—you obeyed your orders.   (Bk. V, Ch. 21)

> —If it be but done right,—said my father, turning to the Section—*de sede vel subjecto circumcisionis,*—for he had brought up *Spenser de Legibus Hebraeorum Ritualibus*—and *Maimonides,* in order to confront and examine us altogether.   (Bk. V, Ch. 27)

A display of Susannah's self-interest, Trim's chivalry and eloquence, uncle Toby's selflessness and martial obsession, and Walter Shandy's attempt at erudite philosophic remove—this is what is made of Tristram's circumcision. Even events possessing veritable objective reality outside the world of the novel are represented within that world uniquely in terms of their relation to characters' psychological tics: "[. . .] The peace of Utrecht was within an ace of creating the same shyness betwixt my uncle and his hobby-horse, as it did betwixt the queen and the rest of the confederating powers" (Bk. VI, Ch. 34). It is in this sense that we are to read Sterne's epigraph to his book, "It is not deeds, but opinions concerning deeds, which disturb men."

In suppressing the logical consequences of the events in order to show the hobby-horses in action, Sterne subordinates the first-level action to the purposes of characterization. The result is to fortify the effect of "amiable humor,"[1] which the characters produce by the combination of an extravagant obsession with the essential good will with which that obsession is expressed. In parallel fashion, Tristram's antics in his role as narrator are chosen so as to dramatize his own hobby-horsed mental processes, which in turn produce this same effect of amiable humor on the novel's second level:

> Here—but why here—rather than in any other part of my story—I am not able to tell:—but here it is—my heart stops me to pay thee, my dear uncle Toby, once for all, the tribute I owe thy goodness.—Here let me thrust my chair aside, and kneel down upon the ground, whilst I am pouring forth the warmest sentiment of love for thee, and veneration for the excellency of thy character, that ever virtue and nature kindled in a nephew's bosom.—Peace and comfort rest for evermore upon thy head!—Thou enviedst no man's opinions—Thou blackenedst no man's character—devouredst no man's bread: gently, with faithful Trim behind thee, didst thou amble round the little circle of thy pleasures, jostling no creature in thy way:—for each one's sorrows, thou hadst a tear,—for each man's need, thou hadst a shilling.
>
> While I am worth one, to pay a weeder—thy path from thy door to thy bowling-green shall never be grown up.—Whilst there is a rood and a half of land in the Shandy family, thy fortifications, my dear uncle Toby, shall never be demolished.   (Bk. III, Ch. 34)

When Tristram thus pays tribute to his uncle Toby, his sentiments are both generous and noble and yet so extravagantly expressed as to yield the same amiable humor created when uncle Toby apostrophizes the fly: "go, poor devil, get thee gone, why should I hurt thee?—This world is surely wide enough to hold both thee and me" (Bk. II, Ch. 12). This effect is further enforced on the novel's third level of action, where the reader's own responses to *Tristram Shandy's* bawdry are dramatized so as to yield yet more amiable humor.

> It is a terrible misfortune for this same book of mine, but more so to the Republic of letters; so that my own is quite swallowed up in the consideration

1. Stuart M. Tave, *The Amiable Humorist* (Chicago: University of Chicago Press, 1960), esp. Ch. III, pp. 91–180.

of it,—that this self-same vile pruriency for fresh adventures in all things, has got so strongly into our habit and humour,—and so wholly intent are we upon satisfying the impatience of our concupiscence that way,—that nothing but the gross and more carnal parts of a composition will go down.
(Bk. I, Ch. 20)

[. . .] Heaven is witness, how the world has revenged itself upon me for leaving so many openings to equivocal strictures—and for depending so much as I have done, all along, upon the cleanliness of my readers' imaginations.   (Bk. III, Ch.31)

We come across a "deleted" phrase in the course of the narrative, or we read a passage that is susceptible of sexual interpretation, and we follow our mind's strongest impulse by interpolating the bawdy expression or smiling at the dirty joke. Then we are told that no such impropriety was intended, and that if we saw smut in what we read, then the smut was in our minds; and we are forced to agree. We recognize, of course, that the ambiguity is intentional, but we cannot deny that we ourselves—hobbyhorsed with thoughts of sex and thirsting for "fresh adventures in all things"—jumped as single-mindedly to the sexual interpretation as uncle Toby jumps to the conclusion that the "bridge" of which Dr. Slop speaks is intended for his own fortifications (Bk. III, Ch. 26). At the end of a lengthy excursus "upon the various uses and seasonable applications of long noses," Tristram warns the reader,

—Now don't let Satan, my dear girl, in this chapter, take advantage of any one spot of rising ground to get astride of your imagination, if you can any ways help it; or if he is so nimble as to slip on—let me beg of you, like an unbacked filly, to frisk it, to squirt it, to jump it, to rear it, to bound it—and to kick it, with long kicks and short kicks, till, like Tickletoby's mare, you break a strap or a crupper, and throw his worship into the dirt.
(Bk. III, Ch. 36)

We cannot when reading this passage but be amused by the sexual connotations of its imagery. And yet at the same time the passage cites our very recognition of those images as evidence of our own sexual obsession. Thus our responses to Tristram's narrative are dramatized so as to make amiably humorous our own obsessive hobby-horse. No doubt it is at least partially for the sake of producing this effect that all of the major events in the novel's first-level action have ultimately to do with sex: Tristram's conception, birth, and circumcision, and uncle Toby's acquisition of modesty.

I have dwelt on *Tristram Shandy* at such length because it is, in so many respects, a self-conscious novel *par excellence*. Its influence upon the later tradition is inestimably great. In foreign literatures alone Shandean self-consciousness may be seen at work in fictions so diverse as Diderot's *Jacques le fataliste* (1773, pub. 1798) and Viktor Shklovsky's *Sentimental-'noye putyeshestviye* (1923, trans. 1970 as *A Sentimental Journey*).[1]

*　　*　　*

For the historian of the self-conscious novel, as for José Ortega y Gasset in "The Dehumanization of Art," the nineteenth century was something of an aberration.[2] It marked the triumph of the "realistic" novel, which eschewed any suggestion of contingency behind the façade of its illusion. Balzac's *Comédie humaine,* for example, was designed to seem as real a world as that in which its readers lived. The esthetic of realism forbade any suggestion that the novelist was inventing his story; rather his role, if it was dramatized at all, was that of observer at a pre-existent scene. In his critical writings, Emile Zola even went so far as to deny that the novelist exercised any imagination at all:

> The greatest praise that could formerly be given to a novelist was to say that "he had imagination." To-day this praise would be looked upon almost as a criticism. This only goes to show that all the conditions of the novel have changed. Imagination is no longer the predominating quality of the novelist. [. . .] I insist upon this fall of the imagination, because in it I see the characteristic of the modern novel. [. . .] All the efforts of the writer tend to hide the imaginary under the real.[3]

We should not allow, of course, the lure of historical generalizations to lead us to overlook those nineteenth-century novelists who did in fact preserve the tradition of self-consciousness handed down by Fielding and Sterne. Trollope's assurances to the reader, as in *Barchester Towers,* that he will take care to have things work out properly, or Thackeray's claims in *Vanity Fair* that his fiction is effectively a kind of puppet show, make clear that the practices of self-consciousness did not fall into com-

1. These works are discussed respectively by Robert Alter, *Partial Magic,* pp. 57–83; and by Ronald Sukenick, "The New Tradition in Fiction," in *Surfiction: Fiction Now . . . and Tomorrow,* ed. Raymond Federman (Chicago: The Swallow Press, 1975), pp. 35–45.

2. José Ortega y Gasset, "The Dehumanization of Art," in *The Dehumanization of Art and Other Essays on Art, Culture, and Literature,* trans. Helene Weyl (Princeton, N.J.: Princeton University Press, 1948).

3. Emile Zola, *The Experimental Novel* (1880), trans. Belle M. Sherman (1893), cited in *The Theory of the Novel,* ed. Philip Stevick (New York: The Free Press, 1967), pp. 394–95.

plete desuetude. The overt moralization that one finds throughout the nineteenth-century infallibly reminds the reader of the presence of the author. And yet it is undeniable that the self-conscious novel was eclipsed[1] in the nineteenth century by the prevailing notion that the novel can and must be a direct imitation of life.

To account for the dominance of this realistic mode, we may briefly consider Wilhelm Worringer's hypothesis, in *Abstraction and Empathy,* as to why all art forms periodically oscillate between the poles of naturalism and non-naturalism.[2] Worringer suggests that naturalistic art expresses a Weltanschauung in which man feels himself to be living in harmony with the cosmos. The arts of classical Greece and of the Renaissance exemplify such naturalism. Non-naturalistic art (Byzantine art, Romanesque sculpture) occurs when the felt relationship between man and the universe is one of disequilibrium and dissonance.[3] From this perspective, the self-conscious novel may be seen as a non-naturalistic mode expressing a disharmonious Weltanschauung, while the naturalistic nineteenth-century novel expresses man's sense of rightful belonging in the cosmos. Efforts such as Worringer's to account for the forms of art by reference to the cultural climate in which they are created illuminate certain issues, but sometimes such "explanations" merely restate the problem in other terms. In this case, for instance, we are left with the question of why the Weltanschauung should have so sharply changed in the first place. One way out of this box might be to consider the historical fluctuations in our confidence in our *knowledge* of the universe, which can be shown to be bolstered by technological advances or sapped by newly found reasons to doubt. Culture in the nineteenth century was charged with a positivistic optimism about its ability to find out what makes man and the universe tick. This optimism may have encouraged the literary culture to use the novel as a tool, one designed both to acquire such knowledge experimentally, and to disseminate it confidently.

The resurgence of self-depicting fiction in the twentieth century may also be viewed in terms of the cultural climate—as a reaction in print to

1. The term is Robert Alter's. See *Partial Magic,* Ch. 4, "The Self-Conscious Novel in Eclipse," pp. 84–137.

2. Wilhelm Worringer, *Abstraction and Empathy: A Contribution to the Psychology of Style* (1908; New York: International University Press, 1953).

3. I have profited from Joseph Frank's discussion of Worringer in "Spatial Form in Modern Literature" (1945), in *The Widening Gyre: Crisis and Mastery in Modern Literature* (New Brunswick, N.J.: Rutgers University Press, 1963), pp. 3–62.

the emergence of film as a narrative medium. As art historians know well, once photography began to furnish ideally realistic images of real life, the art of painting turned inward, forsaking pure depiction so as to explore the possibilities of its medium for its own sake. Similarly, in the narrative arts, film and then TV have to a considerable extent supplanted prose as the most immediately accessible and popular way of being told a story. Innovative prose fiction, I would like to suggest, has turned back to focussing upon its own medium (language and its artifices) in response both to film and to the popular (cinematic) novel. That self-conscious writers are supremely aware of film's pre-emption of story-telling is suggested by the fact that the first person to try to run a commercial cinema in Dublin was none other than James Joyce.

The publication in 1922 of Joyce's *Ulysses* began a new era in the art of the novel, by no means the least significant aspect of which consisted in the readmission of self-depiction as a fictional mode. *Ulysses* is clearly not exclusively a self-conscious novel; or rather, it *is* a profoundly self-conscious novel while it is also, generically, many other things at the same time. We would do well, that is, to keep in mind Northrop Frye's conclusion that *Ulysses* is a "complete prose epic" subsuming all four forms of prose fiction: novel, confession, anatomy, and romance.[1] The crucial importance of *Ulysses* to a study of the self-conscious novel lies in the demonstrably premeditated manner in which the novel's insistence on its own artifice methodically varies from chapter to chapter. (For this reason the next chapter of this study is devoted to a close reading of Joyce's great novel.)

The influence upon subsequent fiction of the self-consciousness of *Ulysses* is not easily exaggerated. In his study entitled *Afterjoyce: Studies in Fiction After* Ulysses, Robert Martin Adams even opines that

> Wherever one finds, in modern fiction, writing that seems aimed at rousing admiration for itself rather than attracting sympathy to characters or opening a clear window on a scene, one can suspect the influence of Joyce.[2]

In many senses Joyce is the horizon beyond which our novelists have yet to go, and countless novels written since *Ulysses* and *Finnegans Wake* have

1. Northrop Frye, *Anatomy of Criticism: Four Essays* (Princeton, N.J.: Princeton University Press, 1957; New York: Atheneum, 1967).

2. Robert Martin Adams, *Afterjoyce: Studies in Fiction After* Ulysses (New York: Oxford University Press, 1977), p. 62.

tended merely to flesh out various possibilities that Joyce had already indicated.

The impetus which Joyce gave to the self-conscious tradition may most immediately be seen in the work of two other Irish writers, Samuel Beckett and Flann O'Brien.

Where Joyce proceeded by addition, Beckett performed subtraction, but the terms of their arithmetic were the same. Where Joyce had shown that the bond between words and the things they name was elastic, and might be stretched and restored at the author's will, Beckett drove in a cutting wedge to show that word and thing were irreparably sundered. The process is best seen in Beckett's English novels, especially *Murphy* and *Watt*.[2] In *Murphy,* the reader is encouraged to share Murphy's solipsistic doubts as to the reality of the world he performs in. Repeated reminders that Murphy's associates are merely "puppets" reinforce the dehumanization of character typical of the self-conscious novel; so too do such descriptions as this of Murphy's girlfriend Celia:

Age.	Unimportant.
Head.	Small and round.
Eyes.	Green.
Complexion.	White.
Hair.	Yellow.
Features.	Mobile.
Neck.	$13\frac{3}{4}''$.
Upper arm.	$11''$.
Forearm.	$9\frac{1}{2}''$.
Wrist.	$6''$.
Bust.	$34''$.
Waist.	$27''$.
Hips, etc.	$35''$.
Thigh.	$21\frac{3}{4}''$.
Knee.	$13\frac{3}{4}''$.
Calf.	$13''$.
Ankle.	$8\frac{1}{4}''$.
Instep.	Unimportant.
Height.	$5'$ $4''$.
Weight.	123 lbs. (p. 10)

For Beckett, characters are less volitional agents than they are figments to be pummelled in effigy; the ultimate fate of Murphy himself is a case in point.

2. Samuel Beckett, *Murphy* (1938; New York: Grove Press, 1957); *Watt* (Paris: Olympia Press, 1953; New York: Grove Press, 1959).

Some hours later Cooper took the packet of ash [Murphy, cremated] from his pocket, where earlier in the evening he had put it for greater security, and threw it angrily at a man who had given him great offense. It bounced, burst, off the wall on to the floor, where at once it became the object of much dribbling, passing, trapping, shooting, punching, heading and even some recognition from the gentleman's code. By closing time the body, mind, and soul of Murphy were freely distributed over the floor of the saloon; and before another dayspring greyened the earth had been swept away with the sand, the beer, the butts, the glass, the matches, the spits, the vomit.   (p. 275)

Beckett's novels are generically self-conscious in that they reflect the appropriate stylistic and structural elements as well as those of theme and character. Beckett is a great and often comic practitioner of parabasis, the marked disruption of style which reminds the reader of the performing artificer. One sentence from *Malone Dies* should suffice as an example:

A stream at long intervals bestrid—but to hell with all this fucking scenery.   (p. 277)

Beckett's novels also characteristically display a conspicuous symmetry of structure, such as the *Wake*-like annularity of *Watt,* which derives not from any natural necessity but from the self-conscious intervention of the implied author.

Flann O'Brien, a writer of lesser stature than Beckett, derived from Joyce the method of simultaneous performances which Beckett eschewed. *At Swim-Two-Birds* uses the frame-tale of a young would-be novelist to enclose three other synchronous narratives, each in a different style and mode, each nested within another. The mythological hero, Finn MacCool, does double duty as an elegiac raconteur whose listeners are co-characters with him in a novel written by one Dermot Trellis, himself a character invented by the unnamed narrator of the frame-tale. The fictionality of this "ground level" narrator is in turn asserted by the notice to the reader on the novel's first page:

All the characters represented in this book, including the first person singular, are entirely fictitious and bear no relation to any person living or dead.[1]

The structure of *At Swim-Two-Birds* thus points towards the infinite regression which becomes even more prevalent in later self-conscious novels, and which may assume the imagery of nesting boxes, wheels within wheels, mirrors reflecting mirrors, a *mise-en-abyme* itself *mise-en-*

1. Flann O'Brien [Brian Nolan], *At Swim-Two-Birds* (1939; New York: Plume, 1976), p. 7.

abyme. When one level not merely duplicates but also parodies the level before, the effect may be a constant undercutting of the novel's own implications,[1] thereby isolating the novel ever more profoundly from the world outside. Such seeming isolation immediately raises the question of narrative plausibility, which the narrator of *At Swim-Two-Birds* addresses, as we have seen, in characteristically direct fashion:

> In reply to an inquiry, it was explained that a satisfactory novel should be a self-evident sham to which the reader could regulate at will the degree of his credulity.   (p. 33)

The first post-Joycean self-conscious novel to use the novel-within-a-novel as a means of challenging the containing novel's suppositions was André Gide's *Les Faux-monnayeurs* (1925). Edouard's concerns, as he composes his novel, echo the concerns of Gide's novel itself, reminding us that it was Gide who first pondered the duplication of novelistic structures *"en abyme," "à l'échelle des personnages."*[2] The version of *Les Faux-monnayeurs* which Edouard contemplates would itself be a generically self-conscious novel, insistent on the irreality of its subject matter and determined to assert the fictitiousness of its own illusion:

> —Est-ce parce que, de tous les genres littéraires, discourait Edouard, le roman reste le plus libre, le plus *lawless . . . ,* est-ce, peut-être pour cela, par peur de cette liberté même (car les artistes qui soupirent le plus après la liberté, sont les plus affolés souvent, dès qu'ils l'obtiennent) que le roman, toujours, s'est si craintivement cramponné à la réalité? Et je ne parle pas seulement du roman français. Tout aussi bien que le roman anglais le roman russe, si échappé qu'il soit de la contrainte, s'asservit à la ressemblance. Le seul progrès qu'il envisage, c'est de se rapprocher encore plus du naturel. Il n'a jamais connu, le roman, cette "formidable érosion des contours," dont parle Nietzsche, et ce volontaire écartement de la vie, qui permirent le style, aux œuvres des dramaturges grecs par exemple, ou aux tragédies du XVIIᵉ siècle français. Connaissez-vous rien de plus parfait et de plus profondément humain que ces œuvres? Mais précisément, cela n'est humain que profondément; cela ne se pique pas de le paraître, ou du moins de paraître réel. Cela demeure une œuvre d'art. [. . .] Eh bien, je voudrais un roman qui serait à la fois aussi vrai, et aussi éloigné de la réalité, aussi particulier et aussi général à la fois, aussi humain et aussi fictif qu' *Athalie,* que *Tartuffe,* ou que *Cinna.*

1. The rhetorical implications of such constant under-cutting, and the vital question of where to stop in the reader's task of reconstructing the author's meaning, are cogently discussed in Wayne C. Booth, *A Rhetoric of Irony* (Chicago: University of Chicago Press, 1974), esp. Ch. 9, "Infinite Instabilities."

2. André Gide, *Journal* of 1893, in *Œuvres complètes d'André Gide* (Paris: N.R.F., 1932), I, 511.

—Et . . . le sujet de ce roman?

—Il n'en a pas, repartit Edouard brusquement. [. . .] Pour obtenir cet effet, suivez-moi, j'invente un personnage de romancier, que je pose en figure centrale; et le sujet du livre, si vous voulez, c'est précisément la lutte entre ce que lui offre la réalité et ce que, lui, prétend en faire.   (pp. 230–33)[1]

Edouard's novel would be "about" a novelist led astray by his own fictional illusions; while the reality of Edouard himself, as well as that of his fellow characters, is similarly destroyed by *intrusions* from the Gidean implied author, such as the chapter in which *"L'auteur juge ses personnages"* (pp. 274–78). By adapting the Sternean and Joycean reflexivity of structure, Gide is thus able to approximate a solution to the challenge of writing a Flaubertian *"livre sur rien"* which does not *"fait mourir d'ennui ses lecteurs."*

While the discussion here has focussed primarily on the extent of the self-conscious tradition in the English-language novel, that tradition has often fed upon equivalent traditions in other literatures, notably the French. That is why I have already mentioned Diderot and Gide and must now briefly mention Marcel Proust. *A la Recherche du temps perdu* is not properly a self-conscious novel, in that it never seeks to rupture the illusion of its narrative to suggest an author freely inventing fictitious creatures and deeds. But in *Le Temps retrouvé,* the novel's final book, a *thematic* self-consciousness comes to the fore, as the novel's "subject matter" becomes the book itself. Proust here combines reminders of the nov-

---

1. "Is it because the novel, of all literary *genres,* is the freest, the most *lawless,*" held forth Edouard, ". . . is it for that very reason, for fear of that very liberty (the artists who are always sighing after liberty are often the most bewildered when they get it), that the novel has always clung to reality with such timidity? And I am not speaking only of the French novel. It is the same with the English novel; and the Russian novel, for all its throwing off of constraints, is a slave to resemblance. The only progress it looks to is to get still nearer to nature. The novel has never known that 'formidable erosion of contours,' as Nietzsche calls it; that deliberate avoidance of life, which gave style to the works of the Greek dramatists, for instance, or to the tragedies of the French XVIIth century. Is there anything more perfectly and deeply human than these works? But that's just it—they are human only in their depths; they don't pride themselves on appearing so—or, at any rate, on appearing real. They remain works of art. [. . .] Well, I should like a novel which should be at the same time as true and as far from reality, as particular and at the same time as general, as human and as fictitious as *Athalie,* or *Tartuffe* or *Cinna.*"

"And . . . the subject of this novel?"

"It hasn't got one," answered Edouard brusquely. [. . .]In order to arrive at this effect—do you follow me?—I invent the character of a novelist, whom I make my central figure; and the subject of the book, if you must have one, is just that very struggle between what reality offers him and what he himself desires to make of it."

—*The Counterfeiters,* trans. from the French by Dorothy Bussy (New York: Vintage Books, 1973), pp. 185–88.

el's composition with assertions that that composition is mimetic. Just as with Stephen Dedalus of *A Portrait,* for whom the task of the artist is to transubstantiate the transient bread of daily existence into the radiant everliving body of art; so, for the Proustian novelist, art may "regain" time by restituting the losses time has inflicted. Like a self-conscious novel, Proust's work contains in explicit form the esthetic theory by which it seeks to be judged; the final book declares what art is good for only after having made dramatically clear what art is not good for. *Un Amour de Swann,* for example, may be read as an apologue designed to show the error of using *esthetic* values to achieve *practical* goals. By dint of such thematic considerations, Proust may be said to have prepared the way for one of the most respected authors of self-conscious novels in English since Joyce, Vladimir Nabokov.

The extent of Nabokov's influence on contemporary fiction is suggested by John Hawkes' remark, "Nabokov is the writer who nourishes and sustains us."[1] All of Nabokov's novels contain aspects of self-consciousness, and several of them contain all the generic elements I have identified. Most characteristic of his novels are the insistent reminders of the implied author lurking playfully behind his creation, no matter how authoritative or reliable the apparent narrator seems to be. On the surface, most of the novels seem acutely mimetic, the faithful and sympathetic rendering of naturalistic detail giving the narratives much of their distinctively rich color and texture. Yet in such hermetically sealed self-conscious works as *Pale Fire* and *The Real Life of Sebastian Knight* the meticulous descriptions are revealed to qualify utterly nonexistent worlds, places heartbreakingly beautiful, perhaps, but of no substance other than that of the author's and reader's imagination. Nabokov's repeated assertions outside his fiction that his work "has no social comment to make, no message to bring in its teeth"[2] underscore the self-conscious novel's denials that it addresses concerns of the external world. Chapter V of this study surveys the whole of Nabokov's oeuvre and focuses on his most complex novel, *Ada.*

Of comparable historical significance as an influence on the contemporary self-conscious novel are the "*ficciones*" of Jorge Luis Borges. Borges's short fictions are not so much stories as they are blueprints for stories—formulae by which any number of distinctive tales might be

---

1. This quote was reported to me by William Veeder.
2. Vladimir Nabokov, "Foreword" to *Despair* (New York: Capricorn, 1970), p. 8.

told. The *ficciones* dramatize the very paradox of fiction's link to life, portraying the world of books as a universe more inexhaustible than the one in which they are written. A fiction, for Borges, is not a representation *of* things, but an addition *to* them. The theme is dramatized in such fictions as "Tlön, Uqbar, Orbis Tertius,"[1] where wholly imaginary objects described in *"The First Encyclopedia of Tlön"* begin to appear in the real world. Behind this conceit, of course, lies Wilde's portrayal of life imitating art. Another typical Borgesian effect is the derealization of character which results when a character learns that he is in fact a fictional creation. Borges has acknowledged his debt to Cervantes for this procedure:

> Why does it disturb us that Don Quixote be a reader of the *Quixote* and Hamlet a spectator of *Hamlet*? These inversions suggest that if the characters of a fictional work can be readers or spectators, we, its readers or spectators, can be fictitious.[2]

Structurally, Borges's *ficciones* frequently take the form of the *regressus ad infinitum,* each narrative referring to potential endo- or exo-narratives which would contain or be contained within it. In the story entitled "The Circular Ruins," for instance, the nameless protagonist, who has spent his life imagining a fictional creature who will believe himself to be actual, suddenly realizes that he himself is precisely such an imagined creature. The story's concentric rings of meaning ripple outward to enclose its reader, challenging in the process our own complacent claim to reality.

The American novelist who has profited most apparently from the example of Borges is John Barth. While Barth's early novels, such as *End of the Road* and *The Floating Opera,* are essentially straightforward realistic narratives, his later work has exploited more and more of the resources of reflexivity. In *The Sot-Weed Factor* and in *Giles Goat-Boy,* the self-consciousness is largely confined to effects of style, and perhaps for this reason seems to be something of a fashionable flourish on otherwise traditional novels. However, in the short fiction of *Lost in the Funhouse,* in the three novellas called *Chimera,* and in Barth's epistolary novel *LETTERS,* the plot structures are themselves self-referential, and the resultant narratives are not only generically self-conscious but more fully satisfying as fictional creations as well. Barth combines (1) dramatizations of im-

1. Jorge Luis Borges, "Tlön, Uqbar, Orbis Tertius" (1941), in *Ficciones,* trans. Alastair Reid (New York: Grove Press, 1962), p. 17–35.
2. Jorge Luis Borges, "Partial Magic in the *Quixote*," cited by Alter, *Partial Magic,* p. 1.

plied authors engaged in the act of writing; (2) reminders to the reader of the activity of reading; (3) stylistic assertions of artifice; (4) ostentatious structural displays; (5) characters whose plights mirror those of the text; and (6) an insistent self-parody that undercuts every assertion *and* its denial. Barth inverts the Joycean practice of casting a modern story in classical shadows; instead, he retells classical stories in an aggressively modern idiom. He follows, perhaps with greater fidelity, Borges's advice that fiction to renew itself must not endeavor to model itself on life with ever greater acuity, but should emulate previous literature with new sophistication.

The central issue raised by these writers—Borges in such tales as "Pierre Menard, Author of *Don Quixote,*" Barth in his retelling of Scheherazade's, Perseus's, and Bellerophon's stories—and of prime importance for *all* self-conscious fiction is the issue of *originality*. Contemporary self-conscious novels regularly confront the perception that there is nothing so unoriginal as the quest for originality. The response of Borges, Barth, and others is to pursue originality by engaging fiction in a retracing of its own *origins*. The quest for originality assumes great thematic importance in William Gaddis's *The Recognitions,* discussed later in Chapter VI.

To document the history of the self-conscious novel into recent decades would require a catalog of several dozen popular and so-called experimental writers.[1] While self-consciousness is far from the dominant literary mode at present, it is clear that self-conscious novels are neither strange nor unfamiliar. What perhaps does go unrecognized is that generic self-consciousness is precisely what many contemporary novels have in common. Every one of Robbe-Grillet's so-called *nouveaux romans* is generically self-conscious. So are Julio Cortázar's *Hopscotch,* Robert Coover's *Pricksongs and Descants,* Richard Brautigan's *In Watermelon Sugar,* Kurt Vonnegut, Jr.'s *Breakfast of Champions,* Donald Barthelme's *The Dead Father,* John Irving's *The World According to Garp,* Tom Robbins's *Still Life with Woodpecker,* and Italo Calvino's *If On A Winter Night a Traveler.*

1. A useful, though far from complete bibliography of self-conscious novels may be found in Steven G. Kellman's interesting study, *The Self-Begetting Novel* (New York: Columbia University Press, 1980). Kellman defines his topic, much more narrowly than I do mine, as those novels that purport to have no human author and affect to have brought themselves into existence. Curiously, most of the texts that Kellman perceptively examines ultimately fail to meet his rather stringent criteria for "self-begetting."

I do not wish to make the imperialistic claim that all interesting contemporary novels fit into my category of the self-conscious, for then such a category would obviously be meaningless. Nor do I wish to claim that any artistic excellence inheres automatically in any generically self-conscious novel solely by virtue of its self-consciousness. Besides, the naturalistic traditions remain vital and productive. But the same interest in self-depiction that has led me to undertake this study is clearly being felt by many current writers of fiction. This is only to be expected, if cultural climates do exist. On the whole I share Robert Alter's estimation that "If this is the moment of the self-conscious novel, that is decidedly a mixed blessing."[1] As a concept and as a genre, though, the self-conscious novel makes salient fiction's dual nature—its ludic *and* its mimetic mission. It may thus enable us, as we next consider five modern exemplars of fiction's self-depiction, to make fine discriminations of effect and of value.

1. Alter, *Partial Magic,* p. 220.

Chapter IV

Getting Back at James Joyce

For his violations of literary propriety, society has taken its revenge upon James Joyce by making him respectable. First, an army of critics heaped upon him all the pomp that accompanies installation in the academic Pantheon. This has amounted to what Max Weber called the "routinization of charisma." Now, even the facts of Joyce's life are being rearranged to bring him into line. The current Penguin editions of *Dubliners, A Portrait of the Artist as a Young Man, Ulysses,* and *Finnegans Wake* inexplicably contain in their first page biographical sketch of Joyce this piece of blatant misinformation:

> He taught at a school in Dalkey until he married in 1904, when he and his wife went to Zurich and later Trieste, where Joyce taught languages in the Berlitz school.[1]

As any reader of Ellmann's life of Joyce knows, Joyce most emphatically did not marry Nora Barnacle before taking her out of Ireland, and made rather a point of "living in sin" with her for the next twenty-seven years.[2] Indeed, in 1905, when Joyce cabled to Dublin "Son born Jim," local wits claimed that the telegram included a second sentence: "Mother and bastard doing well."[3]

We should read the Penguin pseudo-biographical pastiche of Joyce's life, then, the same way that Leopold Bloom listened to the pseudo-sailor's yarns in the cabman's shelter: though paying close attention, "he wouldn't vouch for the actual facts, which quite possibly there was not one vestige of truth in."[4] Close attention and a little paranoia reveal that the revision of Joyce's life on the first page of his own books constitutes the most extreme measure yet in society's "recovery" of James Joyce. "They," as Thomas Pynchon calls them, are routinizing Joyce's charisma

---

1. (Harmondsworth and New York: Penguin Books, 1976, 1977, and 1985), p. 1 in all four books.

2. They also lived in Pola, Rome, and Trieste before, not after, Zurich. Richard Ellmann, *James Joyce* (New York: Oxford University Press, 1959).

3. Ellmann, *James Joyce*, p. 221.

4. James Joyce, *Ulysses* (Paris: Shakespeare and Co., 1922; New York: Random House, 1986), p. 508. All references are to the latter edition, and will be indicated by the letter *U*.

with a vengeance. With the same stolid disregard for particularities that branded Bloom as *l'homme moyen sensuel,* they have made Joyce into *un bon petit bourgeois,* when in fact he was nothing of the kind. He was, at least in his own eyes, closer to "the fiery-hearted revolutionary," as he called young Daedalus in *Stephen Hero.*[1]

Do such details of an author's private life *matter* to a just appreciation of his work? They do, if we accept Stephen's theories as *Ulysses* expounds and partially supports them. Stephen's "account" of *Hamlet* is an emphatically biographical one, as he speculates upon Ann Hathaway's sexual infidelities in order to "explain" the tone of Shakespeare's masterpiece. But even if Stephen's theories were shown to be dangerously reductive when generalized into critical principles, it is still true that *Ulysses* itself invites Stephen's brand of criticism. Few novels draw attention to the performing novelist more persuasively than *Ulysses.* If we are curious about the facts of Joyce's life, if we feel that familiarity with his biography is essential to a full appreciation of his work, it is because Joyce's works themselves portray the circumstances of the artist's life as a matter of key importance to any art he may create. In *Stephen Hero,* Stephen's esthetic theory endeavors

> to establish the relations which must subsist between the literary image, the work of art itself, and that energy which had imagined and fashioned it, that centre of conscious, re-acting, particular life, the artist.   (*SH* 77)

It is worth noting that in this sentence it is the lexical item "the artist" which receives all the rhetorical embellishment.

Whether it be to validate Stephen's theories, then, or for some larger purpose, Joyce's work in general and *Ulysses* in particular make us feel the crucial importance of the artist's identity to any work of art. Stephen's ideal dramatic artist, "invisible, refined out of existence," may absent himself to pare his nails offstage; but the narrator of the 'Cyclops' episode, by urinating onstage in the midst of telling his story (*U* 275), shows himself to be less than refined and his own author not quite refined out of existence. I should like to turn, then, to examine in detail two episodes of *Ulysses,* 'Aeolus' and 'The Oxen of the Sun,' to see how the assertion of the artist's identity takes place, by means of self-consciousness, at the stylistic and structural levels of Joyce's major narrative.

---

1. James Joyce, *Stephen Hero* (New York: New Directions, 1944, 1963), p. 80. All references are to the latter edition of *Stephen Hero,* and will be indicated by the letters *SH.*

'Aeolus': Democratic Ethics

'Aeolus' is the first episode in *Ulysses* that confronts the reader with in-eluctable opacities of style. From 'Telemachus' through 'Hades', the nov-el's prose is essentially transparent, revealing the characters' actions and thoughts without drawing attention to itself. The narration of events until 'Aeolus' has been consistent and reliable; the shifts into *monologue intérieur*, potentially disturbing to the illusion of a realistic novel, have been introduced so gradually as to leave unruffled the semblance of un-mediated reality. Most visible in obtrusive headlines, and more subtly in other self-conscious artifices of style, the prose of 'Aeolus' insistently draws attention to itself as a creation of the artistic imagination.

The headlines, which interrupt the text several times on each page, function in part as chapter titles do: they suggest the presence of an ordering intelligence behind the narrative. In Pater's *Marius the Epicu-rean,* for example, the frequent chapter titles establish a distance between the events and the author's evaluation of these which we would not oth-erwise perceive. Joyce eschewed chapter titles in his novels much as he eschewed inverted commas in the rendering of dialogue; the latter, in his view, impose an unwanted obstacle between the reader and the speech. Yet such obstacles manifestly abound in 'Aeolus.'

There are, furthermore, suggestions that the implied author of the headlines differs in outlook and intention from the narrator of the text itself. Often the headlines bring into prominence something barely men-tioned in the passage so headed, as for example, THE WEARER OF THE CROWN (*U* 96). The resultant incongruity poses in the reader's mind the question of who is writing these headlines and for what pur-pose. The issue is compounded by headlines that draw the reader into complicity with their author, in ironic diminution of the text itself. ONLY ONCE MORE THAT SOAP (*U* 101) implies an author familiar with but archly superior to the whole of *Ulysses'* action, just as LET US HOPE (*U* 118) enlists the reader in the cause of that author, by asking us to hope that he "will live to see it published" (*U* 118).

The answers commonly supplied to the questions raised by the head-lines—that the headline format is appropriate to an episode set in a news-paper office,[1] and that the sequence of headlines roughly follows the

---

1. "They exhibit Joyce's unceasing effort to duplicate the form of his subject-matter in the form of his expression." A. Walton Litz, *The Art of James Joyce* (London: Oxford Uni-versity Press, 1961), p. 49.

history of journalism from the "classically allusive [. . .] Victorian tradition" to "the catch-penny slickness of the modern press"[1]—are helpful
but inadequate. To restrict our observations to the style of the headlines
is to overlook the implications of their content. What is relevant about
the headlines—that is, what justifies their presence in the novel—is the
ultimate effect they produce upon the reader. (This same criterion ought
to be applied to *Ulysses'* Homeric parallels: no matter how ingeniously
these inform the book's structure, characterization, and imagery, they are
meaningful in the novel only to the extent that they affect our reading of
it.) In the case of the headlines, the effect is to drive a wedge between a
heretofore realistic narrative and the reader's belief in that narrative as a
reliable transcription. Our awareness in 'Aeolus' is not of unmediated
reality but of intentional artifice. In *Ulysses,* as I hope to show, a self-
conscious emphasis on artifice serves essentially to assert the presence of
the performing artist.

*   *   *

The imposition of pattern is by nature an exercise of artifice. The intricate patterns which determine every inner and outer event of *Ulysses* thus
serve on one level to assert the supremely conscious artifice of the novel
as a whole. What happens in 'Aeolus' is of course largely determined by
these patterns. The Homeric and Vichian parallels have been amply
noted, and the appointed art, color, organ, et cetera, have all been identified in the substance of the episode. These patterns, which absorb 'Aeolus' into the whole of *Ulysses,* inform the episode with meaning only
insofar as they are perceptible—which they are, solely from an inclusive
overview of the novel. This is not to deny that the apprehension of such
all-embracing patterns contributes to the experience of reading *Ulysses*—
surely it does, at least for the reader who is moderately *rusé*.[2] Within
'Aeolus' itself, however, there are discernible impositions of pattern
which, like the headlines and other opacities of style to be discussed
below, intrude upon the reading experience in conscious assertions of
artifice.

Symmetry, an aspect of beauty abundant in nature but ordinarily alien
to language, is, after the headlines, the ordering device through which

1. Stuart Gilbert, *James Joyce's* Ulysses (New York: Knopf, 1931), p. 162n.
2. To speak of the reader's experience of *Ulysses,* one need not go so far as to posit "that
ideal reader suffering from an ideal insomnia" (James Joyce, *Finnegans Wake* [New York:
The Viking Press, 1939, 1959], p. 120; hereafter *FW*); but clearly the concept of the "naive
reader" has no application here either.

artifice most clearly asserts itself in 'Aeolus.' Spatially, the episode begins and ends at the same point, Nelson's Pillar, IN THE HEART OF THE HIBERNIAN METROPOLIS. 'Aeolus' is thus wrought as a self-contained cycle, premonitory of the story which meets its own end without ending in *Finnegans Wake*, and for which Joyce found intellectual sanction in the Vichian *ricorso*. One function of the unbroken circles in 'Aeolus,' as in all of *Ulysses*, is to draw our attention to the forger of the rings.

Artful symmetries call attention to themselves in the language as well as in the action. There are, of course, the familiar palindromes delivered by Lenehan: "Madam, I'm Adam. And Able was I ere I saw Elba" (*U* 113). Bloom's thoughts less blatantly display palindromic sentences— "Nannan." (*U* 99)—and words—"level" (*U* 100)—and the text is sprinkled with such symmetrical exclamations as "Aha!" (*U* 106), "Oho!" (*U* 109), and the otherwise inexplicable "Ohio!" (*U* 105), a phonic palindrome. Such subtle symmetries are clearly intentional: in *Stephen Hero* young Daedalus "put his lines together not word by word but letter by letter" (*SH* 32). Reversed spellings produce the same symmetrical effect of requiring the reader to retrace his steps from end back to start: "mangiD kcirtaP" (*U* 101). Two sentences near the beginning of 'Aeolus' are nearly completely opaque—that is, rather than furthering the story, they arrest the reader's eye, draw our attention to their specific arrangement of words, and cause us to ponder the artistic reasoning behind that arrangement:

> Grossbooted draymen rolled barrels dullthudding out of Prince's stores and bumped them up on the brewery float. On the brewery float bumped dullthudding barrels rolled by grossbooted draymen out of Prince's stores. (*U* 96)

These sentences constitute in fact as nearly perfect a word-unit palindrome as sense permits.[1] Joyce's method of composition throughout

1. For the concept of the word-unit palindrome I am indebted to Howard E. Bergerson, *Palindromes and Anagrams* (New York: Dover Publications, 1973).

In the earlier version of 'Aeolus' published in the *Little Review* (Oct. 1918), the first of the sentences quoted is repeated without palindromic reversal (Litz, *The Art of James Joyce*, p. 50). It is possible that Joyce recast the passage into its present form in order to add chiasmus to the episode's compendium of rhetorical figures (Gilbert, *James Joyce's* Ulysses, p. 194), to show the novel's invisible body beginning to inhale and exhale (Richard Ellmann, *Ulysses on the Liffey* [New York: Oxford University Press, 1972], p. 72), and to parody Homer's formulaic method of composition (Richard Ellmann, *The Consciousness of Joyce* [New York: Oxford University Press, 1977], p. 25), as well as for the purposes of conspicuous symmetry discussed here.

'Aeolus' seems to parallel that of Martin Cunningham's spellingbee co-nundrum: "Cemetery put in of course on account of the symmetry" (*U* 100).

A final self-conscious technique worth considering in 'Aeolus' is the ineluctable abruptness of shifts in setting which the narrative displays. On the episode's first page alone, for example, four separate locations are rendered without the slightest transition. While in 'Wandering Rocks' this technique loses its obtrusive character by dint of consistent use, the sudden and conspicuous exercise of this narrational liberty in 'Aeolus' strikes the reader perforce as a bold defiance of literary convention. This and every other violation of convention in 'Aeolus' produces these three discernible effects: (1) it draws attention to itself as a literary artifice; (2) it asserts the author's command over space and time; and (3) it expresses the author's individual identity as an artist.

The manner in which 'Aeolus''s sudden shifts in space proclaim the narrative's character as artifice should be clear from the foregoing discussion. Every newspaper headline, every obtrusive symmetry, every conscious innovation in literary technique functions as a rend in the canvas: it destroys the illusion of unmediated reality and asserts in its place the mediating spirit of the artist. As was noted in the previous chapter, the narrator's so-called digressions in *Tristram Shandy* serve the same purpose in that novel as do the opacities of style which are first visible in 'Aeolus' but are at work throughout *Ulysses:* they focus attention on the creation of the book itself, and make of that creative act one of the central subjects of the novel. The crucial if concealed event in Sterne's novel is Tristram's success in telling his story despite yet by means of his Shandy-isms. In like manner, Joyce, by insistently drawing our attention to the self-conscious artifice of his novel, makes the artistic imagination that would create such a work one of the central concerns of *Ulysses.* As S.L. Goldberg has noted in *The Classical Temper,*

> Not only does *Ulysses* become, in one aspect, a symbolistic 'drama of meaning', but since it is also a drama about its own birth, it necessarily includes, as Stephen's argument unmistakably suggests, a hidden character: *the author himself.*[1]

That the Joycean artist enjoys mastery over the categories of time and space, which otherwise both delimit our existence and condition our

---

1. S.L. Goldberg, *The Classical Temper* (London: Chatto and Windus, 1961), p. 35.

perception, is equally clear. In 'Aeolus,' as befits the first episode of a triad, it is mainly *space* that is put through its *paces;* though time, too, is not allowed to *'scape:*

> I have often thought since on looking back over that strange time that it was that small act, trivial in itself, that striking of that match, that determined the whole aftercourse of both our lives.   (*U* 115)

Obtruding conspicuously from an otherwise impersonal third-person narrative, this sentence is unintelligible except as a proclamation of the artist's controlling imagination behind the artifice of narrative, and as a declaration of that artist's mastery over time and space.[1]

This is confirmed both in the rest of *Ulysses* and in Joyce's writings elsewhere as well. In *A Portrait,* Stephen imagines the artist as "a priest of external imagination, transmuting the daily bread of existence into the radiant body of everliving life."[2] Similarly, the responses to the questions of "When?" and "Where?" at the conclusion of the 'Ithaca' episode (*U* 607) suggest that the imagination's womb can, if properly fertilized, conceive the flesh of *allspace* and *alltime.* Art, for Joyce, preserves reality in a timeless solution. The past, the present, and the future are made to live simultaneously in the act of writing and in every *re*reading:

> In the intense instant of imagination, when the mind, Shelley says, is a fading coal, that which I was is that which I am and that which in possibility I may come to be. So in the future, the sister of the past, I may see myself as I sit here now but by reflection from that which then I shall be.   (*U* 160)

In 'Circe,' Bloom's hallucinatory resuscitation of his lost son Rudy is intrinsically artistic; so too is his recollection of "The Halcyon Days," which call out to him, "Mackerel! Live us again. Hurray!" (*U* 447). As the imaginative record of a day in Dublin in 1904, *Ulysses* as a whole announces its own triumph over space and time in its last line of print (following, that is, Molly's much-mentioned "Yes"):

> *Trieste–Zurich–Paris,* 1914–1921   (*U* 644).

Joyce thus reminds the reader that the novel was written at a different time and in a different place from the time and place to which the novel gives life.

---

1. This sentence is also, as Richard Ellmann has pointed out to me, a parody of a fictional technique in Wardour Street novels.

2. James Joyce, *A Portrait of the Artist as a Young Man* (New York: B.W. Huebsch, 1916; The Viking Press, 1961), p. 221. All references are to the latter edition and will be indicated by the abbreviation *A Port.*

The third and final implication that can be drawn from the self-consciousness of 'Aeolus' is the extent to which it serves to assert the author's individual identity as an artist. Clearly, the effect if not the intention of establishing one's independence from the canons of literary tradition must be to distinguish oneself as an individual, to assert, as an artist, one's unique identity. "The artist," Joyce wrote when he was nineteen, "though he may employ the crowd, is very careful to isolate himself."[1] The first step in this assertion of individuality must be a willingness to reject *idées reçues:* "[. . .] to approach the temper which has made art is an act of reverence and many conventions must be first put off."[2]

As the creative imagination transmutes the daily bread of life into the everliving body of art, so does the artist's transient desire to distinguish himself as an individual transform itself into the very substance of his immortal art. The urge to create is inseparable from the assertion of identity. "Let there be life" cries Stephen (*U* 119), rejecting the petrified conventions of hero-worship to spin a tale of two discrete individuals. "I am sure," Joyce wrote in 1905,

> [. . .] that the whole structure of heroism is, and always was, a damned lie and that there cannot be any substitute for the individual passion as the motive power of everything—art and philosophy included.[3]

As for Whitman, so for the Joycean artist, art becomes a Song of Myself:

> I celebrate myself,
> And what I assume you shall assume,
> For every atom belonging to me as good belongs to you.

Here then is the final obstacle which the creative imagination allows the Joycean artist to overleap. As art confers a mastery over space and time, and as it empowers the artist to carve his own identity from the stone of unchallenged convention, so too does it provide a wellspring of sympathy by which the artist is inspired to assert his common identity with all of mankind. Like Whitman, Joyce, by celebrating himself as an

---

1. James Joyce, "The Day of the Rabblement" (1901), in *The Critical Writings of James Joyce,* ed. Ellsworth Mason and Richard Ellmann (New York: The Viking Press, 1964), p. 69.

2. James Joyce, "James Clarence Mangan" (1902), in *Critical Writings,* ed. Mason and Ellmann, p. 75.

3. James Joyce, letter to Stanislaus Joyce, 7 Feb. 1905, quoted in Ellmann, *James Joyce,* p. 199.

individual localized in space and time, affirms in the timelessness of his art the unity of the whole family of man. Shem's esthetic, as rendered in *Finnegans Wake,* recalls this paradox:

> [. . .] (thereby, he said, reflecting from his own individual person life unlivable, trans-accidentated through the slow fires of consciousness into a dividual chaos, perilous, potent, common to allflesh, human only, mortal) [. . .] (*FW* 186).

The considerable deviousness of this view of art—affirming the commonality of all by stressing the singularity of one—is not without parallel in Joyce's philosophy. "Longest way round is the shortest way home," Bloom observes (*U* 309). Joyce writes out of a feeling that "My mind is more interesting to me than the entire country,"[1] and conceives his ideal audience to be himself: "To My own Soul I dedicate the first true work of my life."[2] Yet at the same time he claims to be "trying [. . .] to give people some kind of intellectual pleasure or spiritual enjoyment [. . .] for their mental, moral, and spiritual uplift."[3] Joyce conceived the art so created to participate "in the continual affirmation of the spirit"[4] of all men. Thus the Daedalus of *Stephen Hero* declares that

> every age must look for its sanction to its poets and philosophers. The poet is the intense centre of the life of his age to which he stands in a relation than which none can be more vital. He alone is capable of absorbing in himself the life that surrounds him and of flinging it abroad again amid planetary music. [. . .] It is time for them [the critics] to acknowledge that here the imagination has contemplated intensely the truth of the being of the visible world and that beauty, the splendour of truth, has been born. The age, though it bury itself fathoms deep in formulas and machinery, has need of these realities which alone give and sustain life and it must await from those chosen centres of vivification the force to live, the security for life which can come to it only from them. Thus the spirit of man makes a continual affirmation.   (*SH* 80)

Joyce ironizes this passage by referring in it to Stephen as "this heaven-ascending essayist" and "the fiery-hearted revolutionary;" but he does not undercut Stephen later when he declares, "I wish to bring to the world the spiritual renewal which the poet brings to it" (*SH* 192). Similarly, in *A Portrait,* Stephen wonders

1. Quoted by Ellman, *James Joyce,* p. 81.
2. ibid.
3. ibid., p. 169.
4. First essay on Mangan in *Critical Writings,* ed. Mason and Ellmann, p. 83.

How could he hit their conscience or how cast his shadow over the imaginations of their daughters, before their squires begat upon them, that they might breed a race less ignoble than their own?   (*A Port.*, 238)

It is this same wonderful possibility of making ethical affirmations valid and effective by means of his art that Stephen embraces in *A Portrait's* conclusion:

Welcome, O life! I go to encounter for the millionth time the reality of experience and to forge in the smithy of my soul the uncreated conscience of my race.   (*A Port.*, 252–53)

As the submission to sin is necessary to the discovery of self in *A Portrait,* and as the fall must precede the resurrection in *Finnegans Wake,* so in *Ulysses* must the reliability of the narrative itself be tried in the crucible of doubt before the book's initial affirmations, in Stephen's denials of the nay-sayers, may, in Molly's yea-saying, be finally reaffirmed. The narrative's reliability is brought into doubt by the self-conscious opacities of style which surface at first in 'Aeolus' and persist until Stephen's and Bloom's artistically time-defying visions in 'Circe.' Like the CYNOSURE they bespeak (*U* 123), the assertions of artifice attract attention to themselves by their very brilliance. That *Ulysses'* narrative, like that of *Tristram Shandy,* succeeds both in spite of and by means of its self-consciousness is the great triumph of "this chaffering allincluding most farraginous chronicle" (*U* 345).

'The Oxen of the Sun': Elitist Esthetics

In the episodes that follow 'Aeolus'—'Lestrygonians' and 'Scylla and Charybdis'—the self-conscious effect derives less from opacities of style than from the transparent subordination of the story to artificial principles of structure. The generative principles which Joyce derived from Homer, Vico, and other sources, while they declare their presence throughout *Ulysses,* most overtly do so in these episodes. The spatial disruptions of story in 'Wandering Rocks,' the nonreferential use of language as music in 'Sirens,' and the introduction of strange, unreliable narrators into 'Cyclops' and 'Nausicaa' maintain the novel's intentional artificiality. It is in 'The Oxen of the Sun,' however, that Joyce brings *Ulysses* to its zenith of literary self-consciousness. In 'Circe' and succeeding episodes, the novel is no less subservient to its formulaic generative principles and no less defiant of literary convention. But we must turn to 'The Oxen of the Sun' for the most instructive instance of that disruption of illusion which abounds in all of contemporary fiction.

Let us begin at the beginning:

> Deshil Holles Eamus. Deshil Holles Eamus. Deshil Holles Eamus.
> (*U* 314)

Explicators from Gilbert to Gifford have told us that the first of these words is Irish, the second English, and the third Latin, and that the sense we are to make of the passage is, "Let us go right (or south) to Holles Street."[1] What the explicators do not mention is that to the "implied reader" of *Ulysses* these lines are completely opaque. Immediately we are confronted with an enigma: Joyce's words will produce one effect on a novice to the novel, and another on a reader armed with one of the many guides. As Saul Bellow has said, reading such "works for initiates" as *Ulysses* is like gambling in the Marx Brothers film *A Day at the Races:* "Not only do you bet on the race, but you have to buy the stud-book."[2] The readers that Joyce wrote for, however, had no handy "stud-books" to buy, and therefore could not be counted on to make sense out of "Deshil Holles Eamus." The words are thus chosen for purposes that exceed the merely referential. We have to deal with an inscrutable narrator.

> Send us, bright one, light one, Horhorn, quickening and wombfruit. Send us, bright one, light one, Horhorn, quickening and wombfruit. Send us, bright one, light one, Horhorn, quickening and wombfruit. (*U* 314)

We do recognize these words (although without Gilbert we could not know that "Hawhorn" invokes Helios in the person of Sir Andrew Horne). A narrator has appeared in the first person plural, only to retreat behind phonic rhythms and textures. As before, the triple repetition of the phrase yields harmonies of ear and eye that do nought to advance the story. The incantation embroiders a pattern of abstract (that is, nonreferential) intent.

---

1. Gilbert, *James Joyce's* Ulysses, p. 96. Don Gifford with Robert J. Seidman, *Notes for Joyce: An Annotation of James Joyce's* Ulysses (New York: Dutton, 1974), p. 336. My task here, as with 'Aeolus,' is not to re-explicate the episode but rather to identify and discuss the various devices of self-consciousness which Joyce wrote into it.

2. Quotations from Saul Bellow in this chapter are from his comments in a seminar on *Ulysses,* The University of Chicago, Winter 1977.

Hoopsa, boyaboy, hoopsa! Hoopsa, boyaboy, hoopsa! Hoopsa, boyaboy, hoopsa!

> Universally that person's acumen is esteemed very little perceptive concerning whatsoever matters are being held as most profitable by mortals with sapience endowed to be studied who is ignorant of that which the most in doctrine erudite and certainly by reason of that in them high mind's ornament deserving of veneration constantly maintain when by general consent they affirm that other circumstances being equal by no exterior splendour is the prosperity of a nation more efficaciously asserted than by the measure of how far forward may have progressed the tribute of its solicitude for that proliferant continuance which of evils the original if it be absent when fortunately present constitutes the certain sign of omnipollent nature's incorrupted benefaction.   (*U* 314)

Only the most assiduous exegete can follow from line to line the sense of this, the episode's fourth paragraph. The narrator has changed gears—or, if you will, we have a new narrator altogether, the "implied author" changing tactics for the sake of a larger strategy. What need not take ten words to say is here inflated to a nearly senseless turgidity. It is, however, clear to the initiate and novice alike that the style has become widely inappropriate to the sense. We're reminded of de Man's definition of parabasis: "a sudden revelation of the discontinuity between two rhetorical codes."

'The Oxen of the Sun' proceeds by regularly trading in old narrators for new. Each cluster of paragraphs assumes the diction and syntax of a particular writer, all of whom can be identified by name. At the same time, the sense of each paragraph is conspicuously out of keeping with its style. The incongruity that results offers a wealth of humorous effects. Thus Bloom enters the room:

> And the traveller Leopold went into the castle for to rest him for a space being sore of limb after many marches environing in divers lands and sometimes venery.   (*U* 317)

And thus a can of sardines:

> And there was a vat of silver that was moved by craft to open in the which lay strange fishes withouten heads though misbelieving men nie that this be possible thing without they see it natheless they are so.   (*U* 317)

Ulysses comprises a multitude of simultaneous performances. Scholars may never complete the task of digging out all that is buried in it, so dense is the overlay of patterns.

To translate *Penelope* exactly, Benoîst–Méchin wished to see the scheme of the book. Joyce gave him only bits of it, and protested humorously, 'If I gave it all up immediately, I'd lose my immortality. I've put in so many enigmas and puzzles that it will keep the professors busy for centuries arguing over what I meant, and that's the only way of insuring one's immortality.'[1]

Events, descriptions, and individual words play simultaneous roles in several schema, as we have seen in the case of the word-unit palindrome in 'Aeolus.' Joyce "agreed with Ezra Pound that 'great literature is simply language charged with meaning to the utmost degree.'"[2] Such linguistic "overdetermination" imparts to the text the reflexive character of all polysemous, or many-meaninged, language. This effect is most apparent in 'The Oxen of the Sun.'

> And childe Leopold did up his beaver for to pleasure him and took apertly somewhat in amity for he never drank no manner of mead which he then put by and anon fully privily he voided the more part in his neighbour glass and his neighbour wist not of his wile.   (*U* 317)

The word *beaver,* in the sense of helmet visor, conforms to the diction of the *Travels of Sir John Mandeville* (c. 1336–71), and hence contributes to the stylistic pattern of the episode in which "ontogeny recapitulates phylogeny." Beaver also refers to the hat which Bloom takes off. In the symbolic pattern whereby the hospital represents the womb, the nurse the ovum, and Bloom the sperm, this gesture, as Gilbert delicately puts it, "has, I believe, its significance for the biologist."[3] In American journalist slang beaver also means vagina.[4] Language as polysemous as this, ultimately, is less specifically referential than language not so heavily "charged with meaning." That is, the effect of this passage upon the reader is less the expression of any one of the meanings cited than the assertion by all of them that something fancy is being done with the language.

The reflexive character of polysemous language is more easily seen in the operation of puns. Puns have fascinated such authors as Shakespeare, Joyce, and Pynchon perhaps in part by their paradoxical ability to "mean" two different things at once, by relying upon a Gestalt switch between word-as-sound and word-as-vehicle-of-meaning. "Rose of

1. Ellmann, *James Joyce,* p. 535.
2. Ellmann, *Ulysses on the Liffey,* p. 73.
3. Gilbert, *James Joyce's* Ulysses, p. 299.
4. Wayne Booth has pointed out to me that "beaver" in the sense of "beard" may also be involved.

Castille"/"Rows of cast steel" (*U* 347) says less about either operas or railroads than it does about Lenehan's, *and* Joyce's, peculiar wit. Polysemous language tends to detract from the significance of the thing said, while focussing attention on the performance of the speaker or writer.

The conspicuous subordination of the text to imposed schematic patterns thus disrupts the realistic illusion of story, while asserting the display of artifice. No reader assumes Bloom to have said, "Meseems it dureth overlong" (*U* 318); rather, we recognize the hand of the master putting words in Bloom's mouth. (Of course, *all* the words are Joyce's, but these are chosen for the sake of their express inauthenticity.) Apparent contrivances such as the modelling of the drinking table scene upon that of the Last Supper, and exaggerations of the "pathetic fallacy" such as the rainfall that accompanies the birth, serve further to enforce this effect. In Haines's surreal repetition of remarks made in an earlier episode (*U* 17, 336), Joyce provides an example of the device Bruce Morrissette has identified in Robbe-Grillet's novels as *intertextualité*.[1] As a reflexive assertion of the novel's artifice, intertextuality reigns throughout *Ulysses*.

Beyond such "overdeterminations," the imposed thematic patterns also generate exaggerated expressions of opinion on the part of the various narrators. "The idea [of the whole episode] being the crime committed against fecundity by sterilizing the act of coition,"[2] obtrusive moralizations abound: "Copulation without population! No, say I! Herod's slaughter of the innocents were the truer name" (*U* 345). Narrators apostrophize characters, now in an authoritative "we," now in humble first person singular:

Wherein, O wretched company, were ye all deceived [. . .].   (*U* 324)

You too have fought the good fight and played loyally your man's part. Sir, to you my hand. Well done, thou good and faithful servant!   (*U* 344)

As Sterne discovered, accentuating a narrator's eccentricities helps to dramatize the composition of the fiction itself. Joyce multiplied the power of this effect by multiplying his narrators. Some of these adopt Tristram's procedure of addressing his readers directly: "Did heart leap to heart? Nay, fair reader" (*U* 338). Such narrative obtrusions, conjoined

1. Bruce Morrissette, "Robbe-Grillet Nᵒ 1, 2, . . . , X," in *Nouveau Roman: hier, aujourd'hui* (Paris: Union générale d'éditions, 1972), II, 119–33.
2. Joyce letter to Frank Budgen, 22 March 1920, quoted in Ellmann, *James Joyce*, p. 489.

with references in the text to the text itself, establish beyond question the episode's literary self-consciousness:

> By heaven, Theodore Purefoy, thou hast done a doughty deed and no botch! Thou art, I vow, the remarkablest progenitor barring none in this chaffering allincluding most farraginous chronicle.   (*U* 345)

Joyce wrote of certain lines in 'The Oxen of the Sun' that they were "quite unconvincing and meant to be so."[1] It was, he wrote elsewhere, "the most difficult episode in an odyssey, I think, both to interpret and to execute,"[2] but he capped another description of it with the boast, "How's that for high?"[3] "Virtuoso performance" and "tour de force"— both terms apply, both suggest the extent to which the art displays its own art.

The question to be asked of such a self-conscious art is, as Saul Bellow puts it, "Where is the nucleus of earnestness?" To T.S. Eliot, 'The Oxen of the Sun' "showed up the futility of all the English styles."[4] Is this what it really means for an author self-consciously to parade the whole stylistic history of the English language before his readers? It means rather, I think, that the author has claimed the whole language in all of its synchronic and diachronic expanses as his own. The artist appropriates every style as well as every subject matter as material for his art. For Flaubert, as Saul Bellow has observed, there was nothing heroic in the action of *Madame Bovary;* everything heroic is in the *language* of that novel. Joyce will grant a comic heroism to his characters by casting them into Homeric shadows but, like Flaubert, he claims for himself the role of hero of the language. I am the inheritor of all these traditions, proclaims the implied author of 'The Oxen of the Sun.' By proving my mastery of these traditions I earn the prerogative to impress them into the service of my own ends.

Much though not all of what we have said in the previous chapters about the self-conscious novel as a genre can thus be applied to *Ulysses.* Specifically, we have identified in 'Aeolus' and in 'The Oxen of the Sun,'

---

1. Joyce letter to German translator Georg Goyert, n.d., reproduced in Alan M. Cohen, "Joyce's Notes on the End of 'Oxen of the Sun,'" *James Joyce Quarterly,* 4 (Spring 1967), 198.
2. Quoted by Ellmann, *James Joyce,* p. 489.
3. Ibid., pp. 489–90.
4. Quoted by Ellmann, *James Joyce,* p. 490. Originally quoted by Virginia Woolf in *A Writer's Diary* (New York: Harcourt, Brace & World, 1954; New York: New American Library, 1968), entry for 26 September 192., p. 57.

as disruptions of representational illusion and as implied assertions of authorial artifice, the following twelve devices:

1. parabasis
2. incongruities of sense and style
3. opacities of style
4. use of nonreferential language (including incantations)
5. use of polysemous language (including puns)
6. linguistic and structural overdetermination
7. conspicuous subordination to generative principles:
    of plot (contrivance for the sake of 'theme')
8.   and of language (contrivance for the sake of 'intertextuality')
9. sudden and overt changes of narrator
10. overt and eccentric moralization
11. direct address to characters and readers
12. textual self-reference.

As Richard Ellmann sums it up, "Neither God nor Homer could compete with Joyce in self-consciousness."[1]

Ulysses also demonstrates, however, the total inadequacy of simplistic notions of mimetic and non-mimetic fiction. For all of its self-consciousness, *Ulysses* is minutely, meticulously mimetic. Consider, for instance, this sentence from the novel's opening scene:

> Stephen Dedalus, displeased and sleepy, leaned his arms on the top of the staircase and looked coldly at the shaking gurgling face that blessed him, equine in its length, and at the light untonsured hair, grained and hued like pale oak.   (*U* 3)

That simile—"grained and hued like pale oak"—does not obtrude from the text as a conspicuous contrivance. Rather, its striking acuity and appositeness cause us to see in our mind's eye both the hair on Buck Mulligan's head and the grainy oaken surface to which it is being compared. Similes bear the seeds of self-consciousness, as we will see later in considering Nabokov's playful formulations and Pynchon's "The knife cuts through the apple like a knife cutting an apple." But the "tone of scrupulous meanness" in which Joyce claimed to have written *Dubliners*[2] governs the prose of the opening chapters of *Ulysses* as well, in that it brings to imaginative life a distinctly visualized scene, ahum with psychological and intellectual resonances, without calling attention to the means by

1. Ellmann, *The Consciousness of Joyce*, p. 25.
2. Joyce letter to Grant Richards, 5 May 1906, *Selected Letters*, ed. Richard Ellmann (New York: The Viking Press, 1975), p. 83.

which it does so. The accomplished realism of the novel's opening episodes seems, in the context of the whole novel, almost a defiant exclamation on Joyce's part to the effect that "See! I can write naturalistically if I choose to." Then, beginning with 'Aeolus': "But I choose not to."

By modulating its self-consciousness, *Ulysses* then leads us to respect and remember the capabilities of the author in charge. But exactly what aspect of the performing artist does *Ulysses* place before us? Is it his individual physical existence? No, not if we compare *Ulysses* to the self-conscious novels of Barth and Nabokov: there are no portraits of Joyce himself, such as those given us by the authors of *Chimera* and *King, Queen, Knave*. Does *Ulysses* then express the personal historical aspect of its author's life, as Henry Miller's autobiographical novels may be said to do? Well, in a sense, yes, as many of the incidents in Stephen Dedalus's life may be traced to the experiences of Joyce himself; but also in a sense, no: we are not even sure why 16 June 1904 mattered to Joyce, although it has been conjectured that this date marked the beginning of his liaison with Nora Barnacle.

Does *Ulysses* then assert the political aspect of its artist? Again, yes and no. Joyce seems to have had hardly any politics at all. In his introduction to Stanislaus Joyce's *My Brother's Keeper,* Richard Ellmann quoted James Joyce as saying, Flaubertesquely, "Don't talk to me about politics. I'm only interested in style."[1] But in a more recent work, Mr Ellmann has chosen to consider Joyce as a political writer, and *The Consciousness of Joyce* is consequently a slender book. Ellmann argues that

> The central action of *Ulysses* is to bring together Stephen Dedalus and Leopold Bloom by displaying their underlying agreement on political views which the author thereby underwrites.[2]

If Ellmann is right, the "central action of *Ulysses*" is exceptionally well hidden. When Stephen, just before being knocked down by the soldiers, "taps his brow" and, paraphrasing Blake, says "But in here it is I must kill the priest and the king" (*U* 481), he is in fact dismissing politics as an obstacle to the artistic mentality. Similarly, in *A Portrait,* Stephen had declared to Davin,

> When the soul of a man is born in this country, there are nets flung at it to hold it back from flight. You talk to me of nationality, language, religion. I shall try to fly by those nets.   (*A Port.,* 203)

1. Richard Ellmann, "Introduction" to Stanislaus Joyce, *My Brother's Keeper* (New York: The Viking Press, 1958; McGraw-Hill, 1964), p. xix.
2. Ellmann, *The Consciousness of Joyce,* p. 90.

Bloom cherishes his liberal ideals and his practical connections with politics—"it was Bloom gave the idea for Sinn Fein to Griffith" (*U* 275) and Bloom who recovered Parnell's hat (*U* 535)—but deep down he repudiates the grand gestures of public life and, like Joyce himself, puts his faith in "the individual passion:"

> —But it's no use, says he. Force, hatred, history, all that. That's not life for men and women, insult and hatred. And everybody knows that it's the very opposite of that that is really life.
> —What? says Alf.
> —Love, says Bloom. I mean the opposite of hatred.   (*U* 273)

Earlier in the day Stephen has rejected Mr Deasy's definition of history as a movement "towards one great goal, the manifestation of God" with the formulation that "History is a nightmare from which I am trying to awake" (*U* 28). Mr. Ellmann is therefore right that the views of Stephen and Bloom coalesce on this subject, although they coalesce in a rejection of political action.

In *Stephen Hero,* where Joyce was considerably less guarded, the question of the artist's political engagement is confronted more directly. Exasperated by Stephen's apparent aloofness, Madden exclaims,

> —But surely you have some political opinions, man!
> —I am going to think them out [responds Stephen]. I am an artist, don't you see. Do you believe that I am?
> —O yes, I know you are.
> —Very well then, how the devil can you expect me to settle everything at once? Give me time.   (*SH* 56)

Given time, the Stephen of *Stephen Hero* selects, to go with his artistic self image, "political opinions" of a distinctly Nietzschean, aristocratic cast:

> Stephen had begun to regard himself seriously as a literary artist: he professed scorn for the rabblement and contempt for authority.   (*SH* 122–23)

In *Stephen Hero,* then, Stephen's political views lead back into, not away from, the presentation of himself as an artist. While his snobbery is muted in *A Portrait* and *Ulysses,* as the change in the spelling of his name from Daedalus to Dedalus suggests, Stephen's élitist inversions persist in the later novel in the form of his declaration to Bloom that "Ireland must be important because it belongs to me" (*U* 527), and in his drunken analysis in Nighttown:

A discussion is difficult down here. But this is the point. You die for your country, suppose. *(He places his arm on Private Carr's sleeve.)* Not that I wish it for you. But I say: let my country die for me.   (*U* 482)

If the self-consciousness of *Ulysses* illuminates a set of political views, then, those views have been chosen so as further to set off the artistic temperament from the more mundane temperaments around it. There is thus a strange schizophrenia in the values that Joyce's novel seems to embrace. Ethically, as I have shown in my discussion of 'Aeolus,' *Ulysses* is an essentially democratic book, endorsing the commonality of all men and affecting sympathy for the mundane. Esthetically, however, as consideration of 'The Oxen of the Sun' has revealed, *Ulysses* is an insidiously élitist work; Ireland itself, it intimates, might well perish for the sake of its author. There may be, as Lenehan says, "a touch of the artist about old Bloom" (*U* 193) but to the extent that there is, Bloom is not one of his fellows. That Bloom himself would not read *Ulysses* is perhaps a commonplace, but it is one that cannot be burked. Joyce chose brilliant artifices to depict dull circumstances.

This paradoxical status of *Ulysses* as an ethically democratic but esthetically élitist work has never, to my knowledge, been adequately explored. Is Bloom himself, this novel Odysseus, in fact a figure of Everyman, as critics have traditionally regarded him, or is he rather, in Saul Bellow's phrase, "a genius in ordinary man's clothing"? Joyce's intentions and accomplishments seem to express both views. I would like to suggest, however, that a significant parallelism exists between the apparent contradiction in *Ulysses* and the novel's self-conscious creation-cum-disruption of the fictional illusion. The straightforward telling of an unambiguous yarn is what the mythological "common reader" yearns for, like the sketch, "something quick and neat," that Bloom, on the throne, imagines himself composing (*U* 56). The arcane, incondite, disruptive artifices which make of *Ulysses* such an abundantly self-conscious text, on the other hand, supply precisely those aspects which make it a "work for initiates," since only afficionados can appreciate virtuosi. Self-consciousness presupposes a certain sophistication, at least in the reading of literature. *Ulysses* endeavors to *redeem* the ordinary, the plain, the simple, by exalting it through the artifice of a highly ornate, rigorously structured yet capacious cathedral of language. In so doing it employs the most self-conscious, sophisticated means to celebrate the virtues of unassuming generosity. One of the novel's "missions," then—to give what is profoundly simple the allure of jewels for the jaded—requires it to repudiate those very means by which it is obliged to proceed. Hence our sense that Joyce's parade of successive narrators burn their bridges or, in more Beckettian terminology, pull up their ladders behind them.

From this perspective, *Ulysses* can be read as a drama of narrative reliability. The text begins in the solemn, imperturbable authority of the 'Telemachia,' then suggests a certain relativity of narrative validity as it shifts its locus of perceptions from Stephen Dedalus to Mr Leopold Bloom. The reliability of the text first undergoes serious challenges, as we have seen, in 'Aeolus,' is travestied mercilessly in 'The Oxen of the Sun,' and explodes entirely in the arbitrary and whimsical phantasmagoria of 'Circe.' Ultimately, in the "objective"rendition of Molly's "subjective" monologue, the text's reliability staggers to a precarious balance.

By simultaneously creating and disrupting the narrative illusion, Joyce is thus able to give with one hand and take with the other. He can celebrate the virtues of a seemingly ordinary Dubliner of unassuming generosity while simultaneously elaborating one of the most complex, arcane, and sophisticated works of art of the century. This does not permit him, alas, to be all things to all readers. *Ulysses* renders the mundane accessible to the mandarins, but not vice versa. However, if Bloom, whose two shelves of books are untainted by the likes of Flaubert, would not know what to make of the novel in which he himself appears, it is also true, as the self-consciousness of *Ulysses* reminds us, that we would know nothing of humorous, humane Leopold Bloom (including his reading habits) were it not for the consummate artificer James Joyce. Kierkegaard's *Either/Or,* with its alternate endorsements of the esthetic and ethical approaches to life, reminds us that these two antithetical domains have often resisted attempts at synthesis. But Joyce's presentation of democratic vistas from an élitist perspective may perhaps be best understood as the necessary result of the effort to fashion from the contents of an outwardly ordinary modern consciousness a durable, self-conscious work of art.

I am suggesting that Joyce resolves the rift between his novel's ethics and esthetics by self-consciously making his readers aware of it. First, by the tripartite division of Ulysses, he asserts his own authorial ability to simulate the respectively highbrow, middlebrow, and lowbrow thoughts of Stephen, Bloom, and Molly. But by lodging the faithful mimesis of their *monologues intérieurs* within a disruptively self-conscious text, Joyce then reminds his readers—whoever we are—that we too are imaginatively capable of inhabiting those diverse intellects and sensibilities. As we read (and hence think) their thoughts, we *become* Stephen the metaphysicist, Bloom the physicist, and Molly their earthy affirmer—and, thanks to the text's reflexivity, we become aware that we become them. We find that we know, as readers, how it feels to be *both* as rarefied and effete as a Stephen Dedalus and as common and carnal as a Molly Bloom. Thus, the novel's seeming schizophrenia is in fact a collaboration of effects. By deploying a plot that is essentially mundane and a central character of Bloom's social class, Joyce commends democracy to his audience of initiates; while by its Byzantine structure, stylistic bravado, and such thoughts as Stephen's, *Ulysses* makes not élitists, but esthetes, of us all.

Why Leopold Bloom Masturbates

Two elements of the *action* of *Ulysses* may be regarded as thematically related to the novel's structural and stylistic self-consciousness: Bloom's masturbation and his willingness to be cuckolded. Autoeroticism is sexually reflexive, and it thus shares attributes, for better and worse, of fiction's self-depiction. To the extent that masturbation represents an antisocial short-circuiting of the impulse to love others, it may be seen as a narcissistic self-indulgence. Christopher Lasch, as noted earlier, has in fact viewed self-conscious fiction in precisely these terms.[1] But in *Ulysses,* Bloom's masturbation, besides providing Joyce with an occasion for synchronous figurative pyrotechnics, acquires the dignity of a heroic deed. It serves, for one thing, as a proleptic retaliation for Molly's simultaneous infidelity. Secondly, Bloom's masturbation is seen as an acceptable way of dealing with what the narrator of 'Ithaca' terms "the continual production of semen by distillation" (*U* 604). As Bloom himself thinks of it, "you have to get rid of it someway" (*U* 303). Finally, it is of crucial importance that Bloom does not gratify himself in solitude, but rather while eyeing and being eyed by the innocent, love-starved Gerty MacDowell. Though there is neither physical contact nor a single word passed between the two, Bloom nonetheless thinks of their silent pact of exhibition, observation, and arousal, "Still it was a kind of language between us" (*U* 305). The fact that the episode's locus of narration has in

---

1. Christopher Lasch, *The Culture of Narcissism: American Life in an Age of Diminishing Expectations* (New York: W. W. Norton, 1979).

fact passed from Gerty to Bloom confirms this interpretation: his act of onanism transcends narcissism, by transmitting thoughts and feelings to a consciousness outside his own.

Masturbation's parallels with literary self-consciousness go beyond its ability to transcend its apparent introversion. What stirs Bloom is not Gerty's actual charms but rather the *illusion* of such charms; and he, like the reader of a self-conscious novel, is acutely aware that what has engaged his interest is not fact but fiction. When Bloom realizes, after all the fireworks have "melted away dewily in the grey air," that Gerty MacDowell is crippled, he reflects that he is "glad I didn't know it when she was on show" (*U* 300, 301). Eroticism itself, like the reading of fiction, requires the willing suspension of disbelief; and Bloom, with his "touch of the artist," prizes the role of artifice accordingly: "*Lingerie* does it. [. . .] Fashion part of their charm." Molly, with her comparatively prosaic interest in "that tremendous big red brute of a thing he has" (*U* 611), misses out on the tenderness of intimacy, and Blazes Boylan must inevitably disappoint her: "[. . .] I didn't like his slapping me behind going away so familiarly in the hall though I laughed Im not a horse or an ass am I [. . .]" (*U* 610). Bloom, on the other hand, recognizes and admits the object of his desire to be "A *dream* of wellfilled hose" (*U* 301) (italics mine). Because his autoeroticism, like a self-conscious fiction, thus acknowledges its dependence upon an illusion, its climax and dénouement are gratifying rather than self-abusive: "Did me good all the same. [. . .] For this relief much thanks" (*U* 305). Bloom's masturbation on a public beach, therefore, violates the dictates of propriety, succeeds in communicating thoughts and sentiments despite its apparent insularity, and acknowledges the role of illusion in achieving its ends. The stratagem whereby Dublin's Odysseus spares the modesty of Nausicaa thus serves as a triply appropriate metaphor for the literary self-consciousness of *Ulysses* itself.

The theme of voluntary, or accepted, cuckoldry may similarly be viewed, metaphorically, as a parable of the self-conscious artistic imagination. In *Exiles,* that problematic "problem play" (according to Hugh Kenner, Dublin wits often claim to be "working on a dramatization of *Exiles*"[1]), the hero contrives to put his wife at the disposal of his best friend while insuring his own ignorance of the results, in order to vivify

---

1. Hugh Kenner, *Joyce's Voices* (Berkeley: University of California Press, 1978), p. 24.

his "love" with the sparks of uncertainty and doubt. Leopold Bloom's mixed view of *his* wife's infidelity—"as more than inevitable, irreparable" (*U* 603)—is similarly central to the author's depiction of his hero's mindscape. Biographical speculation has attempted to refer Joyce's apparent preoccupation with sexual jealousy to his own personal experiences, but I would prefer to indicate the peculiar aptness of Poldy's antlers as an emblematic trophy of *Ulysses'* self-conscious esthetic. Voluntary cuckoldry re-enacts on a personal sexual level the relativity of perception in the Joycean universe. A hot-blooded woman like Molly may no more be satisfied by one man than the reality of a single day may be exhausted by literary description from a single point of view. Hence, Bloom allows a variety of men to sleep with his wife just as Joyce allows a variety of narrators to tell his story. Molly, to pursue the analogy still further, is, like Richard Rowan's wife Bertha, a sort of Text; their husband-authors wistfully acknowledge the "more than inevitable" status of multiple readings.

This is not to pretend, of course, that Leopold Bloom actively seeks bedmates for Molly with the same avidity with which Richard Rowan seeks to hand his wife over to Robert Hand. On the contrary, Bloom dodges, as best he can, the thought and sight of Blazes Boylan all day long. But upon finding, as he joins Molly in bed, "the imprint of a human form, male, not his," Leopold Bloom smiles,

> To reflect that each one who enters imagines himself to be the first to enter whereas he is always the last term of a preceding series even if the first term of a succeeding one, each imagining himself to be first, last, only and alone, whereas he is neither first nor last nor only nor alone in a series originating in and repeated to infinity.   (*U* 601)

Bloom recognizes, in other words, the fiction by which we imagine ourselves to "possess" our loved ones to be precisely that, a fiction, at the same time that he allows his domestic life to continue as if that fiction were fact. Again, like the reader of a self-conscious novel, he both willingly and wittingly suspends his disbelief.

Ulysses is, *inter alia*, a tale of three writers. Stephen Dedalus, who intends to "write something" and has been encouraged to "Put us all into it, damn its soul. Father Son and Holy Ghost and Jakes M'Carthy" (*U* III), is the most prominent, but not the only writer-figure in Joyce's novel. Molly, in bed at day's end, wishes "if only I could remember the one half of the things and write a book out of it the works of Master

Poldy yes" (*U* 621). And Poldy himself, to complete the symmetry, has thought of writing a fiction that would draw upon Molly:

> Might manage a sketch. By Mr and Mrs L.M. Bloom. Invent a story for some proverb which? Time I used to try jotting down on my cuff what she said dressing.   (*U* 56)

By tolerating Molly's infidelities and showing her photo to other men, Bloom effectively "publishes" his wife in the way an author publishes a book. In the 'Circe' episode, the three faces of Stephen, Bloom, and William Shakespeare, seen in a mirror, are "crowned by the reflection of the reindeer antlered hatrack in the hall" (*U* 463). The "bullockbefriending bard," the canvasser with "a touch of the artist," and the archetype of the consummate artificer in the English language are thus united in a common cuckoldry, rendered figurative as an avowed (optical) illusion. As masturbator and cuckold, Joyce's hero embodies the paradoxical transcension of private peccadillo and secret shame into durable, fictitious, self-conscious art.

It is fair to ask, of course, whether the reader is *meant* to interpret Bloom's behavior as emblematic of the novel's self-conscious strategy as a whole, as we have just done, or whether such metaphor-mongering isn't a form of disingenuous overreading. "Shakespeare is the happy huntingground of all minds that have lost their balance," says Haines (*U* 204), and Joyce himself may perhaps suffer the same fate. I wonder, however, whether it is not more difficult to overread *Ulysses* than we tend to assume. Joyce once confessed to Beckett, in an unguarded moment, that "I may have oversystematized *Ulysses.*"[1] What this means, in practical terms, is that only a critic more ingenious (or more deranged?) than Joyce himself is likely to put a construction upon *Ulysses* that did not already occur to the novel's author. This is not to say that there is no such thing as an incorrect, or over-ingenious reading. But it does bring us back to the problem of the ideal reader of *Ulysses,* and the role of all those stud-books. It has been said that one must be a Dubliner properly to appreciate Joyce's work.[2] I would go further: to understand *Ulysses* fully, one must *be* James Joyce; and we appreciate his work to the degree that we succeed in making ourselves into his image. (This is even more ob-

---

1. Quoted in Ellmann, *James Joyce,* p. 715.
2. "For Joyce assumes—what is obviously not true—that all his readers are Dubliners [. . .]." Joseph Frank, *The Widening Gyre: Crisis and Mastery in Modern Literature* (New Brunswick, N.J.: Rutgers University Press, 1963), p. 18.

viously the case with *Finnegans Wake*.) All the guidebooks and annotations which seem to have become an indispensable part of our readings of *Ulysses* are in this sense tools designed to help us resemble Joyce—resemble him, at least, in the possession of a particularly broad body of knowledge. Perhaps this is the the best we can hope for.

Joyce claimed, as we have noted, that the inclusion of all the "enigmas and puzzles" in *Ulysses* was a device intended to secure "my immortality." The artist's claims to mastery over space and time, as *Ulysses* endorses them, encourage us to take this remark more seriously than it might otherwise warrant. After all, Joyce was right, we do still continue to puzzle over *Ulysses* and to argue over what it means, with an avidity we bring to no other work of fiction from that period.

This points up, finally, what is perhaps the ultimate appropriateness of fiction's self-depiction to Joyce's novel. *How* do you ensure that your novel will be read and preserved as a work of art? You remind the reader, on every page and with convincing, self-conscious skill, that the author is an artist. In this, by manifestly modulating its modicum of mimesis, *Ulysses* succeeds unmistakably.

Chapter V

Nabokov's Imitations of Mortality

V LADIMIR NABOKOV, who took tea with Joyce in Paris, shared with the Irishman (and with that other tea-drinker, Proust) what has come to be known as the Modernist esthetic. All three were exiles, although the older two had exiled themselves voluntarily—the Irishman to the Continent and the Frenchman to his room. Fiction offered each of them a way of recapturing what had been sacrificed or abandoned. But the relativity of perception, which science had recently corroborated, posed a common threat to their creative enterprises, by strengthening the corollary hypothesis of solipsism. If reality really was what it seemed to each individual, then what was the public worth of the private worlds they were wording? Significantly, each responded to the threat in his own way. Proust dramatized the relativity thematically, by showing, with a minimum of narrative unreliability, how the same entity (a clock tower, a woman) could be perceived differently by others, or by ourselves at other times. Joyce, as was earlier discussed, turned that threat into the thread stringing together the episodes of *Ulysses:* he confronted relativity head-on by diffracting his plot through a colorful spectrum of voices, styles, and points of view. For the Russian exile, however, solipsism became not merely a manner but the very matter of his fiction, the fate that befalls his narrators and protagonists. *Ada's* author felt, as Joyce did, that fiction without its self-depiction was incomplete. Mimesis, essential though it be to recalling a lost time, must not forget its place; imitations must avow their limitations. But Joyce's politics of artistic self-assertion becomes, in Nabokov, a poetics of death and reflexive art.

Self-depiction is of the essence of Nabokov's fictional technique. From *Mary,* his first novel, in which the reflexivity is, as in Proust, confined to the themes, to *Look at the Harlequins!,* his last, in which self-conscious themes and styles are intricately conjoined, his seventeen novels all insist upon their fictivity. Nabokov's fifty-two collected stories (gathered, like the suits of a card deck, into four collections of thirteen stories each) tend equally to inform upon themselves. This is hardly news, of course; the extent to which his fictions display their own artifice has been a staple of Nabokov criticism at least since Vladislav Khodasevich's mile-stone essay of 1937 entitled "On Sirin."[1] But now that his oeuvre has drawn to a close, in the "mumble dying away" of his last novel's last words, we may appropriately take a synoptic view of Nabokov's self-depicting fiction, so as to probe the still unexplained esthetic puzzle that lies at its heart. For, even as they insist on reminding us that they are only fictions, Nabokov's novels nevertheless tell stories that touch us and move us. How is this possible? How can he reveal the strings that bind his characters to the puppeteer's hand, and yet pluck at our own heart-strings as well? To answer this question, I should like to consider in turn the narration, structure, characterization, style, and themes of Nabokov's fiction. Nabokov's handling of each of these resources is both typically and innovatively self-conscious—typical in that he employs practically all of the devices identified in the 'Repertoire of Reflexivity,' and innovative in that he employs them for his own distinctive purposes. What those purposes are, and how they must be judged, will emerge as the discussion proceeds.

* * *

Foremost among Nabokov's techniques of self-consciousness is his draw-ing the reader's attention to the act of writing which produced the book. The first lines of *Despair* (Russian, 1936; English, 1966) are as follows:

> If I were not perfectly sure of my power to write and of my marvelous ability to express ideas with the utmost grace and vividness . . . So, more or less, I had thought of beginning my tale.[2]

Besides pointing out from the very start that this tale has been *written,* these lines also display that exaggerated self-confidence which ultimately undoes Hermann, the narrator, in his role as protagonist. Furthermore,

1. Vladislav Khodasevich, "O Sirine," *Vozrozhdenie* (Paris), 13 Feb. 1937; partially trans-lated by Michael H. Walker, ed. by Simon Karlinsky and Robert P. Hughes, in *Nabokov: Criticism, Reminiscences, Translations and Tributes,* ed. Alfred Appel, Jr. and Charles New-man (New York: Simon and Schuster, 1970), pp. 96–101.
Reference to this essay has become the conventional opening move in Nabokov criti-cism. For example, Andrew Field, "The Artist as Failure in Nabokov's Early Prose," in *Nabokov: The Man and His work,* ed. L.S. Dembo (Madison: University of Wisconsin Press, 1967; hereafter "Dembo"), pp. 57–65; Simon Karlinsky, "Illusion, Reality, and Parody in Nabokov's Plays," in Dembo, pp. 183–94; and Anna Maria Salehar, "Nabokov's *Gift:* An Apprenticeship in Creativity," in *A Book of Things about Vladimir Nabokov,* ed. Carl R. Proffer (Ann Arbor: Ardis, 1974), pp. 70–83, all refer to Khodasevich in their depressingly identical first sentences.

the parabasis, or sudden shift in rhetorical code, of the second sentence asserts the basic arbitrariness of the fictional construct. He began his story one way, we are told, but he could as easily have begun it in another. The story, that is, by no means pre-exists the narrator who merely recounts it; instead, the narrator invents his story as he goes along. The suggestion of possible alternate texts, less prevalent in Nabokov than in, say, Robbe-Grillet, but still a favored device, imparts to the text that we *do* have an essentially "fictional" reality.

Hermann's boastful claims to narrative mastery soon founder, comically, upon his own parenthetical perplexities: "(Don't quite see why I write in this vein)."[1] Even in those novels where the narrator is genuinely in control, however, we are still shown him scratching his head as he strings together his words. In *Bend Sinister* (English, 1947), for example, Krug is given "thick (let me see) clumsy (there) fingers which always trembled slightly."[2]

If dramatizing the process of its composition asserts a story's fictivity, then implying that the apparent narrator is himself a fictional creation further amplifies this effect. When Nabokov interposes a John Ray, Jr. to edit Humbert Humbert's confessions in *Lolita* (1955), or creates a Ronald Oranger to edit Ada's annotations to Van's manuscript of *Ada* (1969), he is in fact setting off with additional sets of inverted commas the depicted ""'"reality"'"" of his fictional creation. The receding series of nesting narrators is frequently given an apparent (but false) vanishing point in the texts' teasing images of Vladimir Nabokov himself. This is done in several ways, all of which are trade marks of Nabokov's work.

There is first of all the physical description of an incidental character whom the reader is meant to identify as the author, in much the same way that the director's distinctive face or profile appears on screen momentarily in many of Alfred Hitchcock's films. I have already cited, in Chapter I above, an example of this seeming physical presence of the author among his characters in *King, Queen, Knave* (Russian, 1928; English, 1968), where Franz observes a couple resembling Nabokov and his wife dancing nearby. However, the connection between the cameo appearances of Nabokov and the actual authorial consciousness of the novels themselves is tenuous at best—hence the merely "apparent" vanishing point which these appearances provide. The problem, from an esthetic

1. Nabokov, *Despair,* p. 14.
2. Vladimir Nabokov, *Bend Sinister* (New York: McGraw-Hill Paperbacks, 1974), p. 6.

point of view, is that there is nothing *within* the texts that obliges the reader to recognize the sly self-portraits as images of the author. Franz's suspicion, in *King, Queen, Knave,* that "this damned happy foreigner knew absolutely everything about his predicament"[1] is, in short, a suspicion which the novel itself cannot substantiate. The characters who impersonate the author rely for their success upon the reader's familiarity with a few public details of Nabokov's private life *outside* his fiction—for example, his lepidoptery. In *King, Queen, Knave,* "sometimes the man carried a butterfly net" (p. 254). At a picnic in *Pnin* (1957), Chateau remarks, "Pity Vladimir Vladimirovich is not here. He would have told us all about these enchanting insects."[2] Similarly, one must have seen a photograph of Nabokov to recognize as images of the author such descriptions as that of "Vladimirov" in *The Gift* (written in Russian, 1935–37; pub. 1952; English, 1963).

That these reminders of authorial presence rely upon information external to the fictions presents an esthetic puzzle to which we must return. But what is even more striking about these seeming self-portraits is how *little* they manage to tell us about Vladimir Nabokov the human being. In fact, for such a self-conscious writer, Nabokov was extraordinarily careful to avoid what he called "the beginner's well-known propensity for obtruding upon his own privacy"[3]—much more careful than, say, John Barth, whose novels claim to proclaim more than one might care to know about the author's succession of marital and post-marital liaisons. Nabokov's practice, however, conforms to his pronouncement that "[t]he best part of a writer's biography is not the record of his adventures but the story of his style."[4] The sudden textual appearance of "the author," which has come to be recognized as a Nabokov trade mark, is in fact no more than just that—a stylized, even conventional sign by which the maker makes known his presence. This explains Nabokov's fondness for sprinkling anagrammatized versions of his own name throughout his fictions—for his name is a sign that conveys no more (but no less) than that *he* is the author.

A few examples will suffice. In *King, Queen, Knave* Dreyer sends Martha a photo of himself skiing taken by "Mr. Vivian Badlook" (p. 153), an

1. Vladimir Nabokov, *King, Queen, Knave* (New York: McGraw-Hill, 1968), p. 259.
2. Vladimir Nabokov, *Pnin* (New York: Avon/Bard Books, 1969), p. 127.
3. Vladimir Nabokov, "Introduction" to *Mary* (New York: McGraw-Hill, 1970), p. xi.
4. Interview with Allene Talmey, *Vogue,* Dec. 1969, quoted by Nabokov in "Introduction" to *Mary,* p. xiii.

anagram of Vladimir Nabokov. *Speak, Memory* (1951, rev. 1966; nonfiction, but penned in Nabokov's novelistic vein) quotes "Vivian Bloodmark, a philosophical friend of mine."[1] Quilty's collaborator in *Lolita* is named Vivian Darkbloom.[2] (These anagrams have been unscrambled by a host of critics before me, but no one to my knowledge has noted that the first name Vivian, common to all three, is itself a pun on the author's initials, VVN.) Nabokov contrives to work his father's name into the historically accurate section of *The Gift:* "The Minister of Justice, Nabokov, made the appropriate report."[3] Similarly, in *Pnin,* we overhear a group of literati "discussing émigré writers—Bunin, Aldanov, Sirin" (p. 116)—Sirin having been, at one time, Nabokov's *nom de plume.* In *Ada,* returning to anagrams, the children are given their treasured "Flavita" (read "Alfavit": Scrabble) game by "Baron Klim Avidov;"[4] and in *Transparent Things* (1972), the name "Adam von Librikov" announces itself as "a sly scramble."[5] In their declarations of authorial presence and in their consequent standing out from the fictional plane, Nabokov's "sly scrambles" of his own name share the intent and effect of a pictorial artist's slightly less than legible signature at the bottom of his canvas. Nabokov specializes in signatures, not self-portraits.

The first words of Nabokov's story "Cloud, Castle, Lake" (Russian, 1937; English, 1941) introduce the protagonist as "[o]ne of my representatives."[6] In what sense, then, if Nabokov is not a self-portraitist, do his dramatized stand-ins "represent" him? Kinbote's promise, at the end of *Pale Fire* (1962), offers a clue:

> I shall continue to exist. I may assume other disguises, other forms, but I shall try to exist. I may turn up yet, on another campus, as an old, happy, healthy, heterosexual Russian, a writer in exile, sans fame, sans future, sans audience, sans anything but his art.[7]

The passage reveals nothing about Nabokov (a heterosexual Russian émigré writer) that we don't already know, but it does assert that the implied Nabokov is happier, healthier, more normal than—in short, su-

1. Vladimir Nabokov, *Speak, Memory: An Autobiography Revisited* (New York: G.P. Putnam's Sons, 1966), p. 218.

2. Vladimir Nabokov, *Lolita* (New York: G.P. Putnam's Sons, 1955), p. 223.

3. Vladimir Nabokov, *The Gift* (New York: Capricorn Books, 1970), p. 304.

4. Vladimir Nabokov, *Ada* (New York: McGraw-Hill, 1969), p. 225.

5. Vladimir Nabokov, *Transparent Things* (New York: McGraw-Hill, 1972), p. 75.

6. Vladimir Nabokov, "Cloud, Castle, Lake," in *Nabokov's Dozen* (New York: Avon/Bard Books, 1973), p. 90.

7. Vladimir Nabokov, *Pale Fire* (New York: G. P. Putnam's Sons, 1962), pp. 300–301.

perior to—his fictional "vicar."[1] The narrator of *Look at the Harlequins!* Vadim Vadimovich N, or "McNab" as he is sometimes called, develops these implications more fully:

> I now confess that I was bothered that night, and the next and some time before, by a dream-feeling that my life was the non-identical twin, a parody, an inferior variant of another man's life, somewhere on this or another earth. A demon, I felt, was forcing me to impersonate that other man, that other writer who was and would always be incomparably greater, healthier, and crueler than your obedient servant.[2]

McNab, like the John Ray, Jr. of *Lolita,* and like the commentator of *Pale Fire* who fancies himself to be an exiled king, is thus a *parodic* image of the implied author, not an image of Nabokov himself. And even this structure of self-parody may be subject to parody, as occurs in the afterword to *Lolita* headed "Vladimir Nabokov: On a Book Entitled *Lolita*":

> After doing my impression of suave John Ray, the character in *Lolita* who pens the Foreword, any comments coming straight from me may strike one— may strike me, in fact—as an impersonation of Vladimir Nabokov talking about his own book.   (*Lolita,* p. 313)

Self-parody is a hard habit to break. In Nabokov's case, it succeeds in corroding all the particularities of his personal biography save the fact of his authorship. In his preface to *Bend Sinister,* Nabokov identifies "the intruder" at the novel's conclusion as "an anthropomorphic deity impersonated by me" (p. xii). The "me" of this explication reveals as little of himself as that same anthropomorphic deity; what Nabokov's vicars, anagrammatic signatures, and parodic stand-ins stand for is the impersonal and omnificent authorial presence itself.

*   *   *

Reminders to the reader of the reading process: this is the second dimension of Nabokov's self-conscious narrative technique. We have already noted that direct address to the reader *as* reader constitutes the most overt form of such reminders. The narrator of *Despair* begins by recommending himself to the "gentle reader" (p. 13); before long he is shouting

---

1. The term is used by Nabokov in his "Introduction" to *Mary,* p. xi.
2. Vladimir Nabokov, *Look at the Harlequins!* (New York: McGraw-Hill, 1974), p. 89.

at us, "you swine, you!" (p. 31). The reader's active participation is not only encouraged but summarily commanded: "Chocolate, as everybody knows . . . (let the reader imagine here a description of its making)" (*Despair,* p. 15). Humbert Humbert, a more sophisticated narrator than Hermann, makes a feint at observing this same self-conscious convention, but then comically demolishes it:

> As greater authors than I have put it: "Let readers imagine" etc. On second thought, I may as well give those imaginations a kick in the pants.   (*Lolita,* p. 67).

Even when the narrator has apparently ceased to address the reader directly, Nabokov still manages to create a fictional version of the reader within the story. In *Bend Sinister,* for example, the dictator Paduk is described as standing with "his back to the reader" (p. 142). The peculiarities of this dramatized reader vary, however, from novel to novel. In *Invitation to a Beheading* (Russian, 1938; English, 1959), the reader is represented as a fundamentally alien spirit, who can be persuaded to understand and sympathize with the narrator's plight only with great difficulty. "You are not I," laments Cincinnatus C to his reader, "and therein lies the irreparable calamity."[1] In *Lolita,* Humbert Humbert's implied audience fluidly shifts from a formal "Ladies and gentlemen of the jury" (p. 11) to a cozy coterie of Humbert fans, by way of such various formulations as "my patient reader whose meek temper Lo ought to have copied" (p. 141) and "my learned reader (whose eyebrows, I suspect, have by now traveled all the way to the back of his bald head)" (p. 50). In fact, the development of Humbert Humbert's relations with his reader, and not those with Lolita, arguably constitutes the real plot of the novel, since Lolita's story is effectively complete in the book's first page. Humbert Humbert, surreptitiously acknowledging his own fictivity, goes so far as to declare that his very existence depends upon the reader's continuing to read:

> Please, reader: no matter your exasperation with the tenderhearted, morbidly sensitive, infinitely circumspect hero of my book, do not skip these essential pages! Imagine me; I shall not exist if you do not imagine me.   (*Lolita,* p. 131)

1. Vladimir Nabokov, *Invitation to a Beheading* (New York: Capricorn Books, 1965), p. 93.

Thus Humbert Humbert resolves, in his own fashion, a Neo-Berkeleyan dilemma: the *fictional* tree does not fall if no reader is present to read about it. Nabokov's most sophisticated narrator, however, *Ada*'s Van Veen, understands that a *spectrum* of variously talented readers, "my un-known dreamers" (p. 129), may be reading any passage of his chronicle at a given time, and that his own image as a narrator is consequently subject to a corresponding spectrum of perceptions. Hence Van refers to himself as "*this* brilliant or obscure V.V. (depending on the eyesight of readers, also poor people despite our jibes and their jobs)" (*Ada*, p. 79).

"V.V.," of course, ostensibly stands for Van Veen, while it also teasingly suggests that V.V. Nabokov is the actual subject of the passage (which goes on to compare V.V.'s "genius" to that of Shakespeare and Proust). The suggestion only teases, however; Nabokov's disclosure of successive narrators behind narrators performs a kind of striptease that never reaches flesh (like the seduction of Oedipa Maas, in Pynchon's *The Crying of Lot 49,* who wears countless layers of clothes so as to defer her surrender, and who falls asleep before she is fully undressed). The ambig-uous use of "V.V." is significant not only for its allowing the author to share in his narrator's boastful claims, but also for its reminding us that that narrator is controlled by an author skilled enough to take his own bow while the narrator proceeds unawares.

If Nabokov's fictions are in some sense "meta-fictional," it is because he focusses the reader's attention beyond the rising-and-falling graphs of the narrated actions, and on to the successive derivatives of these curves (so to speak)—the constantly modulating reliability of the dramatized narrators. Technique *is* recovery, in William Veeder's distortion of Mark Schorer's phrase.[1] In, for example, *The Eye* (Russian, 1930; English, 1965), the narrator starts out as a wholly plausible if somewhat mean-spirited character:

> I met that woman, that Matilda, during my first autumn of *émigré* existence in Berlin, in the early twenties of two spans of time, this century and my foul life.[2]

Life's foulness drives the narrator to attempt suicide by shooting himself through the heart; but

1. William Veeder, "Technique as Recovery: *Lolita* and *Mother Night*," in *Vonnegut in America,* ed. Jerome Klinkowitz and Donald L. Lawler (New York: Delacorte Press, 1977), pp. 97–132.
2. Vladimir Nabokov, *The Eye* (New York: Phaedra, 1965), p. 13.

Some time later, if one can speak here of time at all, it became clear that after death human thought lives on by momentum.   (*The Eye,* p. 30)

The narrator sustains a strangely disembodied existence as an observer of the Berlin émigré scene, obsessed with gathering information about a character named Smurov. Smurov is possibly a Soviet agent, definitely a shady character. While the narrator never confronts Smurov face to face, he questions several common acquaintances about him, especially the girl whose favor Smurov apparently courts. "I could already count three versions of Smurov, while the original remained unknown" (*The Eye,* p. 63). Gradually, the reactions of the narrator's interlocutors reveal to the reader that Smurov himself *is* the narrator. The discovery is corroborated by a line placed just after the suicide attempt: "In respect to myself I was now an onlooker" (*The Eye,* p. 37). The narrative presence, thus, has split into two discrete entitities at the firing of a gun: one, the observing and narrating "eye," and the other, the continued physical existence of the character whose eye it is, now viewed from outside as a mysterious and threatening creature. The "Eye" of the book's title is the "I" of its narrator.

In Robbe-Grillet's *La Jalousie* (1957), the narrative tone is similarly disembodied, similarly concealing the increasingly obvious necessity for the narrator to have been a major participant in the action he impersonally describes—a technique Bruce Morrissette has dubbed that of the "*je-néant.*"[1] In Nabokov's work, however, the status of the narrator is never static, but modulates in response to the turns of the action (hence the analogy to the derivative of a curve). The French might call this elegant shellgame of narrative voices "*le jeu du «je».*"

These modulations of narrative in Nabokov's work achieve all of the principal effects we have associated with literary self-consciousness. The succession of narrators behind narrators yields that infinite regression of structure by which the novel seems endlessly to mirror itself. Narrative, structure, characters, style, and themes are all *mises-en-abyme.* In *The Real Life of Sebastian Knight* (English, 1941), for example, it is never clear whether the narrator's biography of his half brother Sebastian is not "actually" the result of Knight's own invention of an imaginary, narrating half brother. The ludicrous critical battle over whether Shade or Kinbote is the "real" author of *Pale Fire* concerns a similar pair of facing mirrors. Nabokov employs narrative intrusions to produce a kind of

1. Bruce Morrissette, "Le paroxysme du *je-néant: la Jalousie,*" in his *Les Romans de Robbe-Grillet* (Paris: Editions de Minuit, 1963), pp. 111–47.

Verfremdungseffekt, distancing the fictional reality of his characters from the world of his readers by disclosing the narrative voice to be that of a writer at his desk—as in the account of Krug's death at the end of *Bend Sinister:*

> Krug ran towards [the dictator], and just a fraction of an instant before another and better bullet hit him, he shouted again: You, you—and the wall vanished, like a rapidly withdrawn slide, and I stretched myself and got up from among the chaos of written and rewritten pages, to investigate the sudden twang that something had made in striking the wire netting of my window.   (*Bend Sinister,* p. 240)

Narrative modulations are employed further as reminders of the physicality of the text itself, as in *Invitation to a Beheading*'s reference to "the right-hand, still untasted part of the novel" (p. 12). Similarly, our attention is frequently drawn to the physical disposition of ink on the page, as in *The Gift*'s self-illustrative observation, ". . . . It was a life whose portrayal demands from the writer an abundance of dots. . . ." (p. 284). Notably, narrators' reminders of their book's printedness may cover a wide range of *emotional* tones, from humorous, as with those ellipses, to pathetic, as in Humbert Humbert's heartbroken asides:

> Lolita, Lolita, Lolita, Lolita, Lolita, Lolita, Lolita, Lolita, Lolita. Repeat till the page is full, printer.   (*Lolita,* p. 111)

The constant flipping back and forth of pages called for by the cross-referenced Commentary and Index to *Pale Fire* induces a similar awareness that whatever seems to "happen" in its pages, one is, after all, holding a book.

Largely by means of these narrative devices—narrators visibly engaged in the act of composition, reminders of the author in control behind a succession of narrators, direct address to the reader *as* reader, textual self-reference, and so on—the *structures* of Nabokov's fiction are themselves made self-conscious. The neatest example of a "closed" structure is that of Nabokov's story "The Circle" (Russian, 1936; English, 1973). It begins as follows:

> In the second place, because he was possessed by a sudden mad hankering after Russia.[1]

The protagonist, Innokentiy, who loved pretty Tanya when they were children in Russia, one day runs into her—now married, with several

1. Vladimir Nabokov, "The Circle," in *A Russian Beauty and Other Stories* (New York: McGraw-Hill Paperbacks, 1973), p. 255.

children—in émigré Berlin. In the story's last lines Innokentiy walks away from the unexpected reunion with

> a dreadful feeling of uneasiness. He felt that way for several reasons. In the first place, because Tanya had remained as enchanting and as invulnerable as she had been in the past.   ("The Circle," in *A Russian Beauty*, p. 268)

In his preface to the English translation of this story Nabokov points out with distinct pride that it

> belongs to the same serpent-biting-its-tail type as the circular structure of the fourth chapter in *Dar* (or, for that matter, *Finnegans Wake*, which it pre-ceded).   (*A Russian Beauty*, p. 254)

The plots of Nabokov's novels, however, do not generally disclose that "conspicuous subordination to artificial generative principles" which we have identified as characteristic of self-conscious fictional structures, such as that of *Ulysses*. For, Nabokov *tells stories*. The novel *Pnin*, for example, terminates when its eponymous hero drives out of the field of vision of its malicious narrator, as if to prove that Pnin's life is not be subordinated to an autonomous esthetic frame but must remain open-ended. Nabokov is, in various ways, a romantic writer (and thus a practitioner of romantic irony); he tells love stories, stories of loss and of separation, of possession and jealousy, of *Glory* (Russian, 1932; English, 1971) and *Despair.* (Joyce, for one, didn't go in for all that.) There stands, Sphinx-like, at the very center of Nabokov's best fiction this strange and wonderful paradox: that *despite* its relentless insistence on its own fictivity, his preposterous, implausible, transparently fantastic stories touch us, move us, and stir our emotions as the work of few other contemporary writers can do. I am not saying that we turn to Nabokov solely for the sake of his stories—but that without them we would not enjoy turning to him so. This fascinating combination of an anti-mimetic style with the power to move us as events in real life do has perplexed students of Nabokov's work for decades. It is tempting to talk knowingly about the machinery, as Julia Bader does here, without explaining how the machinery works:

> The paradoxical observation that Nabokov's novels constantly invite the reader's emotional participation, while insisting on the self-contained nature of the fictional world, points to the aesthetic center of his work.[1]

The issue is more helpfully viewed by examining the novels themselves from the perspective of characterization. In *The Real Life of Sebastian*

---

1. Julia Bader, *Crystal Land: Artifice in Nabokov's English Novels* (Berkeley: University of California Press, 1972), p. 4. In general this is an excellent study.

Knight, for example, we learn that the "heroes" of Knight's own first novel only *appear* to be people. As the narrator puts it,

> *The Prismatic Bezel* can be thoroughly enjoyed once it is understood that the heroes of the book are what can be loosely called "methods of composition." It is as if a painter said: look, here I'm going to show you not the painting of a landscape, but the painting of different ways of painting a certain landscape, and I trust their harmonious fusion will disclose the landscape as I intend you to see it.[1]

It is not only *tempting* to draw the inference that the heroes of Nabokov's own books are "what can be loosely called 'methods of composition'" but it is also to some extent accurate to do so. When Cincinnatus C is beheaded at the end of *Invitation to a Beheading* (for the crime of "gnostical turpitude"), his fate is not that of human mortality but rather that of a literary device withdrawn from one context, finally acknowledged by "the author" to be inappropriate, to a context more congruous and consistent with the device, and hence more apparently real:

> Everything was coming apart. Everything was falling. A spinning wind was picking up and whirling: dust, rags, chips of painted wood, bits of gilded plaster, pasteboard bricks, posters; an arid gloom fleeted; and amid the dust, and the falling things, and the flapping scenery, Cincinnatus made his way in that direction where, to judge by the voices, stood beings akin to him. (*Invitation to a Beheading*, p. 223)

Similarly, Luzhin, committing suicide (or sui-mate) at the end of *The Defense,* effectively transposes himself from an alien (if thoroughly realistic) world in which he is clearly out of place to an artistic context to which, as a "method of composition," he is much better suited, the serene and orderly matrix of the chessboard:

> Before letting go he looked down. Some kind of hasty preparations were under way there: the window reflections gathered together and leveled themselves out, the whole chasm was seen to divide into dark and pale squares, and at the instant when Luzhin unclenched his hand, at the instant when icy air gushed into his mouth, he saw exactly what kind of eternity was obligingly and inexorably spread out before him.[2]

Nabokov's heroes are thus qualitatively different from the characters by which they are surrounded. To this extent, Nabokov's novels bear

1. Vladimir Nabokov, *The Real Life of Sebastian Knight* (New York: New Directions, 1959), p. 95.
2. Vladimir Nabokov, *The Defense* (New York: Capricorn Books, 1970), pp. 155–56.

comparison to the "monodrama" of Christopher Marlowe and others, in which the play is dominated by a single and often solipsistic central character.[1] Throughout *Invitation to a Beheading* it is repeatedly emphasized that Cincinnatus C possesses a solidity and an opacity which the other characters somehow lack. Cincinnatus declares, for example, "I am the one among you who is alive" (p. 52), and comes to recognize that even his own mother is "just as much of a parody as everybody and everything else" (*Invitation to a Beheading,* p. 132), just as in *Ada* Van describes *his* mother as "essentially a dummy in human disguise" (*Ada,* p. 266). The narrator of *The Eye* observes, "There is no use to dissemble—all these people I met were not live beings but only chance mirrors for Smurov [. . .] created merely for my amusement" (*The Eye,* p. 99).

The key to the differential "reality" between Nabokov's protagonists and his minor characters lies in the fact that the former are all, to varying degrees, artist-figures. Here lies, of course, the crux of Khodasevich's major contribution to Nabokov cricitism:

> The life of the artist and the life of a device in the consciousness of the artist— this is Sirin's theme, revealing itself to some degree or other in almost every one of his writings, beginning with *The Defense.*[2]

Andrew Field, among others, has reduced Khodasevich's insight to a claim that Nabokov "writes only about artists"[3] which, while a typical Field exaggeration, is not so very far from the truth. Dreyer, in *King, Queen, Knave,* shows Franz how neckties "might be sold if the salesman were both artist and clairvoyant" (p. 70), while in *Despair,* Hermann intends the murder of his double, Felix, to be perceived as an act of artistry. In fact it is in pursuit of the recognition which his artistry has failed to achieve that Hermann sets out to tell his story:

> And so, in order to obtain recognition, to justify and save the offspring of my brain, to explain to all the world the depth of my masterpiece, did I devise the writing of the present tale.   (*Despair,* pp. 204–05)

Similarly, Humbert Humbert avers in *Lolita* that "the artist in me has been given the upper hand over the gentleman" (*Lolita,* p. 73), just as in *Ada,* Van "knew he was not quite a savant, but completely an artist" (*Ada,* p. 501).

1. I am indebted to James Schiffer for this comparison (personal communication, 1978).
2. Khodasevich, "On Sirin," p. 100.
3. Field, "The Artist as Failure in Nabokov's Early Prose," p. 57.

With the approximative truth of all such generalizations, we may observe that Nabokov's artist-figures all come to realize in the course of their experiences that the world in which they exist is fictional—and that they themselves, while also fictional, are fictional on a more authentic, "truer" plane; that is, they learn that they represent a superior "method of composition." The protagonist of *Bend Sinister*, the philosopher Krug (whose name, by the way, means "circle" in Russian), offers the clearest exposition of this Nabokovian "coming to knowledge":

> He finally began regarding himself (robust rude Krug) as an illusion or rather as a shareholder in an illusion [. . .]. It was much the same thing as is liable to happen in novels when the author and his yes-characters assert that the hero is a "great artist" or a "great poet" without, however, bringing any proofs (reproductions of his paintings, samples of his poetry); indeed, taking care *not* to bring such proofs since any sample would be sure to fall short of the reader's expectations and fancy. Krug, while wondering who had puffed him up, who had projected him on to the screen of fame, could not help feeling that in some odd way he did deserve it [. . .].   (*Bend Sinister*, p. 173)[1]

Inevitably, a protagonist's discovery that he is a fictional character surrounded by his author's "yes-characters" leads to what, on one fictional plane, appears as his death and on another, as we have seen in Cincinnatus' acceptance of an invitation to a beheading, represents his withdrawal to a new and more appropriate fictional context. Thus Luzhin, the artistic chess genius of *The Defense*, makes his leap from a simulacrum of this world to one of infinite, eternal chess, upon realizing that the apparent events of his life have in fact been chess moves in a game played against an incomparably grander master than he. As Julia Bader has put it,

> For Nabokov and his characters, aesthetic patterns are not a way of escaping from the empirical world but rather a way of creating a self-contained and complete world. When the characters attempt to escape from their aesthetically created selves and circumstances, it is through shifting levels of fictional reality rather than from reality to art.[2]

It is in this sense of fictional death—as a character's transposition between two contexts of unequal fictional reality—that we are to interpret Krug's understanding at the end of *Bend Sinister*, when "it had been proven to him that death was but a question of style [. . .]; a question of rhythm" (p. 241).

1. Let it be noted that Nabokov himself *does* bring proofs of his heroes' artistry, as in Shade's poem in *Pale Fire*.
2. Bader, *Crystal Land*, p. 3n.

Thus the dehumanization of character which we have deemed typical of the self-conscious novel takes place in Nabokov's fiction in a way that does not disrupt the reader's sustained emotional sympathies for the main characters. The reader is reminded that the characters are fictional, *but* the characters who are themselves aware of their fictional status nevertheless retain their integrity as centers of thought and feeling, and thus their power to amuse or sadden us. Nabokov's characters who recognize their fictivity effectively saw off the branch on which they are sitting from the tree that is the novel's apparent "real" world—but it is the tree, not the character, which drops out of sight. When the worlds that condemn Cincinnatus C and Adam Krug to death crumple into bits of plaster and painted wood or are whisked from the projector like an unwanted slide, when the "distant northern land" of Zembla is dismissed as a mad professor's fabrication, we are still left with the memorable and human figures of Cincinnatus and Krug and Charles the Beloved.

"My characters are my galley slaves," as Nabokov has punningly put it.[1] True, and therein lies their tragedy. The contest between self-consciously fictive character and self-consciously authorial author is fixed from the start. "They took a great many precautions—all of them absolutely useless, for nothing can change the end (written and filed away) of the present chapter," begins a chapter of *Ada* (p. 458). Self-depicting fiction proves itself capable of the fatidic overtones of Attic tragedy. At the same time, however, the plight of Nabokov's "galley slaves" is essentially *comic,* as the consciously fictive among them find themselves in an awkward and incongruous, not to say impossible, position: "'Well, and how is our doomed friend today?' quipped the elegant, dignified [prison] director" of *Invitation to a Beheading* (p. 38).

On his *unwitting* galley slaves, his "yes-characters," Nabokov lavishes little but contempt. In *King, Queen, Knave*, Martha reminisces about her childhood, her wedding, "and so on, not very interesting recollections" (p. 66). ("Her autobiography was as devoid of interest as her autopsy would have been," says Humbert of soon-to-die Charlotte Haze [*Lolita*, p. 82].) Oblivious Martha, "who, despite her fine dresses and face lotions, resembled a large white toad" (*King, Queen, Knave*, p. 259), meets a mortal's death while Franz, who acknowledges and resents the image of his author, is, accordingly, "perhaps pitied" and allowed to conclude

---

1. Interview with Herbert Gold, "The Art of Fiction" *The Paris Review,* 41 (Summer-Fall 1967), 96.

the novel "roaring again in a frenzy of young mirth" (p. 272). (The narrator of *Bend Sinister* similarly "felt a pang of pity for Adam" [p. 233].) Characters not in the know, thus, are dehumanized beyond recall; in *Ada* a minor character is introduced parenthetically as "(narrationally a great burden)" (p. 85). What distinguishes Van and Ada, meanwhile, from the rest of that novel's ample cast, what makes of them, as they like to call themselves, "a unique, super-imperial couple" (p. 77), is not their naughty incest, nor even their much vaunted intelligence, but rather the fact that they are the only characters in the book who know that they are characters in the book. Thus their death, as they themselves describe it, is not a "realistically" terminal one, like all the other deaths at the novel's most apparent plane of "reality," but it is rather a "death" that transposes them to another plane of fictional reality, one that is "closer" or "truer" to the narrative process of the book itself:

> One can even surmise that if our time-racked, flat-lying couple ever intended to die, they would die, as it were, *into* the finished book, into Eden or Hades, into the prose of the book or the poetry of its blurb.   (*Ada*, pp. 624–625)

Nabokov's prose style varies from narrator to narrator, and the later narrators vary their own styles from occasion to occasion; but, in general, Nabokov's style is heavily Euphuistic and draws attention to itself accordingly. "You can always count on a murderer for a fancy prose style," as Humbert Humbert assures us on the first page of his narrative (*Lolita*, p. 11). Nabokov's elaborate sentences brachiate Euphuistically, share Lyly's liking for alliteration and his pursuit of parallels from natural science. His similes strike: a "poodlet" in *Ada* "had glistening eyes like sad black olives" (*Ada*, p. 40); a bookseller in *The Eye* had "nerves [. . .] as slack as old suspenders" (*The Eye*, p. 51). The style sticks out like a sore simile.

Nabokov's style draws further attention to itself by its characteristic use of the trope called *phrasal tmesis*, in which, according to Peter Lubin's charming definition, "a semantic petticoat is slipped on between the naked noun and its clothing epithet"[1]—for example, the Arctic no longer vicious Circle" (*Ada*, p. 19) or, in another example, "Memory is a photo-studio de luxe on an infinite Fifth Power Avenue" (*Ada*, p. 109). Alliteration also asserts artifice, as in Van's "final pronouncement, damning all

---

1. Peter Lubin, "Kickshaws and Motley," in *Nabokov*, ed. Appel and Newman, pp. 194–95. Lubin's essay deserves singling out as a particularly delightful *tour de force*.

clowns and clods" (*Ada*, p. 250), or Humbert Humbert's "I spend my doleful days in dumps and dolors" (*Lolita*, p. 45). Zeugma draws attention to itself in Cincinnatus C's efforts to "appear cheerful, crack nuts, crack jokes" (*Invitation to a Beheading*, p. 64), and in Humbert Humbert's mention of "stepfathers with motherless girls on their hands and knees" (*Lolita*, p. 174). This last phrase unpacks to yield at least three relevant meanings: (1) public Humbert burdened by a ward ("stepfathers with motherless girls on their hands"); (2) private Humbert's favorite fondle ("stepfathers with [. . .] girls on their [. . .] knees"); and (3) Lolita's abject position ("motherless girls on their hands and knees"). At its best, as here, Nabokov's polysemous language parades itself self-consciously while simultaneously promulgating the story's human values.

"Tropes are the dreams of speech" (*Ada*, p. 441). Chiasmus flexes its muscles in *Pale Fire*:

> One ear in Italy, one eye in Spain,
> In caves, my blood, and in the stars, my brain.   (ll. 151–52)

Anthropomorphizing like the Dickens he claimed to dislike, Nabokov describes the walls of Cincinnatus' jail cell "with their arms around each other's shoulders" (*Invitation to a Beheading*, p. 32). The tap of a bath tub in *Ada* is "too brutally anxious to emit the hot torrent and get rid of the infernal ardor—to bother about small talk" (p. 26). Anthropomorphization is not necessarily self-conscious—as it is not in Dickens—but like his striking similes, Nabokov's metaphors are intentionally immodest. He means his conceits to seem conceited.

Onomatopoeia offers another neat paradigm of the way in which Nabokov's style achieves a synthesis of both mimetic and ludic effects. "A gong bronzily boomed on a terrace" (*Ada*, p. 49). Assonance ("go*ng* bro*nz*ily") and alliteration ("*b*ronzily *b*oomed") add aspects of ostentatious craft to an otherwise conventional onomatopoetic verb ("boomed"). The sentence successfully evokes the sound of a real gong in the mind's ear while asserting the artifice of the means employed. In somewhat the same way, the "Mrkgnao" of Bloom's cat in *Ulysses* (p. 55) *sounds* like a cat to us, at the same time that it impresses us with Joyce's ability to approximate that sound in printed letters.

Of Van and Ada's mutual father, *Ada* informs us that "Demon's two-fold hobby was collecting old masters and young mistresses. He also liked middle-aged puns" (p. 4). Well-spun puns punctuate Nabokov's prose for a variety of reasons, most of which are fairly obvious by this point in our discussion. For one thing puns are funny, and not infrequently risqué, as in the Spooneristic title of an off-Broadway play in *Transparent Things*, "Cunning Stunts."[1] Frequently, however, they are not funny at all, as in Humbert Humbert calling Dolores Haze, his unhappy Lolita, "my dolorous and hazy darling" (*Lolita*, p. 55). Trilingual Nabokov tends to pun across languages, an affectation no doubt offensive to readers confined to one tongue, but strangely exhilarating to those who can follow him across. There are, of course, evaluative distinctions to be made. When, for example, in *Ada*, "three young ladies in yellow-blue Vass frocks" (p. 199) are seen to conceal, more or less, the я люблю вас [*ya lyub-lyu vass*] of Russian's "I love you,"[2] we may well feel confronted, in the words of *Pnin*, by "one of those random likenesses as pointless as a bad pun" (p. 113). But, on the other hand, *Ada*'s version of King Lear's famous monologue is surely as durable a piece of translingual punning as it is possible for such frippery to become:

> Ce beau jardin fleurit en mai;
> Mais en hiver
> Jamais, jamais, jamais, jamais, jamais
> N'est vert, n'est vert, n'est vert, n'est vert,
> n'est vert.   (*Ada*, p. 98)

Nabokov plays similar games when offering English transliterations of Russian pronunciations of French words, as in Marina's request to "let me put on a *penyuar*" (*Ada*, p. 17).

Helpfully (for my purposes), the narrator of *Despair* explains his fondness for puns as a desire "to make words look self-conscious":

> I liked, as I like still, to make words look self-conscious and foolish, to bind them by the mock-marriage of a pun, to turn them inside out, to come upon them unawares. What is this jest in majesty? This ass in passion? How do God and Devil combine to form a live dog?   (*Despair*, p. 56)

Of course by "self-conscious" Hermann means socially awkward, but the effect he is describing is that of language used reflexively—when the "accidental properties" of a word's sound or spelling, as we discussed in

---

1. Vladimir Nabokov, *Transparent Things* (New York: McGraw-Hill, 1972), p. 34.
2. This has been pointed out by Carl R. Proffer, "*Ada* as Wonderland: A Glossary of Allusions to Russian Literature," in *A Book of Things about Vladimir Nabokov*, ed. Proffer, p. 262.

Chapter 1, are treated as if they were "essential properties," and thus bearers of their own meaning. "You look quite satanically fit, Dad," says Van to Demon. "I suppose you have not been much in Manhattan lately—where did you get its last syllable?" (*Ada*, p. 252). While revealing the man in a tan hat hidden in Manhattan, Van's "homespun pun in the Veenish vein" (p. 252) further asserts that the accidents of a word's physical composition may be mined for new (and posibly even germane) meanings.

As puns mine meanings in the sounds of words, so anagrams make use of their spelling. Both tropes treat language less as the "gray inaudible wife who services the great man" of William Gass's offensive formulation, than as the athlete whose body is exercised in games.[1] Puns opacify, anagrams reify language. They are both liable to be used frivolously, since they need not make any particular point in order to qualify as puns or anagrams, and they accordingly suffer from a general disesteem. We groan at puns, though not at anagrams, perhaps because we read anagrams but hear puns uttered by grinning punsters. Nabokov's anagrams, at their best, rise above these accusations of frivolity when, like his best puns, they contribute to the characterization or enforce the emotional themes of his novels' plots. One such happy combination of ludic and mimetic effects occurs in the scene in *Ada* in which Ada "played anagrams with Grace" (both her friend and a pun). The girls begin with *insect,* then proceed to *scient* ("Dr. Entsic was scient in insects" [p. 91]); and when Ada "instantly" comes up with *incest* the reader recognizes her contribution as, thematically speaking, the *nicest.* At the same time the game's progress neatly dramatizes Ada's considerable intellectual superiority over her playmates, an important aspect of Ada's characterization. Nabokov anagrammatizes thematically; "Eros, the rose and the sore" (*Ada*, p. 389) is not only crystalline in itself but an appropriate emblem for "the Ardors and Arbors of Ardis" (p. 625). Vekchelo, an inversion of the Russian word for man, человек [chelovyek], is the name of the man in *Ada* who stands on his hands (p. 88).

1. "[. . .] Ordinarily language ought to be like the gray inaudible wife who services the great man: an ideal engine, utterly self-effacing, devoted without remainder to its task; but when language is used as an art it is no longer used merely to communicate. It demands to be treated as a thing, inert and voiceless. Properties that it possesses accidentally as a sign it suddenly possesses essentially." William H. Gass, "Gertrude Stein: Her Escape from Protective Language," in his *Fiction and the Figures of Life* (New York: Knopf, 1970), pp. 92–93.

Palindromes, which are anagrams of fearful symmetry, produce an analogous reflexive effect but of a greater magnitude, corresponding to the apparently greater difficulty of composing palindromes. Lending orthographic amplification to the novel's uniquitous mirror imagery, *Pale Fire*'s good Odon is given an evil twin brother Nodo (p. 150); Yakob Gradus is matched by Sudarg of Bokay (p. 111). "Nova Avon" materializes in *Bend Sinister* (p. 113), and in order to complete that novel, the narrator turns Adam Krug into "mad Adam" (p. 145). Nabokov's most ambitious novel sports a palindromic title.

Palindromes are words that survive passage across the looking glass. Humbert Humbert's name, as a word-unit palindrome, retains its identity back-to-front.[1] The initials of *Lolita*'s "editor," John Ray, Jr., are likewise mirror twins (JR, JR). HH and VV, the initials by which Humbert and Van often refer to themselves, would physically survive transposition across mirrors in a variety of planes. Like "the shadow of the waxwing" immortalized in the first stanza of *Pale Fire*, these characters and titles "Lived on, flew on, in the reflected sky."

It is hard to use palindromes to make a point (although Nabokov did enjoy turning *T.S. Eliot* into *toilest*). Acrostics, however, are easier to compose, and much more manageable. Nabokov's story, "The Vane Sisters," concerns Cynthia and Sybil, two dead sisters whom the narrator tries to contact telepathically.[2] (Sybil Vane has not changed her name since playing another dead sister in Wilde's *The Picture of Dorian Gray*.) The narrator wanders about town, observing melting icicles and the moving shadow of a parking meter, as he listens for ghostly voices. In the story's final sentences he laments his failure to receive any intelligible message from beyond the grave:

> I could isolate, consciously, little. Everything seemed blurred, yellow-clouded, yielding nothing tangible. Her inept acrostics, maudlin evasions, theopathies—every recollection formed ripples of mysterious meaning. Everything seemed yellowly blurred, illusive, lost.   ("The Vane Sisters," p. 238)

The lament itself, however, conceals an acrostic message signed by Sybil, which reveals that she and her sister had a mysterious hand in the com-

1. Humbert Humbert's name may also be, as William Veeder has pointed out to me, a clever allusion to Umberto Eco, with a play on "echo." Both Humpty Dumpty and "humbug" are more definitely implied.

2. Vladimir Nabokov, "The Vane Sisters," in *Tyrants Destroyed and Other Stories* (New York: McGraw-Hill, 1975), pp. 217–38.

position of the whole story (the acrostic spells "Icicles by Cynthia; meter from me—Sybil"). Pointless acrostics, like cheap puns, are not difficult to compose. In this story, however, Nabokov uses the physical "accident" of the initial letters of words to conceal a secondary meaning which comically controverts the apparent sense of the passage. The acrostic not only makes sense but makes sense of the story.

Like the games of "word golf" which *Pale Fire* invites the reader to play—for example, go from hate to love in three moves, "lass-male in four, and live-dead in five (with 'lend' in the middle)" (*Pale Fire*, p. 262)—Nabokov's word play is generally of a visual sort that relies on the body as well as on the spirit of its words. Van, for example, refers to "the still existing but rather gaga *Kaluga Gazette*" [my emphasis] (*Ada*, p. 6). Marina's Spanish vocabulary, Van informs us, is limited to "*aroma* and *hombre*, and an anatomical term with a 'j' hanging in the middle" (*Ada*, pp. 49–50). (Hemingway taught Americans about *cojones*, but that flaccid "j" is pure Nabokov.) Obviously the potential for humor in such wordplay is great. "There is always a danger," as *The Gift* warns us, "that one letter will fall out of the cosmic" (p. 256). With less frequency, but with equal success, however, Nabokov also "reifies" language in the interests of pathos. In *Invitation to a Beheading*, for example, the language of grief falls apart, then pulls itself back together:

> It was plain that he was upset by the loss of that precious object. It was plain. The loss of the object upset him. The object was precious. He was upset by the loss of the object.   (*Invitation to a Beheading*, p. 36)

Abject gratitude has a similar distorting effect: "Cincinnatus said: 'Kind. You. Very.' (This still had to be arranged)" (*Invitation to a Beheading*, p. 15).

Nabokov's playing fields are the paradoxical extremes of language where words either seem to mean but do not, or seem not to mean but do. Cincinnatus sees an example of the former painted on the wall of his cell: "Testing brush, testing bru——" (*Invitation to a Beheading*, p. 72). A foolish character in *Ada* replies to a question to which he doesn't know the answer by saying, "That is what we are going to find out;" as if, smirks the narrator, everything one can say must contain a thought. "*That which does not have a name does not exist.* Unfortunately everything had a name" (*Invitation to a Beheading*, p. 26). Language which, deceptively, seems not to mean but does, is one way of defining *code;* the lovers' coded messages in *Ada* permit the inclusion of ideally opaque language which can nonetheless be made to yield a sense conducive to the plot:

> Van plunged into the dense undergrowth. He wore a silk shirt, a velvet jacket, black breeches, riding boots with star spurs—and this attire was hardly convenient for making *klv zdB AoyvBno wkh gwzxm dqg kzwAAqvo* a *gwttp vq wjfhm* Ada in a natural bower of aspens; *xlic mujzikml,* after which she said [. . .].   (*Ada,* p. 168)

The reader is not taught until the following chapter how to decode these words. (Decoded, they read: "his way through the brush and crossing a brook to reach;" and "they embraced.") The reader must carry with him for several pages these unintelligble husks which spring to life only when their secret is revealed.

Nabokov's predilection for the most *recherché* of diction produces this same pattern of effects: initially opaque language which disrupts the smooth flow of the narrative, when properly understood, is then seen actually to participate in the narrative process. The following sentence from the "Night of the Burning Barn" scene in *Ada* offers perhaps the best example of Nabokov's playfully opaque diction:

> He caressed and parted with his fleshy folds, *parties très charnues,* in the case of our passionate siblings, her lank loose, nearly lumbus-length (when she threw back her head as now) black silks as he tried to get at her bed-warm splenius.   (*Ada,* p. 125)

Van's "fleshy folds" and *"parties très charnues"* allude elliptically (and hence teasingly) to the various definitions of "lips" in dictionaries which the children have consulted in an earlier chapter (dictionaries constitute quite a theme in *Ada*). "Lumbus" is Latin, not English, for loin; but the reader is certain to be intrigued by "her bed-warm splenius," which may sound pudic to all but the medically educated. In fact, according to the *OED,* the splenius is "a broad muscle [. . .] which occupies the upper part of the back of the neck." Like Tristram Shandy's unconvincing protests that his innocent tale of noses is being misread as bawdry, Nabokov's obscure diction seems to promise salaciousness and to disdain it at the same time. The coded passages quoted above are likewise designed to seem pornographic until they are decoded; Van's attire, we read, "was hardly convenient for making [coded blank] Ada in a natural bower of aspens" (*Ada,* p. 168). Nabokov characteristically places obscure but precise diction in contexts which make it seem naughty to the unknowing reader; only recourse to a reference book can dispel the illusion of naughtiness founded upon the word's unfamiliarity. We can find another example in *Invitation to a Beheading:* "Marthe, when she was a bride, was frightened of the frogs and cockchafers" (p. 19). This is what Hermann, in *Despair,* called, as we have noted, "coming upon words unawares," but most often it is the reader who is caught.

We should also note, before leaving the subject of Nabokov's diction, his habit of coining his own words. Like the coded messages and the foreign and domestic words which can be looked up, Nabokov's neologisms initially jar the reader but eventually, through consistent use, yield a meaning whose relevance becomes clear. "Humbertish" is a typical example, as in *Lolita*'s narrator's description of himself "imagining in all possible detail the enigmatic nymphet I would coach in French and fondle in Humbertish" (p. 37). Nabokov's use of "nymphet" has even worked its way into our own lexicon; *Webster's Third New International Dictionary Unabridged* defines "nymphet" as "2. a sexually precocious young girl: a loose young woman."

*   *   *

The manner in which Nabokov's novels enforce their themes partakes of the same radical ambivalence that we have discerned in his treatment of narration, structure, characterization, and style. That is, certain recognizably human values are promulgated at the same time that their bearing upon the "real world" outside the fiction is denied. Despite their claims of esthetic insularity, Nabokov's novels nonetheless dramatize a contest between serious ethical values. His novels are not allegories, nor are they morality plays, but they do pit the forces of Good against those of Evil. Like the pitiable plight of characters enslaved to a self-conscious author, Nabokov's themes furnish another means by which the author engages our emotions while insisting on his own artifice. In order to understand how this can be so, it is first necessary to disabuse ourselves of some of Nabokov's own disclaimers on the subject of his themes. Nabokov himself, in conformity with his *fin de siècle* esthetic of art for art's sake, of course, consistently denied that he had anything to say. *Despair* has "no message to bring in its teeth," Nabokov declares in the Preface (p. 8). "Few things are more boring than a discussion of general ideas" (Preface to *Bend Sinister,* p. vi). He welcomed the chance to publish his *Strong*

Opinions because "my fiction allows me so seldom the occasion to air my private views."[1]

Notwithstanding these protestations, Nabokov's fiction is muscle-bound with "strong opinions" and "private views." The esthete who narrates the story "Spring in Fialta" (Russian, 1936; English, 1957) may announce, with a martyr's vainglory,

> I will contend until I am shot that art as soon as it is brought into contact with politics inevitably sinks to the level of any ideological trash.[2]

Fine. Still, Nabokov is, in his way, an ethical, and even an intensely political writer.

Nabokov's fiction is, for instance, fiercely anti-Soviet. The description which the narrator of *Look at the Harlequins!* offers of his relations with the Soviet Union only slightly parodizes the relations of Nabokov himself with the tyrannical government of his lost homeland:

> I had escaped from Russia at the age of not quite nineteen, leaving across my path in a perilous forest the felled body of a Red soldier. I had then dedicated half a century to berating, deriding, twisting into funny shapes, wringing out like blood-wet towels, kicking neatly in Evil's stinkiest spot, and otherwise tormenting the Soviet regime at every suitable turn of my writings. In fact, no more consistent critic of Bolshevist brutality and basic stupidity existed during all that time at the literary level to which my work belonged.   (*Look at the Harlequins!*, pp. 203–04)

The passage describes Nabokov's writings as well as those of V.V. McNab, save for that mock-heroic felled Red who, like *Pnin's* "old Miss Herring, Professor of History, author of *Russia Awakes* (1922)" (*Pnin*, pp. 27–28), is certainly another "red herring." In his 1975 introduction to his 1938 story "Tyrants Destroyed," Nabokov acknowledged that he had particular tyrants in mind, and even described the story and its development into the novel *Bend Sinister* as a kind of political action:

> Hitler, Lenin, and Stalin dispute my tyrant's throne in this story—and meet again in *Bend Sinister*, 1947, with a fifth toad. The destruction is thus complete.   (*Tyrants Destroyed*, p. 2)

The ethical combat which Nabokov's fiction thematically enacts, however, is much broader in scope than the specifically political issues raised by his native Russia's fate. Throughout his fiction, the values of his cre-

---

1. Vladimir Nabokov, *Strong Opinions* (New York: McGraw-Hill, 1973), p. xii.
2. Vladimir Nabokov, "Spring in Fialta," in *Nabokov's Dozen*, p. 25.

ated worlds are threatened by the undeniably "real" Evils of cruelty, madness, time's passage, and death; while the positive values that resist and ultimately triumph over these threats are those of love, imagination, memory, and art. Schematically, these Manichean dichotomies may be arrayed as antithetical pairs: love versus cruelty, imagination versus madness, memory versus time's passage, and art versus death. However, the final value of art, as we shall see, ultimately encapsulates, redeems, and immortalizes all the other values and threats. As Proust did, thematically, in the last volume of *A la Recherche du temps perdu,* and as Joyce did, through the repertoire of resources we have examined in *Ulysses,* Nabokov thus composes art that displays its own art *in order to* address that very art as its subject.

The repugnant cruelty of Van Veen, though often overlooked, is central to the ethical impact of his narrative,

> for no sooner did all the fond, all the frail, come into close contact with him (as later Lucette did, to give another example) than they were bound to know anguish and calamity [. . .].   (*Ada,* p. 22)

Similarly, although Part One of *Lolita* works rhetorically to convince us that Humbert Humbert's sexual liaison with little Dolly Haze is morally acceptable, Part Two renders ethically intolerable his depriving her of a normal childhood. What Humbert cruelly violates is, as William Veeder puts it, "not Lolita's maidenhead, but her maidenhood."[1] The cruelty of Paduk, the dictator of *Bend Sinister,* and that of Axel Rex in *Laughter in the Dark* (Russian, 1933; English, 1938), are similarly presented not with the esthete's requisite dispassion, but with unmistakable signs of authorial indignation and repudiation. Van, the artist *manqué,* and Ada, the would-be naturalist, are not only totally sterile but satisfied by their sterility: Ada vaunts her "acarpous destiny" (p. 231), while

> all the doctors agreed that Van Veen might be a doughty and durable lover but could never hope for an offspring. How merrily little Ada clapped her hands!   (*Ada,* p. 417)

With their mutual father named Demon, and Ada's name the locative case of "hell" (*iz ada* means "out of hell" in Russian), the ethical repudiation of Van and Ada's elegant, "romantic" cruelty is thus clear.

"When I hear a critic speaking of an author's sincerity," says John

1. William Veeder, "Technique as Recovery," p. 99.

Shade, "I know that either the critic or the author is a fool" (*Pale Fire*, p. 156). In the Preface to *Bend Sinister*, similarly, Nabokov declares that

> I am not "sincere," I am not "provocative," I am not "satirical." I am neither a didacticist nor an allegorizer.   (*Bend Sinister*, p. vi)

Despite these denials, in Nabokov's fiction *art expresses love. Lolita,* viewed in one light, is a heartrending cry of loss, and of undying love for "*Dolorès disparue.*" Humbert's greed to possess his beloved is both grotesque and eloquent:

> My only grudge against nature was that I could not turn my Lolita inside out and apply voracious lips to her young matrix, her unknown heart, her nacreous liver, the sea-grapes of her lungs, her comely twin kidneys.   (*Lolita,* p. 167)

In *Lolita,* as in the play-within-the novel *The Enchanted Hunters,* "mirage and reality merge in love" (*Lolita,* p. 203). In *Ada,* similarly, it is frequently made clear that Van's and Ada's incest is spurred by love as well as by lust. Van suggests, for example, that his love for Ada renders masturbation inadequate as a satisfaction:

> If the relief, any relief, of a lad's ardor had been Van's sole concern; if, in other words, no love had been involved, our young friend might have put up—for one casual summer—with the nastiness and ambiguity of his behavior. But since Van loved Ada, that complicated release could not be an end in itself; or rather, it was only a dead end, because unshared; because horribly hidden; because not liable to melt into any subsequent phase of incomparably greater rapture which, like a misty summit beyond the fierce mountain pass, promised to be the true pinnacle of his perilous relationship with Ada. (*Ada,* p. 107)

Shade's poem *Pale Fire* is in large part a moving expression of love for his tragically unhappy daughter Hazel. Nabokov wrote with atypical candor about the importance of love in his work, in his preface to *Bend Sinister:*

> The main theme of *Bend Sinister,* then, is the beating of Krug's loving heart, the torture an intense tenderness is subjected to—and it is for the sake of the pages about David and his father that the book was written and should be read.   (*Bend Sinister,* p. viii)

Feelings are thus central to Nabokov's fictional creations, which only pretend to be heartless. The description, in "Spring in Fialta," of the books written by Nina's husband, parodies Nabokov's own reputation in 1938, and exemplifies his studied pretense at heartlessness:

> At the beginning of his career, it had been possible perhaps to distinguish some human landscape, some old garden, some dream-familiar disposition of trees through the stained glass of his prodigious prose . . . but with every new book the tints grew still more ominous; and today one can no longer see anything at all through that blazoned, ghastly rich glass, and it seems that were one to break it, nothing but a perfectly black void would face one's shivering soul. ("Spring in Fialta," pp. 16–17)

Unfortunately, some readers accept Nabokov's claims to heartlessness at face value, to the detriment of his books. R.A. Sokolov's response to *Ada* is a case in point: "there has never been a more cerebrally constructed, less emotionally involving book than this geometric study of lifelong illicit passion."[1] But the death of Lucette, to take a single example, is, for most readers of my acquaintance, immensely involving emotionally, for all its "cerebral construction." Nabokov may disclaim messages, but he has gone out of his way to insist that his writings express feeling.

> The main favor I ask of the serious critic is sufficient perceptiveness to understand that whatever term or trope I use, my purpose is not to be facetiously flashy or grotesquely obscure but to express what I feel and think with the utmost truthfulness and perception.[2]

Though their author claimed to pursue an amoral "esthetic bliss," Nabokov's novels thus engage in considerable moral suasion. Rhetorically his fictions *repudiate* the cruelty that, however "artistic" its motives, abuses the helplessness of others, and, equally, they endorse the love that respects its object as a consciousness independent and whole.

Madness is a constant threat to Nabokov's artist-heroes, and more than a few of them succumb. Humbert Humbert says that "You have to be an artist and a madman" to recognize a nymphet (*Lolita*, p. 19), and, like those of Hermann in *Despair*, Humbert's problems arise mainly from an inability to distinguish between the two. Sometimes, as the title of *Despair* suggests, suicidal depression beckons. Before eventually killing herself, Van's mother Aqua, for instance, treks from one asylum to the

1. R.A. Sokolov, review of *Ada* in *Newsweek*, 5 May 1969, p. 110.
2. Interview with Alden Whitman, "Vladimir Nabokov, 72 Today, Writing a New Novel," *New York Times*, 23 April 1971; quoted in Bobbie Ann Mason, *Nabokov's Garden: A Guide to* Ada (Ann Arbor, Mich.: Ardis, 1974), p. 176n.

next, hoping for "just a little grayishness, please, instead of the solid black" (*Ada,* p. 22). Most often, however, his heroes' sanity is sabotaged by solipsism.

Saving notable Pnin, in fact, Nabokov's hero-characters are all solipsists. Nabokov's novels make solipsism, as a system of thought, tangible as a dramatic situation through the greater fictional reality of the hero and the cardboard qualities of the "yes-characters" around him. But something goes wrong as soon as these "artistic" types carry their solipsistic imaginings out of the realm of imagination and put them into practice in the "real" world around them. Hermann's "artistic" murder of Felix results in a critical and criminal failure, just as Humbert Humbert comes to understand that Lolita was not so "safely solipsized" after all. Luzhin's surrender to the world of abstract chess concepts proves fatal. Kinbote the dreamer kills Shade the poet. Van and Ada kill Lucette. "You can always count on a murderer for a fancy prose style" (*Lolita,* p. 11). Yes, but must one kill to be an artist? These novels make it look that way, by showing what can happen when the mad imaginings of solipsism are not contained by imagination's proper domain: dreams and art. When solipsism enacts itself in the external world of action, the results may kill, as Felix and John Shade are killed; but when imagination transforms and channels the potential madness of solipsism into art, the results may, on the contrary, engender a kind of life, as in the self-conscious texts of *Despair* and *Pale Fire.*

In his quirky and rather irritating biography of the author, Andrew Field quotes Nabokov as saying, "If I had been born four years later, I wouldn't have written all those books."[1] Time perhaps seemed such a precious commodity to Nabokov because small units had such a huge impact on his life. "I wish to caress time," Van announces in *Ada* (p. 571), devoting Part IV of his chronicle to a demonstration that "time is a fluid medium for the cultivation of metaphors."

Time proves to be a more recalcitrant medium for Van than for earlier Nabokov heroes. Cincinnatus C, for example, is most conscious of his own life in the instant of hypothetical lag time between the movement of an object and that of its shadow:

1. Andrew Field, *Nabokov: His Life in Part* (New York: The Viking Press, 1977), p. 105. As 'Walter Walkarput,' I have pretended to discover that Andrew Field is one of Nabokov's own fictional creations, in "Nabokov: His Life *is* Art," *Chicago Review,* 29:2 (Autumn 1977), 72–82, excerpted in *Contemporary Literary Criticism,* XI, 392–93. See also M. Marks, "Index to Volume 29," *Chicago Review,* 29:4 (Spring 1978), 125–31.

Here is what I want to express: between his movement and the movement of the laggard shadow—that second, that syncope—there is the rare kind of time in which I live.   (*Invitation to a Beheading*, p. 53)

The narrator of the story "The Vane Sisters" shows a similar interest in the shadows of drops falling from melting icicles as compared with the fall of the drops themselves, just as in the poem *Pale Fire* Shade is fascinated by the reflections of leaves in a pond which never fail to meet their falling originals as they hit the water. Describing in his nonfictional memoir *Speak, Memory* the instant of inspiration for his first poem, Nabokov seems to share his characters' fascination with durationless time: "Tip, leaf, dip, relief—the instant it all took to happen seemed to me not so much a fraction of time as a fissure in it [. . .]" (*Speak, Memory*, p. 217). Nabokov continues:

Vivian Bloodmark, a philosophical friend of mine, in later years, used to say that while the scientist sees everything that happens in one point of space, the poet feels everything that happens in one point of time.   (*Speak Memory*, p. 218).

Similarly, as Nabokov's first novel in English tells us, "Time for Sebastian was never 1914 or 1936—it was always year 1" (*The Real Life of Sebastian Knight*, p. 65). "Time and space were to him measures of the same eternity" (p. 66)—in other words, in Sebastian Knight's view one ought to sympathize equally with a calamity of long ago as with one of today in a distant land.

The power of art, and especially literary art, to give back to us what time has taken away is perhaps made most clear in a passage of *Ada* which exposes the metaphorical dimension of Van's performances as Mascodagama, the magician who walks on his hands:

The essence of the satisfaction belonged rather to the same order as the one he later derived from self-imposed, extravagantly difficult, seemingly absurd tasks when V.V. sought to express something, which *until* expressed had only a twilight being (or even none at all—nothing but the illusion of the backward shadow of its imminent expression). It was Ada's castle of cards. It was the standing of a metaphor on its head not for the sake of the trick's difficulty, but in order to perceive an ascending waterfall or a sunrise in reverse: a triumph, in a sense, over the ardis of time.   (*Ada*, p. 197)

Art, then, reverses the arrowheads of time (as Lucette's governess told her, "ardis" means "the point of an arrow" in Greek [*Ada*, p. 327]). Humbert is able to bring back his lost Lolita, Van and Ada recapture their vanished childhood. *Ada* as a whole asserts its "triumph, in a sense, over the ardis of time" by the emphatic anachronisticity of its created world: Antiterrans fly magic carpets and drive automobiles, study micro-films and fight duels, ban electricity and send telegrams. The setting of *Invitation to a Beheading* is likewise rendered ahistorical by its patent anachronisms; the action takes place at a "time" when "those splendid lacquered stream-lined automobiles" have been replaced by "degenerate [wind-up] descendants" (p. 74). The novel's time is not "our" time, not *any* time.

"Imagination is a form of memory," Nabokov told Alfred Appel, Jr. "Both memory and imagination are a negation of time."[1] In *Speak, Memory,* the author put the matter more dramatically:

> I confess I do not believe in time. I like to fold my magic carpet, after use, in such a way as to superimpose one part of the pattern upon another. Let visitors trip. (*Speak, Memory,* p. 139)[2]

With scientific (or sophistic) skepticism, however, Godunov–Cherdyn-tsev in *The Gift* opines that art's ultimate defeat of time may be only hypothetical at best:

> The theory I find most tempting—that there is no time, that everything is the present situated like a radiance outside our blindness—is just as hopeless a finite hypothesis as the others. "You will understand when you are big," those are really the wisest words that I know. (*The Gift,* p. 354)

Memory, ancilla to art in Nabokov's novels, is naturally art's primary resource in the combat with time. "An artist's memory [. . .] beats all other kinds, I imagine," marvels the narrator of *Despair* (p. 213). "The real author is not I," Hermann states, "but my impatient memory" (p. 47). In *Speak, Memory*'s description of memory's "supreme achievement," Nabokov employs the same imagery of superimposing folded patterns as in his denial of time quote above:

> I witness with pleasure the supreme achievement of memory, which is the masterly use it makes of innate harmonies when gathering to its fold the suspended and wandering tonalities of the past. (*Speak, Memory,* p. 170)

1. Alfred Appel, Jr., "An Interview with Vladimir Nabokov," in *Nabokov,* ed. Dembo, p. 32.
2. Nabokov's characteristic "re-ply" to a Jamesian figure has been adopted by Susan Fromberg (now the novelist Susan Fromberg Schaeffer) in the title of her interesting study, "Folding the Patterned Carpet: Form and Theme in the Novels of Vladimir Nabokov," Ph.D. dissertation, The University of Chicago, 1966.

Memory, for better or worse, is intensely artistic. "Remembrance, embers, and membranes of beauty make artists and morons lose all self-control," runs Van's "apology" to Lucette for his and Ada's attempt to rape her (*Ada,* p. 164). Memories of an earlier "princedom by the sea" similarly inspire Humbert Humbert "poetically" to imprison Lolita (*Lolita,* p. 11). Van's moral authority is greater when he declares that "You lose your immortality when you lose your memory" (*Ada,* p. 622), but his remark applies to his art, not his life. In Nabokov's first novel, *Mary,* memory threatens to disrupt the lives of several characters, but becomes benign again when the main character ultimately decides not to act out his reminiscences. When memory, like imagination, re-enacts itself in life, the results may kill (Lolita, Lucette); but when memory reconstructs itself in art, the results may be immortal (*Lolita, Ada*).

Death assumes such an enormous importance in Nabokov's fiction because it is the one obstacle which neither the solipsism of madness nor that of art can overcome. As *Invitation to a Beheading* puts it,

> The only real, genuinely unquestionable thing here was only death itself, the inevitability of the author's physical death.   (p. 124)

The narrator of Nabokov's story "The Assistant Producer" (English, 1943) makes a similar point (with a significant addition):

> We have a saying in Russian: *vsevo dvoe i est; smert' da sovest'*—which may be rendered thus: "There are only two things that really exist—one's death and one's conscience."[1]

Death is a constant presence in Nabokov's fictional world; it is always there right from the start. The epigraph to *The Gift* comes from Smirnovski's *Textbook of Russian Grammar:*

> An oak is a tree. A rose is a flower. A deer is an animal. A sparrow is a bird. Russia is our fatherland. Death is inevitable.

Death is formidable in its ubiquity, in the impossibility of knowing when it will strike; to cite Kinbote's (also inevitable) classical allusion, "Even in Arcady am I, says Death in the tombal scripture" (*Pale Fire,* p. 174). Cincinnatus's appointment with the executioner thus spares him *one* of death's terrors: as he wittily puts it,

---

1. Vladimir Nabokov, "The Assistant Producer," in *Nabokov's Dozen,* p. 71.

> The compensation for a death sentence is knowledge of the exact hour when one is to die. A great luxury, but one that is well earned. (*Invitation to a Beheading*, p. 16)

From this perspective, suicide promises, in Kinbote's words, "the perfect safety of wooed death" (*Pale Fire*, p. 221). Hazel Shade "deserves great respect, having preferred the beauty of death to the ugliness of life" (*Pale Fire*, p. 312).

But the ultimate and irremediable horror of death, as it looms as a constant presence in Nabokov's work, is its complete unknowability, its complete inaccessibility to rational thought—at least, on this side of mortality. The philosopher-hero of *Bend Sinister* is, with *Ada*'s Van, the most intellectually astute of Nabokov's characters;

> Krug could take aim at a flock of the most popular and sublime human thoughts and bring down a wild goose any time. But he could not kill death. (*Bend Sinister*, p. 31)

Krug recognizes death as the crux of all philosophical questions, including that of solipsism, because death is the ineluctable point of contact between the "inner" and "outer" worlds of our experience:

> What is more important to solve: the "outer" problem (space, time, matter, the unknown without) or the "inner" one (life, thought, love, the unknown within) or again their point of contact (death)? (*Bend Sinister*, pp. 173–74)

Even though Nabokov disclaimed any didactic intentions in the writing of his novels, it must be recognized that his novels do have the effect of educating and persuading the reader of the ubiquitous presence of death in the world around us. There is much that is meant to seem invented in the "Antiterra" of *Ada*, but the characters' passions and their deaths are recognizble imports from our own "Terra the Fair." The first sentence of *Pale Fire* mentions the death of John Shade. The first line of *Ada* (a note from "[Ed.]" preceding Chapter 1) informs us that, with certain obscure exceptions, "all the persons mentioned by name in this book [. . .] are dead" (p. [xi]). Humbert significantly objects to the imaginary world created by Hollywood musicals as "an essentially grief-proof sphere of existence wherefrom death and truth were banned" (*Lolita*, p. 172). For Humbert (at least in his role as critic of popular culture), death *is* truth.

For the narrator of *Pnin*, death threatens the loss of individual identity: "Death is divestment, death is communion. It may be wonderful to mix with the landscape, but to do so is the end of the tender ego" (*Pnin*, p. 20). It is this obliteration of the concept of self, so precious to such a selfish solipsist as himself, that Van has in mind when he calls death "the master madness" (*Ada*, p. 232).

Disquietingly (for readers raised in an age when the term "soul" is nearly taboo save as an epithet for food or music), Nabokov's novels hint repeatedly at the possibility of continued spiritual existence after death. Like Aqua, many of Nabokov's characters have "sudden dreams of eternity-certainty" (*Ada*, p. 24). Nabokov attributes the epigraph to *Invitation to a Beheading* to "the altogether delightful Pierre Delalande, whom I invented" (p. 6); the epigraph reads

> *Comme un fou se croit Dieu, nous nous croyons mortels.* (*Invitation to a Beheading*, p. [10])

Cincinnatus himself reflects that, were he given longer to live,

> I would write also about the continual tremor—and about how part of my thoughts is always crowding around the invisible umbilical cord that joins this world to something—to what I shall not say yet . . .[.] (*Invitation to a Beheading*, p. 53)

The issue of death as it is faced by a character of sensitivity and intelligence has always posed considerable technical difficulties for the novelist. As *Look at the Harlequins!* rhymingly puts the problem,

> The I of the book
> Cannot die in the book. (p. 239)

We have already noted how many of the deaths of Nabokov's hero-characters take the form of a transition from one plane of fictional reality to another. Making a characteristic analogy with nature, Nabokov has also frequently compared death to the emergence of a butterfly from a cocoon (as in the story "Christmas").[1] Van, after describing the "prepupational locomotion" of Ada's moth larvae, remarks, "Aqua had walked through a wood and into a gulch to do it last year" (*Ada*, p. 62). This metaphor of death as emergence from the chrysalis is reinforced by the last line of *Despair*—"I'm coming out now" (p. 222)—and by the final lines of *Transparent Things*:

---

1. Vladimir Nabokov, "Christmas," in *Details of a Sunset and Other Stories* (New York: McGraw-Hill, 1976), pp. 151–61.

> This is, I believe, *it*: not the crude anguish of physical death but the incomparable pangs of the mysterious mental maneuver needed to pass from one state of being to another.
>
> Easy, you know, does it, son.   (p. 104)

This sense of death as the start of a journey toward things greater than this life has revealed lies behind *Pale Fire*'s statement that "human life is but a series of footnotes to a vast obscure unfinished masterpiece" (p. 272). In much the same spirit, the narrator of *Look at the Harlequins!* conjures up a vivid picture of his own posthumous journey:

> Imagine me, an old gentleman, a distinguished author, gliding rapidly on my back, in the wake of my outstretched dead feet, first through that gap in the granite, then over a pinewood, then along misty water meadows, and then simply between marges of mist, on and on, imagine that sight!   (*Look at the Harlequins!*, p. 246)

Cincinnatus, the most visionary of Nabokov's heroes, conceives a fully developed dream of the world where death takes us and, like a true solipsist, is wholly convinced of his vision's reality: "It exists, my dream world, it must exist, since, surely, there must be an original of the clumsy copy" (*Invitation to a Beheading*, p. 93). Cincinnatus's enchanting dream of an afterworld where the wrongs of this life are righted makes of Nabokov's *Invitation to a Beheading* a beautiful Baudelairean *Invitation au voyage*:

> *There, tam, là-bas*, the gaze of men glows with inimitable understanding; *there* the freaks that are tortured here walk unmolested; *there* time takes shape according to one's pleasure, like a figured rug whose folds can be gathered in such a way that two designs will meet—[. . .] *There, there* are the originals of those gardens where we used to roam and hide in this world [. . .]; *there* shines the mirror that now and then sends a chance reflection here . . . And what I say is not it, not quite it [. . .].   (*Invitation to a Beheading*, pp. 94–95)

I am not suggesting that Nabokov's novels recommend belief in an afterlife. I would as soon call *Ulysses* a manifesto for metempsychosis. The afterlife exists in the minds of the characters who believe in it in the same way that the work of art exists in the consciousness of the artist. Cincinnatus's destination, like the heavenly Terra to which Aqua "trusts" she'll go (*Ada*, p. 22), is a world of perfect order, perfect pattern. "For me a work of fiction exists only insofar as it affords me what I shall bluntly call aesthetic bliss," Nabokov wrote in the afterword to *Lolita* (pp. 316–17).

The continued existence of the spirit after death exists for Nabokov's characters and for his readers in the same way.

Nabokov's novels *are* persuasive when it comes to the matter of making readers feel the immanence of death in our *own* lives. Near the end of *Ada*, the sibling-lover-narrators overtly discuss the technical challenge of maintaining death always as a palpable background to their narrative, and agree that they have met the challenge successfully:

> One great difficulty. The strange mirage-shimmer standing in for death should not appear too soon in the chronicle and yet it should permeate the first amorous scenes. Hard but not insurmountable (I can do anything, I can tango and tap-dance on my fantastic hands).   (*Ada*, p. 621)

Like *Bend Sinister, Lolita,* and *Pale Fire, Ada* thus succeeds in making the reader *feel,* as well as intellectually apprehend, "the final tragic triumph of human cogitation: I am because I die" (*Ada,* p. 164).

Against death, as against all threats to human value in his work, the Nabokovian hero's most potent weapon is art. In contrast to the perils posed by misplaced pseudoartistry, Nabokov's fiction attributes awesome powers to well-placed, effective art—especially, of course, its own. Nabokovian art is capable, we have already noted, of communicating thoughts and feelings and expressing love, but its powers and attributes go much further. Charles Kinbote recreates the Zembla from which he imagines himself to have been exiled with the same vividness with which Cincinnatus C imagines countless escapes from prison. Van's re-creation of "a perfectly normal trilingual childhood" similarly gives life to a lost world (*Ada,* p. 77). Of "the pangs of exile," Nabokov wrote in his memoir *Speak, Memory* that "the writing of a novel relieved me of that fertile emotion" (pp. 244–45). *Art palliates exile.*

In a passage of his memoir addressed to "the particular idiot who, because he lost a fortune in some crash, thinks he understands me," Nabokov declares

> The nostalgia I have been cherishing all these years is a hypertrophied sense of lost childhood, not sorrow for lost banknotes.   (*Speak, Memory,* p. 73)

The matter is put similarly in *The Defense* by "a charming old general who always maintained that it was not Russia we expatriates regretted but youth, youth" (*The Defense,* p. 129). In his necrologue for Nabokov,

Herbert Gold describes "his enormous nostalgia [as] a paradigm of what all living creatures must lose."[1] *Art celebrates youth.*

The Gift begins with a description (albeit a quirky one) of a tractor hitched to a moving van in a seedy section of Berlin. The milieu is modest, the details, while devoid of cliché, mundane. Similarly, *Bend Sinister* begins with a description of "an oblong puddle inset in the coarse asphalt" (p. 1). The narrators of both novels pride themselves on their ability to turn such inauspicious openings into refined works of art. In the somewhat Joycean view of Godunov–Cherdyntsev, narrator of *The Gift*, art's raw material is

> all the trash of life which by means of a momentary alchemic distillation—the "royal experiment"—is turned into something valuable and eternal.   (*The Gift*, p. 176)

Art redeems trash.

The great advantage of the ideal chess world over the "real" world from which Luzhin flees in *The Defense* is that the chess world is one of carefully defined rules and orderly systems of play. In his Introduction to *Poems and Problems* (1970), Nabokov wrote that

> Chess problems demand from the composer the same virtues that characterize all worthwhile art: originality, invention, conciseness, harmony, complexity, and splendid insincerity.[2]

Art imposes order. The order, however, must be unique; and the subtler (i.e., the better hidden), the better. Thus, as Nabokov put it in *Speak, Memory,* "Deceit, to the point of diabolism, and originality, verging upon the grotesque, were my notions of strategy" in the composition of chess problems (*Speak, Memory*, p. 214). *Art is original:* "Now I shall do what none has done," promises John Shade (*Pale Fire,* the Poem, l. 838). Van pursues "that originality of literary style which constitutes the only real honesty of a writer" (*Ada,* p. 501). *Art deceives.* "I discovered in nature the nonutilitarian delights that I sought in art," Nabokov wrote in *Speak, Memory.* "Both were a form of magic, both were a game of intricate enchantment and deception" (*Speak, Memory,* p. 125). "The most enchanting things in nature and art are based on deception," opines *The Gift* (p. 376), and the "red herrings" of *Pnin* and the other novels put this theory

1. Herbert Gold, "Vladimir Nabokov, 1899–1977," *New York Times Book Review,* 31 July 1977.

2. Vladimir Nabokov, *Poems and Problems* (New York: McGraw-Hill, 1970), p. 15.

into practice. As *Despair* sums it up (p. 188), "every work of art is a deception."

Humbert Humbert, who insists that "The gentle and dreamy regions through which I crept were the patrimonies of poets—*not* crime's prowling ground" (*Lolita*, p. 133), earns his claim to the title of artist by composing the narrative of *Lolita*. His sole artistic justification for existence, as he tells Lolita in his narrative's final sentences, is his power to

> make you live in the minds of later generations. I am thinking of aurochs and angels, the secret of durable pigments, prophetic sonnets, the refuge of art. And this is the only immortality you and I may share, my Lolita.   (*Lolita*, p. 311)

The reader of these lines knows, as Humbert does not, what were the circumstances of "Mrs. Richard F. Schiller"'s death—yet Nabokov's novel does give an immortal (or at least rereadable) kind of existence to Lo-lee-ta. As Anthony Burgess has put it,

> That nymphet's beauty lay less on her bones
> Than in her name's proclaimed two allophones [. . .].[1]

For Nabokov, then, *art transcends time and redeems death*.

The strongest resistance that any non-medical art can offer against physical death can never, of course, be more than symbolic; and by its self-consciousness, Nabokov's fiction never pretends otherwise. But in focusing upon the powers and perils of art as their principal theme, his novels nonetheless proclaim art's ability to immortalize itself as it invents and commemorates its subject. If, as *Ada* asserts, "artists are the only gods" (p. 553), it is because, as Nabokov portrays it, art may indeed achieve an authentic victory over the oblivion of death, by subsuming love, imagination, and memory to an explicit awareness of its own essentially imaginary existence.

Nabokov's novels may thus be said to be *about* art, *about* solipsism, *about* passion, *about* death—but it would be equally true to say that they are *about themselves*. Nabokov's nesting narrators, involuted structures, consciously fictive characters, reflexive styles and metafictional themes create a world that resembles our own at the same time that it denies the resemblance. The author is thus able simultaneously to move his reader's emotions by dramatizing the fates of sympathetic characters, and to re-

1. Anthony Burgess, "To Vladimir Nabokov on his 70th birthday," in *Nabokov*, ed. Appel and Newman, p. 336.

mind his readers not to confuse the sophisticated game of art with the author's and readers' real, mortal lives. These reminders, I would note further, take place at the stylistic and thematic levels simultaneously. Although his protagonists are nearly all solipsists, Nabokov's novels ultimately repudiate solipsism by dramatizing the ethically unacceptable consequences of acting out one's solipsism upon the world. His fictional plots thus enact the tragedy of would-be artists who mistake other human beings for their canvas or paper. At the same time, Nabokov's narrative styles discourage readers from mistaking *his* paper constructions for other human beings. Ethically and esthetically, then, the novels are all of a piece: the proliferation of artist-figures who kill in life but immortalize in art (Hermann, Humbert, Van) corresponds thematically to Nabokov's stylistic insistence that art and life are not to be confused.

Nabokov's fiction thus "teaches" that fiction does not "teach." Parody is, of course, the most appropriate form for such a message, since parody is essentially reflexive, and battens onto literature, not life, as its "subject." The esthetic parodoxes which Nabokov's synthesis of ludic and mimetic effects raise are, in fact, the same as those raised by literary parody. Nabokov himself has emphasized that parody is not a didactic medium, and he has distinguished it from satire on these grounds: "Satire is a lesson, parody is a game."[1] At the same time, however, Nabokov has glossed the parodic opening of *Ada* as if there were no such distinction:

> The opening sentences of *Ada* inaugurate a series of blasts directed throughout the book at translators of unprotected masterpieces who betray their authors by "transfigurations" based on ignorance or self-assertiveness. (*Strong Opinions*, p. 123)

A more useful distinction, perhaps, would be that satire treats life, while parody treats treatment of life; Nabokov's approach is clearly the latter. The fictions he invented resemble the butterfly he discovered,

> the newly described, fantastically rare vanessian, *Nymphalis danaus* Nab., orange-brown, with black-and-white foretips, mimicking, as its discoverer Professor Nabonidus of Babylon College, Nebraska, realized, not the Monarch butterfly directly, but the Monarch *through* the Viceroy, one of the Monarch's best known imitators. (*Ada*, p. 169)

Ada itself, that is, mimicks, not life directly, but life *through* some of its "best known imitators."

1. Appel interview, in *Nabokov*, ed. Dembo, p. 32.

Parody is nonrealistic, particularly in its spirit of exaggeration, but it still picks its targets in the outside world. I made note of this dimension of "external reference" in the parodic images of Nabokov himself within the novels, in the extent to which they depend for their success upon the reader's familiarity with a few salient details of Nabokov's life outside the novels. Similarly, the reader must be familiar with the other books in Nabokov's oeuvre to enjoy the self-parodic mock bibliography prefixed to *Look at the Harlequins!*

I. Other Books by the Narrator

In Russian:
Tamara 1925
Pawn Takes Queen 1927
Plenilune 1929
Camera Lucida (Slaughter in the Sun) 1931
The Red Top Hat 1934
The Dare 1950

In English:
See under Real 1939
Esmeralda and Her Parandrus 1941
Dr. Olga Repnin 1946
Exile from Mayda 1947
A Kingdom by the Sea 1962
Ardis 1970 (*Look at the Harlequins!*, p. [ix])

While parody is essentially ludic, it still maintains relations with the world outside the book. In this way it is able to parade as a game while treating seriously things that matter to us in life. Shade's poem may ruthlessly parody Robert Frost, while touching us with its terror and rage over mortality. The hero of Nabokov's first English novel significantly resembles his author in this respect:

As often was the case with Sebastian Knight he used parody as a kind of springboard for leaping into the highest region of serious emotion. (*The Real Life of Sebastian Knight,* p. 91)

Godunov-Cherdyntsev makes the point even more emphatically in *The Gift:* "the spirit of parody always goes along with genuine poetry" (p. 24). *The Real Life of Sebastian Knight* and *The Gift* may parody literary biographies, *Lolita* ("or the Confession of a White Widowed Male" [p. 5]) may parody the confessional memoir, *Pale Fire* may parody the critical apparatus, *Ada* may parody the family chronicle, and *Look at the Harle-*

quins! may parody the memoirs of a distinguished author—but all of these novels contain the moving stories of sympathetic humans caught in the momentum of great passions, or locked in a struggle with madness or death. Bobbie Ann Mason, in her excellent study of *Ada* entitled *Nabokov's Garden,* has observed the capacity of Nabokovian parody for "drawing the reader in closer":

> This trick of parody, annoyingly diverting to some minds, is actually a way of drawing the reader in closer to the emotional reality of the story by another route. By reminding the reader that the characters are only characters, Nabokov calls attention to emotions deeper and more painful than one expects from cardboard characters. [. . .] Pain or grief becomes suggestively more intense because it is in the process of being toned down from raging torrents of tears and shrieks of pain. Authorial distance saves it from sentimentality and also makes it bearable for the reader.[1]

Parody thus allows the self-conscious author not to take himself too seriously as he treats, movingly, the most serious of human concerns.

At the same time, parody allows Nabokov to emulate his most admired predecessors while preserving his most cherished "originality." Possessing, as we have noted, much the same esthetic and some of the same talents as the early Modernists, Nabokov nonetheless suffered from a disadvantage that Proust and Joyce did not share: the published works of Proust and Joyce. His reponse was to make fun of both of them. As *Ada* observes in the margin of Van's manuscript, for instance, "(On fait *son grand Joyce* after doing one's *petit Proust*)." Van Veen responds, "(But read on; it is pure V.V.)" (*Ada,* p. 181). This same tension between imitation and originality, between what is Joycean or Proustian (or Tolstoyan, or "Chateaubriandesque") and what is "pure V.V.," crackles and hums through all of V.V. Nabokov's fiction.

It is in his role as parodist, finally, that Nabokov is most manifestly élitist in his stance towards his readers. I observed in Chapter I, for example, how the parodic first lines of *Ada* function as an "opening dismissal of catechumens," and noted Nabokov's claim, "I write mainly for artists, fellow-artists and follow-artists." While this is clearly an exaggeration, it is certainly true that Nabokov's densely allusive parodies demand well-read readers, if those readers are to understand what is going on. Upon those who have not attained a certain, relatively high degree of literary culture, the implied author of Nabokov's fictions lavishes the

---

1. Mason, *Nabokov's Garden,* p. 143.

proud man's contumely, and this brand of condescension may be viewed, not unfairly, as a regrettable form of intellectual snobbery.

For, it must be admitted, not everything about Nabokov's work is admirable. The sensibility behind *Laughter in the Dark,* for example, can seem unwontedly cruel. No less a critic than Frank Kermode has written on the unpleasantness of Nabokov's published persona:

> Probably he will not be greatly loved; the personality that presides over his work is not amiable. We do not much care to be objects of an author's contempt and—to simplify for a moment—that is the way Nabokov seems to feel about us.[1]

Joyce Carol Oates has written that for writers such as herself, Nabokov is "deadening to retain for very long in one's imagination," largely because "Nabokov exhibits the most amazing capacity for loathing that one is likely to find in serious literature."[2] The feud with Freud, for example, is lamentably shrill.

If I find fault with Nabokov's sensibility, however, I find none with his craft. And his heart, even if it seems not always to be in quite the right place, is prodigiously abundant. His novels make us laugh, and they disturb us; they satisfy our appetites for the dramatic and the romantic, and they challenge our intellects; they are as unassuming as toys, yet focus on the most crucial issues of existence and mortality. Nabokov's fiction, then, from the shortest story to the longest novel, manifests its artifice in order to isolate its fictional world from our own. That fictional world, however, is composed of a myriad of details taken "from life"—from natural and human phenomena minutely observed and meticulously described. That fictional world, further, is energized by the same passions that engage vital moral issues in our own mortal lives, outside the book, outside *all* fictions. He thus draws our thoughts to the things that matter, even as he acknowledges, in ways that pay respect to the reader's sophistication, the limitations of imitations. With elegance and grace Nabokov's finest fiction accomplishes all of this "and" (in *Ada*'s self-depicting final words) "much, much more."

1. Frank Kermode, "Aesthetic Bliss," *Encounter,* 14 (June 1960), 81; quoted in Peter J. Rabinowitz, "The Comedy of Terrors: Vladimir Nabokov as a Philosophical Novelist," Ph.D. dissertation, University of Chicago, 1972, p. 13.
2. Joyce Carol Oates, "A Personal View of Nabokov," *Saturday Review of the Arts,* 1 (Jan. 1973), 37.

Chapter VI

Plagiarizing *The Recognitions*

W ILLIAM G ADD IS is no devotee of art-for-art's sake. His novel *The Recognitions* is an intensely moral book, one which bears as close a relation to Dante's *Inferno* and Bunyan's *The Pilgrim's Progress* as it does to the work of Joyce and Gide. Gaddis's theme is the way we live and what is wrong with it. He is primarily a satirist, and hence exaggeration and incongruous juxtaposition predominate among his techniques. "*The Recognitions* is a novel about forgery," as the jacket copy to the first edition has it,[1] but it is also one about salvation, about damnation and redemption, unpunished sin and undeserved suffering, profanity and sanctity, and the rightful place of faith in life and in art. If Joyce wrote (however indirectly) of what is, and Nabokov wrote (with similar indirection) of what might be, then Gaddis writes (with the satirist's obliquity) of what ought to be. (There is no "ought" about Joyce's all-embracing "Yes," nor in Nabokov's playful invitation to "Imagine.") Gaddis's first two novels are much too deeply involved in exposing what is wrong with the world to content themselves with contemplating their own fictivity. *The Recognitions* and *JR* are only faintly, just suggestively self-conscious. Yet they do implicate themselves in their own design.

Critical attention has been slow in coming to Gaddis. In the first twenty years after the publication of *The Recognitions*, only three articles on his work appeared in the journals.[2] There is still no book-length study

1. William Gaddis, *The Recognitions* (New York: Harcourt, Brace, 1955). Future references are to this edition.

2. The first major appreciation did not appear until 1965: Bernard Benstock, "On William Gaddis: In Recognition of James Joyce," *Wisconsin Studies in Contemporary Literature*, 6 (Summer 1965), 177–89. The entire corpus of Gaddis criticism through the 1970s may be included in this note: Charles Leslie Banning, "William Gaddis' *JR:* The Organization of Chaos and the Chaos of Organization," *Paunch*, 42–43 (Dec. 1975), 153–65; Susan Strehle Klemtner, "'For a Very Small Audience': The Fiction of William Gaddis," *Critique*, 19:3 (1978), 61–73; Peter William Koenig, "Recognizing Gaddis' *Recognitions*," *Contemporary Literature*, 16 (Winter 1975), 61–72; "David Madden on William Gaddis' *The Recognitions*," in *Rediscoveries*, ed. David Madden (New York: Crown, 1971), pp. 291–304; Joseph. S. Salemi, "To Soar in Atonement: Art as Expiation in Gaddis's *The Recognitions*," *Novel*, 10 (Winter 1977), 127–36; John Stark, "William Gaddis: Just Recognition," *The Hollins Critic*, 14 (April 1977), 1–12; James J. Stathis, "William Gaddis: *The Recognitions*," *Critique*, 5 (Winter 1962–63), 91–94; and Tony Tanner, "Conclusion" to *City of Words: American Fiction*

of Gaddis's work, though this situation seems soon likely to improve. Since the task has yet to be undertaken, I will begin my discussion of *The Recognitions* with a summary account of what happens in the novel, before attempting to say what the novel *means* (for it most certainly has a meaning), and ultimately assessing the contribution of the novel's self-consciousness to that meaning.

What Happens in The Recognitions

The central character of *The Recognitions* is named, at least when we first meet him, Wyatt Gwyon. However, Wyatt is less a character than the dark outline of a character, inviting the reader to fill him in. Wyatt exists more as a presence reflected in the lives of the characters around him than as a character in himself.

Like *The Adventures of Augie March* (1953) and Ellison's *Invisible Man* (1952), *The Recognitions* (1955) is a Bildungsroman, the picaresque story of an education. (More technically, it is a Künstlerroman, "a novel which shows the development of the artist from childhood to maturity and later."[1]) As in those novels, as in *Marius the Epicurean* and *The Adventures of Huckleberry Finn,* the hero's course exposes him to the influence of a consecution of strong-willed characters who offer him—and usually try to impose upon him—a catalogue of ways of seeing the world and of uses to which the world may be put. Like Augie and like Pater's Marius, Wyatt fights his way through, *lives* his way through, to, if not the Final Answer, at least Freedom from constraining dogma. "Now at last," declares Wyatt near the end of the novel, "to live deliberately" (p. 900).

The first two influences on Wyatt's life are his father, Reverend Gwyon, and Wyatt's Aunt May. Gwyon is a minister in an unnamed New England town, who divides his time between studying ancient religions, haranguing his docile congregation on the bonds between Christianity and the savage pagan religions which preceded it, and drinking from a bottle of schnapps which he keeps hidden in a gutted copy of St. John of the Cross's *Dark Night of the Soul.* Reverend Gwyon faces backward into the past,

---

1950–1970 (London: Jonathan Cape, 1971), pp. 393–415.

More recent Gaddis criticism is discussed below in Chapter IX.

1. J.A. Cuddon, *A Dictionary of Literary Terms* (New York: Doubleday, 1977), s.v. "Künstlerroman," p. 346. By use of the terms *Bildungsroman* and *Künstlerroman*, I mean to imply only a specific structure, not (yet) a specific effect.

as though he could recall, and summon back, a time before death entered the world, before accident, before magic, and before magic despaired to become religion.   (pp. 11–12)

His favorite text is not the Bible, but Sir James George Frazer's *The Golden Bough,* the great study of "our debt to the savage," particularly to the ageless rights of sacrifice and sacrament.[1] Not only do excerpts from Gwyon's readings in *The Golden Bough* appear verbatim in *The Recognitions*—for example, the passage on the treatment of the public scapegoat among the Garos of Assam, on page 49 of *The Recognitions*—but much of the action of the novel as a whole is based upon Frazer's findings. Thus, for example, in accordance with Frazer's description of the sacrifice of the *Entellus* monkey (*The Golden Bough,* pp. 658–59), Reverend Gwyon butchers Heracles, the Barbary ape he brought back from Gibraltar, so as magically to cure Wyatt of a mysterious disease. Wyatt immediately recovers.

As an influence upon Wyatt, Reverend Gwyon oversees his son's preparation for the ministry. Although Wyatt eventually rejects his father's priestly example, Reverend Gwyon's influence endures nonetheless in the priestliness of Wyatt's chosen career as an artist. "You are a priest!" his wife Esther accuses him (p. 116), just as Basil Valentine, another ex-divinity student, more moderately observes, "You have something of a priest in you yourself, you know" (p. 261).

Yet even as a boy, Wyatt's calling is to art, not religion (for the two are seen, at this point, as clearly distinct). His first creative efforts meet the opposition of his puritanical Aunt May, who declares original artistry to be a sin against God; "moral creative work was definitely one of His damnedest things" (p. 33).

[. . .] Wyatt's first drawing, a picture, he said, of a robin, which looked like the letter *E* tipped to one side, brought for her approval, met with —Don't you love our Lord Jesus, after all? He said he did. —Then why do you try to take His place? Our Lord is the only true creator, and only sinful people try to emulate Him [. . .]. To sin is to falsify something in the Divine Order, and that is what Lucifer did. His name means Bringer of Light but he was not satisfied to bring the light of Our Lord to man, he tried to steal the power of Our Lord and to bring his own light to man. He tried to become original, she pronounced malignantly, shaping that word round the whole structure of

1. Sir James George Frazer, *The Golden Bough: A Study in Magic and Religion,* abridged ed. (New York: Macmillan, 1922). References in the text are to this edition. "Our Debt to the Savage" is the title of Frazer's Chapter XXIII.

damnation, repeating it, crumpling the drawing of the robin in her hand, — original, to steal Our Lord's authority, to command his own destiny, to bear his own light! That is why Satan is the Fallen Angel, for he rebelled when he tried to emulate Our Lord Jesus. And he won his own domain, didn't he. Didn't he! And his own light is the light of the fires of Hell! Is that what you want? Is that what you want? Is that what you want?   (p. 34)

Thus Wyatt is told, from the start, that creative "emulation" is sinful and that originality leads to damnation. He reacts to this advice, as we learn later in the novel, by forging a perfect copy of a painting owned by his father, and substituting his forgery for the original,

> a painting by Hieronymus Bosch portraying the Seven Deadly Sins in medieval (meddy-evil, the Reverend pronounced it, an unholy light in his eyes) indulgence.   (p. 25)

Quitting divinity school and New England, Wyatt goes (in Chapter 2) to Paris. Here he paints his own pictures, original ones, to little attention and no success. One art critic, named Crémer, does offer Wyatt good notices in exchange for ten percent of the ensuing sales. But Wyatt refuses and his show naturally flops, suggesting that a man of integrity cannot succeed by doing original work.

Wyatt now moves (in Chapter 3) to New York where, in earnest, he begins his career as a forger of paintings by men whose names mean big money. Unlike the people he works for, however, Wyatt is less interested in the financial value than in the artistic faithfulness of his copies. His wife Esther, whom he soon leaves, resembles the wife who advised her husband, Job, "Dost thou still retain thine integrity? curse God, and die."[1] Alarmed by Wyatt's great devotion to his art, Esther asks him, more than once, "Why do you fight it all so hard?" (pp. 86, 118). Perhaps inevitably, the Book of Job is one of Gaddis's many literary models, and the experience of reading *The Recognitions* indeed compares to "reading alternatively the Book of Job and the Siamese National Railway's *Guide to Bangkok*" (p. 5).

At a point barely an eighth of the way into his story (p. 118), Wyatt's name drops out of the novel for good. The remaining narrative refers to him, when need be, by the impersonal pronouns "he" or "him":

> He took the hand and said his own name in reply, distantly, as though repeating the name of an unremembered friend in effort to recall him.   (p. 140).

1. Job 2:9, King James version.

Frazer's account of "personal names tabooed" partially explains the suppression of Wyatt's name.[1] More importantly, Gaddis has here marshalled even syntax into reducing Wyatt to a kind of nonexistent hero, nearly invisible but for his reflection in the lives of the characters who surround him. Wyatt himself offers the best explanation of the kind of hero he is, when it occurs to him (in classic self-conscious fashion) that he may be a fictional character in somebody's novel:

> But, do you know how I feel sometimes? [. . .] as though I were reading a novel, yes. And then, reading it, but the hero fails to appear, fails to be working out some plan of comedy or, disaster? All the materials are there, yes. [. . .]
> —The half-known people, Valentine interrupted easily [. . .].
> —Yes, while I wait. I wait. Where is he? Listen, he's there all the time. None of them moves, but it reflects him, none of them . . . reacts, but to react with him, none of them hates but to hate with him, and loving . . . none of them loves but loving . . .
> —Loving?
> The cab swerved suddenly.   (p. 263)

Wyatt reappears near the end of the novel under a variety of names, including Stephan, Stephan Asche, and (at his most Joycean) Stephen, and also as an anonymous drowned man. His constant vacancy at the center of the novel, however, makes of *The Recognitions* "a whole Odyssey without Ulysses" (p. 816). We recall that Joyce, too, rejected the traditional conception of the hero; "the whole structure of heroism is, and always was, a damned lie," as he wrote in a letter to his brother Stanislaus (7 Feb. 1905).[2] Gaddis out-minimalizes Joyce's diminution of heroic stature by hiding his protagonist. Pynchon, as will be seen, goes further still by letting his hero dissolve into thin air. I am not satisfied that I know why this is happening, but it should be recalled that in *To the Lighthouse,* Virginia Woolf had experimented, successfully, with a similarly absent central character, by showing the influence of the late Mrs. Ramsay upon a periphery of survivors. *The Recognitions'* many minor characters likewise continue to reflect Wyatt's influence long after his death.

The least distorting reflector is a character named Otto, who mimics Wyatt meticulously, even to the point of taking his place in Esther's bed. Otto's palindromic name reflects his talent for mirroring. When we first meet him, he has just "repeated" one of Wyatt's observations (p. 119),

1. Frazer, *The Golden Bough,* pp. 284–89.
2. Joyce, *Selected Letters,* p. 54.

and he continues throughout the novel to play Wyatt's most sedulous ape. Otto takes down in shorthand Wyatt's *obiter dicta,* and assigns them to Gordon, the hero of the play he is composing:

> Grdn: Orignlty not inventn bt snse of recall, recgntn, pttrns alrdy thr, q. You cannt invnt t shpe of a stone.   (p. 123)

Otto's cadgings from Wyatt rely upon the reader's own "snse of recall, recgntn, pttrns alrdy thr," for Gaddis never identifies Otto's borrowings as such. The reader is required to recognize stolen goods upon sight. Thus when Otto entitles his completed play "The Vanity of Time" (p. 162), the alert reader (if we are to follow what is going on) must remember that Otto picked up this expression from Wyatt ("About the whole of creation working to be delivered from the vanity of time, about nature working for this great redemption" [p. 148]), that Wyatt, in turn, was quoting one of his father's sermons, and that Reverend Gwyon had himself "thundered the lines of William Law":

> —O man, consider thyself! Here thou standest in the earnest perpetual strife of good and evil. All nature is continually at work to bring forth the great redemption; the whole creation is travailing in pain and laborious working to be delivered from the vanity of time; and wilt thou be asleep?   (p. 41)

Perhaps not even finally, we may discern behind William Law the theme of Ecclesiastes: "Vanity of vanities, saith the Preacher, vanity of vanities; all *is* vanity."[1] The proper reading of *The Recognitions,* as any reader of the novel soon learns, thus depends upon one's ability to recognize the repetition of statements or actions that have gone before. Reading *The Recognitions* is itself an exercise in recognition.

Recognition is, further, the only way of identifying the dozens of characters who reappear in the novel without mention of their names, or tags to their dialogue. Wyatt himself, for example, must be recognized by his hesitant, abrupt speech patterns and by the abstraction of his ideas. We learn that beautiful and fragile Esme models for Wyatt by recognizing the smell of lavender which clings to her body (for Wyatt, like the counterfeiter Mr. Sinisterra, uses oil of lavender in his work). When Wyatt's copyist Otto and his model Esme spend the night together, they each dream of someone else:

> —I dreamt about someone.
> —Who?

1. Ecclesiastes 1:2.

—Someone you don't know, she said. Then she said to herself, —He was in a mirror, caught there.

—Now I remember who it was I saw in the park [in my dream], Otto said.

—Who?

—Someone I used to know, someone you don't know, he said [. . .].
(p. 220)

The reader must figure out that Otto and Esme both dream of Wyatt, who is himself absent from this part of the novel. *The Recognitions* is thus itself that novel which Wyatt imagines himself to be reading, in which none of the other "half-known" characters "moves but it reflects him, [. . .] none of them loves, but loving . . . [the absent hero]."

The next influence on Wyatt's life is that of Recktall Brown, whose name, as John Stark delicately puts it, is "a scatological pun."[1] Brown serves as a surrogate father-figure for Wyatt, as his possession of the original Bosch which Wyatt removed from his father's house suggests. Indeed, the chords between parents and children echo many times in this novel, in a series of variations which subsume all types of filial bond, from the sublime to the incongruous. A character named Stanley devotes himself sublimely to his mother, for example, and composes a Mass in her honor. Otto, at the other extreme, arranges to meet his father for the very first time in the bar of a New York hotel, and then fails even to connect. Through a concatenation of bizarre but perfectly logical circumstances, Otto mistakes for his father the counterfeiter Mr. Sinisterra, who in turn takes Otto to be the bill-passer he expects to meet. Otto's true father, Mr. Pivner, has meanwhile had a diabetic attack in the hotel lobby, and has been carted off by the police, who mistake him for another Christmas drunk. Astonished Otto receives "five G's in perfect twenties" (p. 518), while in exchange for his son Mr. Pivner gets the cane from Mr. Sinisterra's discarded disguise. Later Mr. Pivner adopts his own son-figure in the person of Eddie Zefnic, while Mr. Sinisterra despises *his* son Chaby, Esme's lover and a heroin addict. Near the end of the novel Mr. Sinisterra, posing as Mr. Yák, adopts Wyatt as his son, renaming him Stephan. Thus Otto and Esme are linked to Wyatt both directly and through each other, while Mr. Sinisterra is triply tied to Wyatt: directly, through Otto, and through Chaby through Esme. Thus do all the characters of this novel weave a coherent if convoluted web, with Wyatt Gwyon, prismatic, at the center.

Recktall Brown's relation to Wyatt is Mephistophelean as well as pa-

1. Stark, "Just Recognition," p. 4.

ternal. During his association with Brown, Wyatt figuratively works for the Devil. (Recktall Brown's name recalls both Dante's attention to the Devil's anus, and Carlyle's "Teufelsdröckh" figure in *Sartor Resartus*.) Allusions to Goethe's *Faust* abound in *The Recognitions,* beginning with the epigraph to the first chapter; a very British art critic, for example, compares the greaves of Brown's suit of armor to the "false calves" worn ("to cover his cloven feet") by "Mephistopheles, don't you know, in mfft that ponderous thing by Goethe" (p. 676). Brown pays Wyatt for his forgeries, in exchange for what amounts to ownership of Wyatt's soul:

—God damn it, my boy. Did we make a bargain or didn't we. We're in business, you and me.   (p. 362)

Recktall Brown has been given such a patently implausible name in part to suggest his kinship to allegorical figures, such as Mr. Worldly-Wiseman or Lord Hate-good in Bunyan's *Pilgrim's Progress*. In the allegorical reading which his name thus invites, Recktall Brown may be said to "stand for" a view of life as unregenerate matter. "Art today is spelled with an *f,*" Recktall Brown says (p. 143). "Money," on the other hand, "gives significance to anything" (p. 144). This white man named Brown has "bought" a black man named Fuller (which means, in this case, whitener). Fuller practices homeopathic magic (as described in Frazer's *Golden Bough*), by burning scraps of paper bearing Recktall Brown's name and bits of his hair, with the result that Brown, encased in his favorite "work of art," the suit of armor, falls down a flight of stairs and dies. Wyatt is freed from Brown's onus.

Minutes later Wyatt escapes from the influence of Basil Valentine, by stabbing him with Recktall Brown's penknife and leaving him for dead. Valentine, a dropout from divinity school and hence a fallen angel like Lucifer, has stood at Recktall Brown's side during the exploitation of Wyatt. Named after Basilius Valentinus, the seventeenth-century ecclesiastic who poisoned his fellow monks in the interests of science, Basil Valentine "stands for," in an allegorical reading, the application of reason unguided by human sympathy. His face is described as "strong, unsympathetic, bearing all of the force which sympathy lacks" (p. 263). When Valentine reappears, as if risen from the dead, near the end of the novel, Esme calls him "the Cold Man" (p. 767). He dies, eventually, in a state of perfectly lucid, rational insomnia, "reason doomed to itself,"[1] just as

1. Koenig, "Recognizing Gaddis' *Recognitions*," p. 67. Koenig has profited by access to Gaddis's own notes, but his readings do not always coincide with the published novel (e.g., Koenig portrays Esther as a goad to Wyatt to "do more," p. 66).

Recktall Brown's silver-clad death enacts the fate of money pursued in itself.

Valentine adds another element of self-consciousness when he solipsistically declares to Wyatt and Recktall Brown, "I am the only person in this room who exists. You are both projections of my unconscious, and so I shall write a novel about you both" (p. 247). Like Lucifer's presumption, however, Valentine's surreptitious claim to have authored *The Recognitions* is false. Gaddis pretends instead to repose the authorship of his novel upon a half-glimpsed character named Willie—so called, no doubt, to suggest William Gaddis himself. As the reader learns from Basil Valentine's half of a telephone conversation (a "Belled chat," as Peter Lubin would call it[1]), Willie is writing a novel based upon the Clementine *Recognitions:*

> [. . .] but what in heaven's name do you want to know this sort of thing for? A novel? But . . . yes, perhaps he can, if he thinks it will do any good. But you can tell your friend Willie that salvation is hardly the practical study it was then. What? . . . Why, simply because in the Middle Ages they were convinced that they had souls to save. Yes. The what? The *Recognitions?* No, it's Clement of *Rome*. Mostly talk, talk, talk. The young man's deepest concern is for the immortality of his soul, he goes to Egypt to find the magicians and learn their secrets. It's been referred to as the first Christian novel. What? Yes, it's really the beginning of the whole Faust legend. But one can hardly . . . eh? My, your friend is writing for a rather small audience, isn't he. (pp. 372–73)

Willie appears briefly on two other occasions in *The Recognitions*. On the middle page of the novel, we overhear this conversation in a Greenwich Village cafe:

> —Scatological?
> —Eschatological, the doctrine of last things . . .
> —Good lord, Willie, you are drunk. Either that or you're writing for a very small audience.
> —So . . . ? how many people were there in Plato's Republic? (p. 478)

In the novel's last third, Willie reappears as "a young man with a thin face, a slightly crooked nose, and a weary expression which embraced his whole appearance" (p. 734), a description which, it so happens, matches fairly well the single public photograph of Gaddis himself.[2]

1. Peter Lubin, "Kickshaws and Motley," in *Nabokov: Criticisms, Reminiscences, Translations and Tributes,* ed. Alfred Appel, Jr. and Charles Newman (New York: Simon and Schuster, 1970).
2. First published in *Time* Magazine, 14 March 1955, p. 112.

—There, there's the guy who was working on this, he's one of the writers. Hey, Willie . . . But the weary figure went on. He was carrying two books, one titled, *The Destruction of the Philosophers,* the other, *The Destruction of the Destruction.*   (p. 734)

Note that *W*yatt *G*wyon's name, central but barely there, shares the same initials and trochaic meter as that of its author.

When Mr. Sinisterra, alias Mr. Yák, comes upon Wyatt in Spain and renames him, "Stephan" submits to the influence of yet another form of dishonesty. Mr. Sinisterra, the same counterfeiter whom Otto took for his own father, has heard that a Mr. Kuvetli is searching for a Fourth Dynasty Egyptian mummy in Spain. Mr. Yák cajoles and pesters a very reluctant Stephan into helping him counterfeit such a mummy, using an actual disinterred cadaver. The plan succeeds; Mr. Kuvetli agrees to buy the mummy, and then (as only careful reading reveals) Mr. Kuvetli assassinates Mr. Yák. For 'Mr. Kuvetli' is the pseudonym of Mr. Inononu, Basil Valentine's colleague in a clandestine assassination bureau linked to both the Devil and the Roman Catholic Church. Mr. Inononu's intended victim, the real Mr. Yák, is a Rumanian Egyptologist whose stolen passport supplied the unfortunate Mr. Sinisterra with his assumed name. Gaddis's satirical technique thus relies upon such incongruous juxtapositions as a social impostor—"Nobody's named Otto any more, he must be an impostor" (p. 173)—mistaking a counterfeiter for his father, and a very venal Church using evil methods to punish the wrong man for no crime, with the right results.

The final influence Wyatt comes under is that of a "distinguished novelist," whose writings make easy affirmations of the eternal verities but who in his own life has avoided any experience of a real sort. Wyatt, who is now engaged in "restoring" old paintings by chipping away at them, introduces himself to the writer, Ludy (whose name has ludi-crous connotations), with "—People I've never seen before in my life call me Stephen" (p. 867). Stephen ultimately shares with Ludy (afterwards described as "a man having, or about to have, or at the very least valiantly fighting off, a religious experience" [p. 900]) the fruits of his lifelong education. Life, with all its possibilities for sin and for suffering, is to be "lived through," not avoided; nor is it to be wished away by utopian art-for-art's sake:

Look back, if once you're started in living, you're born into sin, then? And how do you atone? By locking yourself up in remorse for what you might have done? Or by living it through. By locking yourself up in remorse with what you know you have done? Or by going back and living it through. By locking yourself up with your work, until it becomes a gessoed surface, all prepared, clean and smooth as ivory? Or by living it through. By drawing lines in your mind? Or by living it through. If it was sin from the start, and possible all the time, to know it's possible and avoid it? Or by living it through.   (p. 896)

[. . .] if the prospect of sin, draws us on but the sin is only boring and dead the moment it happens, it's only the living it through that redeems it. (p. 898)

Stephen leaves Ludy with a final motto.

—Do you have a pencil? Then write this. Dilige et quod vis fac.
Stephen rose slowly above him, standing, watching the pencil move.
—e . t . . qu . o . o . d . . v . i . s . . fac, and what does it mean? I studied Vergil but I've forgotten . . .
—Love, and do what you want to.   (p. 899)

Finally Stephen decides, "Now at last, to live deliberately." Just as Esther, Recktall Brown, and Mr. Yák did, Ludy tries to impose himself on Stephen:

—You and I . . .
—No, there's no more you and I, Stephen said withdrawing uphill slowly, empty-handed.   (p. 900)

As we learn later, Stephen then sets out by ship from Spain back towards the United States.

Meanwhile, on another ship, Stanley is taking Esme to Rome on a religious pilgrimage. Stanley is chaste and pious in the virtuous, not the self-righteous sense; he shares his cabin with Esme without taking advantage of her sexually. Unlike all the novel's other false artists, Stanley has composed a veritable Christian Mass, which he means to play on the Fenestrula organ.

In the middle of the ocean, the ship on which Esme, Stanley, and Basil Valentine (incognito) are sailing rams and sinks Wyatt's boat. As Esme, Stanley, and Basil Valentine look on, sailors pull from the water "his" nameless and senseless form (which readers must recognize from "that square face all screwed up around the eyes" [pp. 795, 833]). Separately, the three witness the death of "the man they took out of the sea" (p. 834). After last rites are administered, Wyatt's body is returned to the sea, in a weighted canvas sack. Esme, forgetting all the Christian lore which Stanley has been trying to teach her, becomes convinced that Wyatt is her god; her pleas to be allowed to see Wyatt's body constantly elide between "him" and "Him" (p. 841). Ultimately, Esme sacrifices her life in religious devotion to Wyatt, her saint-in-the-boat:

—She's dead, Stanley insisted suddenly, then was silent again.
—But . . . what happened? What happened?
—She died, she . . . she had a place on her lip, a sore, a . . . and it got infected, it was just something like . . . staphylococcic infection, and it happened just like that almost, in a couple of days, she . . .
—How'd she pick up something like that just like that, she . . .
—She wasted away, so quickly as though she . . . she had no will to live, and she . . . she said, Stanley shuddered, —from kissing Saint-Peter-in-the-Boat, she said, For some fishes, the sea, the sea . . .   (p. 953)

Stanley meets his own death soon thereafter, while playing his just-completed Mass in an old church whose walls cannot withstand the sound. In the novel's final words,

[. . .] he did not stop. The walls quivered, still he did not hesitate. Everything moved, and even falling, soared in atonement.

He was the only person caught in the collapse, and afterward, most of his work was recovered too, and it is still spoken of, when it is noted, with high regard, though seldom played.   (p. 956)

In the world according to Gaddis, even the best are crushed.

Wyatt as a Hero

Just as Joyce bases the action of *Ulysses* loosely and covertly upon episodes from the Homeric *Odyssey,* so Gaddis loosely and covertly molds the narrative of *The Recognitions* upon the cycle of the birth, death, and resurrection of the god, as this is described in Frazer's *Golden Bough.* Gaddis travesties the *Recognitions of Clement* by grafting *The Golden Bough* upon it.[1] The novel itself, that is, implicitly validates Esme's recognition of Wyatt as a god.

The Recognitions begins with the funeral of Wyatt's mother, who died on board ship while she and Reverend Gwyon were making the crossing from Boston to Spain:

1. Gaddis's adherence to the Clementine *Recognitions* as a structural model seems no more than general. *The Recognitions of Clement,* trans. Thomas Smith, in *Ante-Nicene Christian Library: Translations of the Writings of the Fathers Down to A.D. 325,* ed. Alexander Roberts and James Donaldson (Edinburgh: T. & T. Clark, 1867), III, 135–471.

> Even Camilla had enjoyed masquerades, of the safe sort where the mask may be dropped at that critical moment where it presumes itself as reality. (p. 3)

Camilla's funeral is a "masquerade" because it treats Wyatt's mother as if she were a virgin:

> Camilla had borne Gwyon a son and gone, virginal, to earth: virginal in the sight of man, at any rate. The white funeral carriage of San Zwingli was ordained for infants and maidens. (p. 14)

The novel sustains the theme of Camilla as Wyatt's virgin mother even after her death has left Reverend Gwyon and Wyatt on their own:

> The father and son faced one another across the stark declivity of their different heights, the man staring wordless at this incarnation of something he had imagined long before, in a different life; the child staring beyond at his virgin mother. (ρ. 19)

The term 'incarnation' in this passage further suggests Wyatt's mythological status as a god. Camilla herself may be named after Camilla the Volscian, the "virgin warrior" in Vergil's *Aeneid* (vii, 800f.). The very uncertainty, however, over whether allusions are being made to things outside the book is a virtue in this *kind* of book, the self-conscious satire.

Wyatt's father, in his embrace of Mithraism and his general attunement to a world that is long gone, may be said to represent, albeit ambiguously, the old god who must be supplanted by the new. Reverend Gwyon's mythological status is dramatized, almost gruesomely, by the fate of his body after death. Every year since his wife's death, Reverend Gwyon had sent parcels of food, especially flour, to the Spanish monastery where he took refuge after her burial. When Gwyon himself dies, his body is cremated, and through another bizarre but wholly logical set of misunderstandings, his own ashes are included, without notice, in the last food parcel which had been prepared for mailing to Spain. At the monastery, where Wyatt, as Stephen, is engaged in "restoring" old paintings and conversing with Ludy, Reverend Gwyon's ashes are baked in with the daily bread. Stephen and the others then eat this bread communally. Wyatt is thus the son of a virgin mother and a father whose body is eaten as a sacrament.

The fate of Reverend Gwyon's ashes, by the way, helps to explain the relevance of the unattributed epigraph to the first chapter of Part III, "There are many Manii at Aricia" (p. 723). The line is in fact a Roman proverb which Frazer glosses in a chapter of *The Golden Bough* headed "Eating the God":

> We are now able to suggest an explanation of the proverb "There are many Manii at Aricia." Certain loaves made in the shape of men were called by the Romans *maniae,* and it appears that this kind of loaf was especially made at Aricia.　(*The Golden Bough,* p. 569)

Frazer goes on to explain the significance of the sacramental meal in the ensuing chapter, headed "Homeopathic Magic of a Flesh Diet":

> [. . .] we have found a widespread custom of eating the god sacramentally, either in the shape of the man or animal who represents the god, or in the shape of bread made in human or animal form. The reasons for thus partaking of the body of the god are, from the primitive standpoint, simple enough. The savage commonly believes that by eating the flesh of an animal or man he acquires not only the physical, but even the moral and intellectual qualities which were characteristic of that animal or man; so when the creature is deemed divine, our simple savage naturally expects to absorb a portion of its divinity along with its material substance [. . .]. The doctrine forms part of the widely ramified system of sympathetic or homeopathic magic.　(*The Golden Bough,* p. 573)

The Recognitions most consistently hints at the deity of Wyatt himself in the periodic repetition of a parable which proves prophetic of Wyatt's own fate. The parable, when Wyatt first hears it from his father, relates to Saint Clement of Rome (fl. ca. A.D. 96), the putative author of the *Recognitions* from which Gaddis's novel takes its name:

> —Yes, Gwyon murmured catching it under his thumb, —Clement's monogram, he was martyred, yes here, gettato a mare con un'ancora . . . they tied an anchor to his neck and threw him into the Black Sea.
> —Yes into the sea with an anchor? like the man you told me about? The anchor caught on a tombstone, and the man coming down the rope in the celestial sea to free it, and he drowned?　(p. 44)

Years later Wyatt retells the parable while Esme models for him, and she remembers it still later when Wyatt drowns:

> —[. . .] O friars minors, is he in Purgatory if he drowned? Down, on a rope, did he tell you that story? Drowned, in the celestial sea came down the rope to undo the anchor caught there on a stone with no one's name on, and a date, inclined against the bottom by the darkness, and so no wonder that the anchor caught, and he came down the rope. If there were time . . .
> (p. 922)

The parable of the man who came down through the celestial sea to earth and drowned, in short, fits Wyatt Gwyon as well as it does Jesus Christ. Wyatt's whole life, in fact, is punctuated with discreet but distinct Christological allusions. Recktall Brown, for example, defending his habit of talking only "business" to Wyatt, says, "—Somebody has to nail him down to it" (p. 235).

To simulate Wyatt's myth-dictated resurrection, Gaddis has even violated the otherwise strictly chronological order of his narrative. Chapters 4 and 5 of Part III have been intentionally switched around, so that we read of "the man they pulled from the sea" *before* we see Stephen leaving Ludy behind. The omission of any number at all from the novel's twenty-second and final chapter (Part III, Ch. 6) hints at the tampering that has taken place. So our last view of Wyatt is not of his burial at sea, but of his (temporally prior) "withdrawing uphill slowly, empty-handed," to live "deliberately" (p. 900). In defense, perhaps, of this willful distortion, *The Recognitions* alludes to those "oriental carpets made with a conscious flaw, in order not to offend the creator of Perfection by emulating his grand design" (p. 906). Again, the uncertainty as to whether the book is actually referring to itself works in the book's favor.

At the same moment that Stanley is sounding the triumphant chords of his Mass, on the last page of the novel, a new saint is being canonized nearby in Rome. Supposedly, the new saint is a young girl who was brutally assaulted and killed in San Zwingli, Spain, and whose seeming intervention in various miracles is mentioned periodically throughout the novel. In the burial with which the novel opens, Wyatt's mother Camilla is in fact laid next to this little girl. Forty years later, when 'Stephan' and 'Mr. Yák' meet at that same cemetery—Wyatt there to visit his mother's grave, Mr. Sinisterra to get a cadaver for his counterfeit mummy—they hear from the townspeople

> all about this patron saint they're getting. When they took her out of the graveyard here to put her somewhere else when she was beatified they thought she looks kind of big for an eleven-year-old girl [. . .].   (p. 791)

And when Stephan and Mr. Yák open what ought to be Camilla's coffin, they find instead "the little girl who had been left behind" (p. 792). So the body about to be canonized in Rome is Camilla's. *The Recognitions* thus begins with the burial of Wyatt's mother as a virgin "in the sight of man," and it concludes with the Church's recognition of Camilla as a sainted virgin in the eyes of God. These are the necessary first and last steps in Wyatt's mythological apotheosis.

The Recognitions Self-Implied

The diametrical juxtaposition of Camilla's body and soul at the beginning and end of *The Recognitions* defines only the outermost in the novel's *Inferno*-like construction of concentric rings. John Stark has pointed out "oblique" allusions to Dante in "this concentric ice-ridden chaos" (p. 695), and in such snippets of dialogue as

—Look, Leroy . . .
—Dis city . . .
—Leroy . . .
—Dis   (p. 696)[1]

On the third page of the novel, Gaddis refers specifically to "Dante's eyewitness account of the dropsical torments being suffered even now in Malebolge by that pioneer Adamo da Brescia, who falsified the florin" (p. 5). The allusion is to Canto XXX of the *Inferno*, of which Dorothy L. Sayers has written: "*The Falsifiers*. In this canto we have the images of impersonators (falsifiers of person), perjurors (falsifiers of words) and coiners (falsifiers of money)."[2] Otto, for example, impersonates; Ellery perjures; Mr. Sinisterra coins.

On the novel's third from last page, the reference to Dante finds its symmetrical response in "a little round hat with ribbons, and the name of the first Italian dreadnought, *Dante Alighieri*, embroidered in gold round the band" (p. 954). Such a ship was in fact "laid down" in 1909;[3] but, more significantly, "the name of the first Italian dreadnought" *poet* is thus neatly embroidered round the band of this novel as well.

Even the detail of Adamo da Brescia is symmetrically mirrored in the disclosure in the final pages of the name of the ship on which Otto, Esme, and Basil Valentine crossed to Italy: "the *Conte di Brescia*" (p. 951). For the sake of achieving this crafty symmetry, Gaddis is obliged to with-

1. Stark, "Just Recognition," p. 3.
2. Dorothy L. Sayers, "Commentary" to Dante's *Divine Comedy*, trans. D.L. Sayers (Harmondsworth: Penguin Books, 1949, 1974), I: *Hell*, 262.
3. *Encyclopedia Britannica*, 11th ed., s.v. "Ship," XXIV, 904.

hold the name of the ship during the actual narration of the voyage, which is certainly an artificial procedure and perhaps a kind of dishonesty. Like the disordering of two chapters so as to simulate a myth of apotheosis, however, this juggling of details into an order neater than that of narrative logic suggests the extent to which *The Recognitions,* like other self-conscious novels, is translucently (if not quite "transparently") "subordinated to artificial principles of organization."

For the structure of events in *The Recognitions* is as scrupulously symmetrical as that of its literary allusions. Rings of counterfeiters, of diamonds, and of churchbells encircle the novel like the ouroboros depicted on its title page. Mr. Sinisterra, masquerading as the ship's surgeon, causes Camilla's death at the novel's start; it is he, posing as an archaeologist, who uncovers her "resurrection" at the end. Wyatt's mother dies in midocean aboard the *Purdue Victory;* Wyatt himself dies, forty years later, at the same spot, when the same ship is sundered and sunk.

In its overall design, *The Recognitions* is a triptych, in which, as in a fourteenth-century Italian altarpiece, "the central panel is twice the width of the wings;"[1] Part II of *The Recognitions* is indeed roughly twice as long as Parts I and III. Furthermore, the novel's two "wings" mirror each other in details large and small, with interest and humor enhanced by the principle of *mutatis mutandis.* For example, a scene in Part I set in Paris begins as follows:

> On the terrace of the Dôme sat a person who looked like the young George Washington without his wig (at about the time he dared the Ohio territory). She read, with silently moving lips, from a book before her. She was drinking a bilious-colored liquid from a globular goblet [. . .]. Anyone could have seen it was *transition* she was reading, if any had looked. None did.   (p. 63)

The corresponding passage in Part III goes like this:

> On the terrace of the Flore sat a person who resembled the aging George Washington without his wig (at about the time he said farewell to his troops). She was drinking a bilious cloudy liquid and read, with silent moving lips, from a small stiff-covered magazine. Anyone could have seen it was *Partisan Review* she was reading, if anyone had looked.   (p. 938)

Recognition of these symmetrical patterns becomes a challenging game for the reader—the novel *demands* annotation—and the effort proves re-

1. Peter and Linda Murray, *A Dictionary of Art and Artists* (Baltimore: Penguin Books, 1959), p. 324.

warding, naturally, according to one's tastes. Some of the interlocking details are, however, incontestably delightful in their ingenuity. At one gathering of miscellaneous characters we overhear this bit of social imposture:

—He's still in Paris. He wrote that he's just bought one of those delightful Renaults . . .
—Oh yes, I do love them. An original?   (p. 569)

The joke's interlocking mirror image near the end of the book is, when recognized, even funnier:

—We've just bought a lovely big Pissarro . . .
—My uncle had one, it was so big he couldn't park it anywhere.
(p. 940)[1]

The triptych's central panel, further, is itself symmetrical. The openings of Chapters II,3 and II,9, for example, echo each other faithfully:

Above the trees, the weathercock atop the church steeple caught the sun, poised there above the town like a cock of fire rising from its own ashes. (p. 390)

The sun rose at seven, and its light caught the weathercock atop the church steeple, epiphanized it there above the town like a cock of fire risen from its own ashes.   (p. 700)

At the precise center of the book, as we have noted, appears the character named "Willie," talking about his novel "*The Recognitions*" (p. 478). The book really is "this perfectly ordered chaos" (p. 18).

The Recognitions implicates itself as part of its inquiry into the validity of art. By its teasing images of its own author, its sneaky shell game with its characters, and its craftily wrought symmetrical structure, Gaddis's novel puts itself at stake in its own debate over art's real value. As *The Recognitions* is emphatically literary in its allusiveness, and painterly in its scope and attention to detail, so too is it self-consciously musical in its rhythmic repetition of details. For example: like Pope, who "uses the term [wit] forty-six times in at least five different senses" in his *Essay on Criticism*,[2] Gaddis repeats the word "recognition" twenty-eight times. Each time the word appears, the whole book seems to vibrate in one's

---

1. It must be admitted that these two jokes are not quite so symmetrically disposed in the novel as one might wish.
2. Cuddon, *A Dictionary of Literary Terms*, s.v. "wit," p. 739.

hands (the literary equivalent, perhaps, of acoustical "sympathetic vibration").

*　　*　　*

Art forgery, as *The Recognitions* documents, began in Roman times; it has flourished, that is, upon the private ownership of art. Not an appreciation of a work's esthetic merits but greed for the selling price of a "recognized" art work prompts most forgeries. But Wyatt insists (and the novel endorses his claims) that his own forgeries are inherently valuable, and that they are so *precisely* because they are such faithful copies. Other forgeries are based upon superficial resemblances, whereas Wyatt's work is based upon "recognitions" that "go much deeper" (p. 250). In an amusing juxtaposition, Wyatt complains that a magazine's photographic reproductions of his forged paintings are "cheap fakes" and "a calumny, that's what it is, on my work." When Basil Valentine suggests, reasonably enough, that "every piece you do is calumny on the artist you forge," Wyatt responds, stirringly,

> —It's not. It's not, damn it, I . . . when I'm working, I . . . Do you think I do these the way all other forging has been done? Pulling the fragments of ten paintings together and making one, or taking a . . . Dürer and reversing the composition so that the man looks to the right instead of left, putting a beard on him from another portrait, and a hat, a different hat from another, so that they look at it and recognize Dürer there? No, it's . . . the recognitions go much deeper, much further back, and I . . . this . . . the X-ray tests, and ultraviolet and infra-red, the experts with their photomicrography and . . . macrophotography, do you think that's all there is to it? Some of them aren't fools, they don't just look for a hat or a beard, or a style they can recognize, they look with memories that . . . go beyond themselves, that go back to . . . where mine goes.
> —Sit down, my boy.
> —And . . . any knock at the door may be the gold inspectors, come to see if I'm using bad materials down there, I . . . I'm a master painter in the Guild, in Flanders, do you see? And if they come in and find that I'm not using the . . . gold, they destroy the bad materials I'm using and fine me, and I . . . they demand that . . . and this exquisite color of ultramarine, Venice ultramarine I have to take to them for approval, and the red pigment, this brick-red Flanders pigment . . . because I've taken the Guild oath, not for the critics, the experts, the . . . you, you have no more to do with me than if you are my descendants, nothing to do with me, and you . . . the Guild oath, to use pure materials, to work in the sight of God . . .　　(p. 250)

Wyatt goes on to explain that, like a Flemish painter, "I take five or six or ten" perspectives, whereas the camera takes only one (p. 251). The only good forgery, then, is a perfect forgery, which surpasses even photography in the depth of its "recognitions."

Plagiarism, according to the *Oxford English Dictionary,* is

> the wrongful appropriation or purloining, and publication as one's own, of the ideas, or the expression of the ideas (literary, artistic, musical, mechanical, etc.) of another.

A character named Max, for example, plagiarizes the *Duino Elegies* by publishing Rilke's poetry under his own name. The term's etymology, however, gives "plagiary" even broader relevance to *The Recognitions.* Plagiary comes from the Latin *plagiārius,* "one who abducts the child or slave of another" (*OED*). Thus, Arny and Maude Munk "plagiarize" when they take home with them an infant found wandering through Esther's Christmas party. Mr. Sinisterra plagiarizes not only when he forges official currency, but also when he "abducts" Otto from Otto's proper father, Mr. Pivner. Otto himself plagiarizes both when he tries to publish Wyatt's ideas in his own play and when he helps Ed Feasley to "abduct" Stanley's mother's amputated leg. Even Camilla's body is plagiarized by abduction.

Yet, as Wyatt's advocacy suggest, there are some kinds of borrowing that the novel endorses. For her own appreciation, Esme copies into her notebook verses from the first Duino Elegy. This is not the same thing as Max publishing it for money. Quotations can be stolen, or used as padding; but quoting can also be an act of homage. When Mr. Feddle goes about forging signatures on the flyleaves of books he admires—such as "autographing" a copy of *Moby Dick* (p. 574)—he is in fact testifying to his recognition of these books' *spiritual* value. Mr. Feddle even carries his personal copy of Dostoyevsky's *The Idiot* inside a dustjacket which identifies the author as "Feodor Feddle" (p. 937).

Both Wyatt and Stanley, here as elsewhere the halting, almost reluctant spokesmen for the novel's positive values, defend this kind of appreciative appropriation founded upon true recognitions. According to Stanley,

> —Everybody has that feeling when they look at a work of art and it's right, that sudden familiarity, a sort of . . . recognition, as though they were creating it themselves, as though it were being created through them while they look

at it or listen to it and, it shouldn't be sinful to want to have created beauty?   (pp. 534–35)

Stanley admires the work of Bach, Palestrina, the Gabriellis, and Corelli "beyond all else in this life, for they had touched the origins of design with recognition" (p. 322). ("Classical" music gives Mr. Pivner, on the other hand, "a sense of recognition which he did not understand" [p. 501].) Stanley says of composing, "—But it isn't making it up, inventing music, it's like . . . remembering [. . .]" (p. 461). Meanwhile Wyatt, who, as noted earlier, defends his forged paintings by pointing out that "the recognitions go much deeper, much further back" (p. 250), experiences the same epiphanic sense before the works of other great painters. Wyatt says of Picasso's *Night Fishing in Antibes,* for example, "When I saw it, it was one of those moments of reality, of near-recognition of reality" (p. 91). As Otto's notes put Wyatt's idea, originality itself is "not inventn bt snse of recall, recgntion, pttrns alrdy thr" (p. 123). (Comical Otto himself fails to recognize that the remainder of the quote, "You cannt invnt t shpe of a stone," as he copies it, is in fact a "line of Ben Shahn's" [p. 463].)

Wyatt's pursuit of deep recognitions also suggests how profoundly Platonic Gaddis's novel really is. The Platonic form, "the permanent reality which makes a thing what it is, in contrast with the particulars which are finite and subject to change,"[1] constitutes the real goal of Wyatt's painterly quest. *The Recognitions* self-consciously asserts its Platonism in "Willie"'s defense of "writing for a very small audience": "—So . . . ? how many people were there in Plato's Republic?" (p. 478).

The Recognitions thus withholds the praise traditionally due originality. Originality was Satan's crime, Aunt May taught. Wyatt's old painting instructor Herr Koppel refers to originality as "that romantic disease," and reminds us that two hundred years ago "to be original was to admit that you could not do a thing the right way" (p. 89). Basil Valentine even suggests that truly "talented" people would rather "plagiarize" than be "original":

> —Originality is a device that untalented people use to impress other untalented people, and protect themselves from talented people . . . Most original people are forced to devote all their time to plagiarizing. Their only difficulty is that if they have a spark of wit or wisdom themselves, they're given no credit. The curse of cleverness.   (p. 252)

1. *Encyclopedia Britannica,* 11th ed., s.v. ' Form."

Like Boss Tweed, who, according to *The Autobiography of Lincoln Steffens,* distinguished between "dirty" graft and "clean" graft, Gaddis's novel distinguished between good and bad plagiarism. Uncomprehending material greed motivates "bad" plagiarism (e.g., most counterfeiting and social imposture), whereas "good" plagiarism is inspired by recognition of the subject's abiding value (e.g., learning to emulate the masters). "Pythagoras Socrates Plato Homer & Hesiod, all plagiarized from Moses, one and all," thinks Wyatt (p. 393). His own disciple Esme quotes Wyatt, "—He even said once, that the saints were counterfeits of Christ, and that Christ was a counterfeit of God" (p. 483).

*   *   *

Given so much consideration of the value of art, it is inevitable that *The Recognitions* should investigate the role of the critic. We have already noted that criticism-of-the-novel-itself is a characteristic feature of self-conscious novels, and Gaddis's work is no exception. Basil Valentine observes that "your friend [Willie] is writing for a rather small audience, isn't he" (pp. 372–73), just as Gide's Laura criticizes Edouard's plan for "*Les Faux-monnayeurs,*" "*Mon pauvre ami, vous ferez mourir d'ennui vos lecteurs.*"[1]

Gaddis's portrait of most critics of art and literature is caustically satiric. The narrator's attitude resembles that of Anselm, who says, "—I keep myself busy sawing toilet seats in half for half-assed critics" (p. 134). In the most sharply satiric scene, two book reviewers discuss a book which sounds suspiciously like *The Recognitions:*

> —You reading that? both asked at once, withdrawing in surprise.
> —No, I'm just reviewing it, said the taller one [. . .], —all I need is the jacket blurb to write the review.
> It was in fact quite a thick book. A pattern of bold elegance, the lettering on the dust wrapper stood forth in stark configurations of red and black to intimate the origin of design. (For some crotchety reason there was no picture of the author looking pensive sucking a pipe, sans gêne with a cigarette, sang-froid with no necktie, plastered across the back.)   (p. 936)

The critic's work, as *The Recognitions* displays it, partakes of both good and bad plagiarism. For surely in publishing explications of and commentaries on other people's work, the critic effectively retails the ideas of others for his own financial or professional profit. But at the same time,

1. André Gide, *Les Faux-monnayeurs* (Paris: Gallimard, 1925), p. 233.

criticism, when it is sensitive, may uncover the deep recognitions which underlie great works of art, and may *share* those recognitions with others. Wyatt avers to Basil Valentine that such a criticism, based upon "disciplined recognitions," is "the art we need most today":

> —I came down to ask a favor of you. But if you are so painfully sensitive to criticism, such a self-conscious artist that . . .
> —No I, it's just, listen, criticism? It's the most important art now, it's the one we need most now. Criticism is the art we need most today. But not, don't you see? not the "if I'd done it myself . . ." Yes, a, a disciplined nostalgia, disciplined recognitions but not, no, listen, what is the favor?   (p. 335)

A faithful copy inspired by recognition is thus to be valued in itself as art; and criticism at its best is the best form of plagiarism.

*   *   *

There remains to consider the demands which *The Recognitions* places upon its readers. These are heavy demands indeed. The novel refuses to translate quotes and epigraphs from a half-dozen foreign languages, and relies symptomatically upon hundreds of more or less abstruse allusions. The shattering of syntax into the jagged and ill-fitting fragments which we are accustomed to hear but are unaccustomed to read makes for still more difficult reading. The two characters who jocosely tell Willie that he must be "writing for a very small audience" (pp. 373, 478) are not really joking. Wyatt's conviction that "being obvious" is "fatal" (p. 96) is definitely at work.

The novel itself, however, defends its own difficulty. In a long but crucial passage, Wyatt attacks authors who "write for people who read with the surface of their minds":

> —[. . .] most writing now, if you read it they go on one two three four and tell you what happened like newspaper accounts, no adjectives, no long sentences, no tricks they pretend, and they finally believe that the way they saw it is the way it is, when really . . . why, what happened when they opened Mary Stuart's coffin? They found she'd taken two strokes of the blade, one slashed the nape of her neck and the second one took the head. But did any of the eye-witness accounts mention two strokes? No . . . it never takes your breath away, telling you things you already know, laying everything out flat, as though the terms and the time, and the nature and the movement of everything were secrets of the same magnitude. They write for people who read with the surface of their minds, people with reading habits that make the smallest demands on them, people brought up reading for facts, who know

what's going to come next and want to know what's coming next, and get angry at surprises. Clarity's essential, and detail, no fake mysticism, the facts are bad enough. But we're embarassed for people who tell too much, and tell it without surprise. How does he [Hemingway] know what happened? unless it's one unshaven man alone in a boat, changing I to he, and how often do you get a man alone in a boat, in all this . . . all this . . .   (p. 113)

An anonymous character complains of most contemporary writing,

—It's like the movies because there's everything spread out for you, and you just have to react, like at the movies you don't have to pay with your *real* emotions, you don't have to *do* anything . . .   (p. 577)

Explaining his Mass to Agnes Deigh, Stanley offers a similarly compelling defense of art which does not shirk the complexity of life but embraces it in all its fragmented diffusion:

—Because we get time given to us in fragments, that's the only way we know it [. . .]. And now it's impossible to accomplish a body of work without a continuous sense of time, so instead you try to get all the parts together into one work that will stand by itself and serve the same thing a lifetime of separate works does, something higher than itself [. . .].   (p. 616)

The lengthy and vitriolic satire which Gaddis directs against Dale Carnegie's best-selling manual *How to Win Friends and Influence People* (pp. 497–503) treats with particular sarcasm Carnegie's complete omission of the very sort of challenges to the reader's intellect upon which Gaddis's own literary method depends:

It was written with reassuring felicity. There were no abstrusely long sentences, no confounding long words, no bewildering metaphors in an obfuscated system such as he [Mr. Pivner] feared finding in simply bound books of thoughts and ideas. No dictionary was necessary to understand its message; no reason to know what Kapila saw when he looked heavenward, and of what the Athenians accused Anaxagoras, or to know the secret name of Jahveh, or who cleft the Gordian knot, the meaning of 666. There was, finally, very little need to know anything at all [. . .].   (p. 499)

The Recognitions thus passionately repudiates both the superficiality of facile entertainment and the artificiality of art-for-art's sake. As Stanley expresses it, Gaddis's art serves "something higher than itself":

—When art tries to be a religion in itself, Stanley persisted, —a religion of perfect form and beauty, but then there it is all alone, not uniting people, not . . . like the Church does but, look at the gulf between people and modern art . . . It isn't for love of the thing itself that an artist works, but so that through it he's expressing love for something higher, because that's the only place art is really free, serving something higher than itself, like us, like we are . . . (p. 632)

The Recognitions asserts the value of love, and displays love's rightful context in both life and art. Satire traditionally implies a standard to which men's behavior is compared and found wanting; for Gaddis, this standard is furnished by the precepts of love: "Dilige et quod vis fac." Life and art are nearly synonymous for Gaddis; and in both spheres right is to be distinguished from wrong. Reason, like money, may be put to good uses; but if pursued as an end in itself it produces evil results. Love, however, is not only the sole rightful guide to life, but it is also the only rightful inspiration for art—an art whose *duty* it is to reflect life as it is lived, through an enhancing filter that distinguishes right life from wrong, good deeds from evil. As Esther quotes Wyatt,

—The boundaries between good and evil must be defined again, they must be re-established, that's what a man must do today, isn't it? (p. 590)

Wyatt responds,

—[. . .] the only way to reality is this moral sense . . . (p. 591)

Such a moral art can *redeem* the otherwise lost time which it commemorates, by affirming what is good in it and condemning what is evil, only if it itself is redeemed by a significant pattern. Such is the case with "this perfectly ordered chaos."

As a self-conscious satire, *The Recognitions* necessarily asserts its own artifice less aggressively than self-conscious fictions that are not satiric, such as those of Joyce and Nabokov. There are several reasons for this. The satirist refers, however obliquely, to conditions that exist in the real world; and for his project to succeed he therefore cannot afford to cast doubt upon literature's capacity to "render" the real world in a meaningful fashion. An utterly reflexive, self-regarding text cannot draw our attention to the rights and wrongs of the world in which we purchase and read that text—and this, transcendently, is Gaddis's aim. Therefore, the self-consciousness of *The Recognitions* must be restrained by the dictates of the satiric genre to which it belongs.

We should also note that although Gide's Edouard is a self-conscious novelist, and Humbert Humbert and Van Veen are similarly self-conscious artists, the painter-hero of *The Recognitions* is emphatically *not* self-conscious in his art. In his forgeries of old masters, Wyatt endeavors to conceal, rather than to display, his own hand in the composition. He strives to create and maintain, rather than to disrupt, the illusion that the work exists (and has long existed) separately and independently from his own identity. To his sharpest critics, it is true, Wyatt's success in extinguishing his personality and presence from his paintings is never wholly complete; as Basil Valentine tells him,

> Your work, it's old, isn't it, but a little always shows through, yes something, semper aliquid haeret? something always remains, something of you.
> (p. 336)

But what "remains" of Wyatt in his work is always earnest, never game-playing; and what he displays of himself in his forgeries, even if Valentine is correct, appears inadvertently, not deliberately. As a novelistic character who imagines himself to be a character in somebody's novel, Wyatt Gwyon stands squarely within the tradition of literary self-consciousness. But as an artist-hero who repudiates self-consciousness in his own art, Wyatt must be seen as standing apart from that tradition, aloof and indifferent to it.

Gaddis thus succeeds in adding a new wrinkle to the repertoire of reflexivity, by using self-conscious devices in order to repudiate the esthetic premises of self-consciousness itself. For, all of the appointed artful ruses are here: the mirrors that duplicate and reduplicate the self-regarding characters, the palindromic names (Otto, Hannah), even palindromic restatements of the novel's central theme: "Trade ye no mere moneyed art" (p. 177). Gaddis's first novel refers to itself just as his second novel refers to the first; *JR* devotes several pages, for example, to mock reviews of a dozen or so novels, the titles of all of which are anagrams of the title of *The Recognitions: I Chose Rotten Gin, The Onion Crest GI*, etc. Informed by a manifestly artificial symmetrical structure, incondite and recondite in its reliance upon foreign languages and abstruse literary allusions, peopled by characters who suspect their own fictional status and haunted by a writer named Willie who is writing *The Recognitions, The Recognitions* nonetheless renounces "art that tries to be a religion in itself," and asserts, in Stanley's words, that "nothing is self-sufficient, even art" (p. 617). Gaddis dons the esthete's guise so as to display its inadequacy; he re-orchestrates the repertoire of reflexivity in order to sound a call for Art-for-Humanity's-Sake. Self-consciously he demands our consciousness of others.

Both despite and because of its many self-conscious challenges to the reader, *The Recognitions,* like Stanley's Mass, is still spoken of, when it is noted, with high regard, though seldom read. As John Stark cleverly notes in the title of his appreciative essay, however, William Gaddis is beginning to get his "just recognition." Critical attention, it seems, is about to explode all around him. The implied author of *The Recognitions,* of course, does not crave success in terms of numbers of readers. As one particularly astute anonymous character observes,

> —What I get a kick out of is these serious writers who write a book where they say money gives a false significance to art, and then they raise hell when their book doesn't make any money.   (p. 749)

Art's task is to distinguish the good from the bad and not worry about how many copies sell. But as more and more people are led to read Gaddis, one cannot help feeling that more and more good is being done.

Chapter VII

Paradoxical Pynchon; or, The Real World Inside *Gravity's Rainbow*

I F self-consciousness can sustain satire, as in William Gaddis, Thomas Pynchon shows us how it can also sharpen the edge of a particular wedge of paradox.

Gravity's Rainbow creates a paradoxical effect: some readers rave about the book, while others cannot read it. Although the Fiction Jury of the Pulitzer Committee unanimously recommended Pynchon's novel for the 1973 Pulitzer Prize, the Committee at large found it "turgid," "obscene," and "unreadable," and voted to withhold its fiction prize that year. Books have already been written on Pynchon, critical studies calling him "the greatest living writer in the English-speaking world"; and even the semi-official gate-keeper, *PMLA,* admitted Pynchon's four-year-old novel into the Academy. Other critics, meanwhile, have called his work "American plastic" and "a failure." *Gravity's Rainbow* is highly controversial; even the fact of its authorship is in dispute.[1]

I would like to suggest that the response to *Gravity's Rainbow* has been paradoxical because the novel is itself paradoxical in *genre*. The entire

---

1. Thomas Pynchon, *Gravity's Rainbow* (New York: The Viking Press, 1973). All references are to this edition. Peter Kihss, "Pulitzer Jurors Dismayed on Pynchon," *New York Times,* 8 May 1974, p. 38, cited in Scott Simmon, *"Gravity's Rainbow* Described," *Critique,* 16:2 (1974), 54. "The greatest": Edward Mendelson, "Introduction" to *Pynchon: A Collection of Critical Essays,* ed. Edward Mendelson (Englewood Cliffs, N.J.: Prentice-Hall, 1978), (hereafter *Pynchon Essays*), p. 15. Lawrence C. Wolfley, "Repression's Rainbow: The Presence of Norman O. Brown in Pynchon's Big Novel," *PMLA,* 92:5 (Oct. 1977), 873–89. Gore Vidal, "American Plastic: The Matter of Fiction," *New York Review of Books,* 23:12 (15 July 1976), 31–39, reprinted in his *Matters of Fact and of Fiction: Essays 1973–1976* (New York: Random House, 1977), pp. 99–126 ("To compare Pynchon with Joyce, say, is to compare a kindergartener to a graduate student," p. 37). David H. Richter, "The Failure of Completeness: Pynchon's *V.,"* in his *Fable's End: Completeness and Closure in Rhetorical Fiction* (Chicago: University of Chicago Press, 1974), pp. 101–35. A New York tabloid ran a photo of *Gravity's Rainbow* on its front page and asked, "Did J.D. Salinger Write This Book?": John Calvin Batchelor, "Thomas Pynchon is not Thomas Pynchon," and "The Ghost of Richard Farina," *Soho Weekly News,* 22 April 1976 and 28 April 1977, pp. 19–26. I am indebted to Kermit Frazer for sending me Batchelor's article, which I nonetheless do not take seriously.

novel, that is, seeks to produce the specific esthetic effect which I shall call the Power of Paradox: the peculiar suspension of the intellectual and emotional faculties between two equally plausible but mutually exclusive modes of perception or belief. The novel's self-consciousness reinforces its paradoxical effect.

We are already familiar with paradox as an esthetic power—as the "final cause," the "intended effect"—of works of art in other media. In drawing, for example, paradox is sought as the final power in much of the work of M.C. Escher. In the folk art of verbal humor, the power of paradox underlies many jokes, especially puns. Paradox is rarer as the intended effect of literature since it is primarily a local effect, not easily sustained without becoming tedious. Poems, though, are often generically paradoxical; some of John Donne's, for example, in M.H. Abrams's account, are "paradoxical in the overall structure as well as in the component statements."[1] John Lyly's *Euphues* (1579) is an early example of book-length paradox, a string of varied and elaborate antitheses balanced between wisdom and wit. Paradox has consistently interested philosophers, as the titles of *Either/Or* and *Beyond Good and Evil* suggest.

Gravity's Rainbow creates its own paradoxical effect by offering the reader two antithetical perspectives on everything that happens in its pages. Everything in it can be seen either as related *caus*ally, or as related *casu*ally: the novel provides evidence for both conclusions. If events in *Gravity's Rainbow* are related *caus*ally, then a massive conspiracy envelopes Tyrone Slothrop and the other characters. This is confirmed by the novel. If events are related *casu*ally, however, then the apparent links are no more than the characters' (and reader's) paranoid imaginings. This, too, is confirmed by the novel.

Slothrop's amorous successes coincide point for point with the rocket strikes in London: surely cause-and-effect, either precognition or psychokinesis. But both patterns conform to a Poisson distribution: perfect randomness, each point ideally independent of any other. Where does Slothrop see the most pervasive web of conspiracy surrounding him? In a casino—hazard's home. This is the essence of the paradoxical effect of what happens in the novel: the insistence, in every episode, that everything is fixed; inseparable from the insistence, in those same episodes, that everything is random. Does Slothrop escape into the anarchic chaos

---

1. M.H. Abrams, *A Glossary of Literary Terms* (New York: Holt, Rinehart and Winston, 1957), s.v. "Figurative language," p. 37.

of "the Zone," asserting his independence of plots and conspiracies? Then the first person he meets there will spontaneously offer him information on "the one rocket out of 6000" that he seeks (p. 292). Death by bombardment is surely the most random and pointless of fates; but what if voices from the dead say that it all makes sense? Is the world watched over by a spiritual divinity? Or are the conventional restraints on man's bestiality wholly arbitrary? Rhetorically, the novel endorses both Christ and coprophilia. To every question, the action of *Gravity's Rainbow* offers two plausible answers, each a contradiction of the other.

The structure of the novel, although enormously elaborate, may be reduced to two simple opposite movements: the assembly of the Rocket, and the disassembly of Tyrone Slothrop. The more he (and we) learn about the Rocket, the less of Slothrop remains as a character, until there are left only a "few who can still see Slothrop as any sort of integral creature any more" (p. 740). The Rocket, by contrast, first appears in the novel in dispersed fragments, and is only gradually reassembled:

> What it is is a graphite cylinder, about six inches long and two in diameter, all but a few flakes of its Army-green paint charred away. Only piece that survived the burst.   (p. 20)

Slothrop, until his own dispersal, collects the fragments of rocket information that ultimately coalesce in the twin rocket sagas of Blicero's Rocket No. 00000 and its repetition, Enzian's No. 00001. The Schwarz-kommando's reconstruction of Rocket No. 00001 from scattered debris coincides with the reader's reconstruction of Rocket No. 00000 from scattered details. Just as the reader puts the whole story together, its hero (paradoxically) falls apart.

Pynchon juxtaposes antitheses in the small details of characterization as well as in the broad outlines of plot. The debates between Roger Mexico and Ned Pointsman, two researchers into Slothrop's "case," typify the particular kind of paradox at work throughout *Gravity's Rainbow*:

> If ever the Antipointsman existed, Roger Mexico is the man. [. . .] In the domain of zero to one, not-something to something, Pointsman can only possess the zero and the one. He cannot, like Mexico, survive anyplace in between. Like his master I.P. Pavlov before him, he imagines the cortex of the brain as a mosaic of tiny on/off elements. [. . .] Each point is allowed only the two states: waking or sleep. One or zero. [. . .] But to Mexico belongs the domain *between* zero and one—the middle Pointsman has excluded from his persuasion—the probabilities.   (p. 55)

Pointsman seeks the mechanical cause for every effect: "No exceptions. When we find it, we'll have shown again the stone determinacy of everything, of every soul" (p. 86). Mexico argues for the contrary perspective:

> "[. . .] There's a feeling about that cause-and-effect may have been taken as far as it will go. That for science to carry on at all, it must look for a less narrow, a less . . . sterile set of assumptions. The next great breakthrough may come when we have the courage to junk cause-and-effect entirely and strike off at some other angle."   (p. 89)

The novel simultaneously endorses and repudiates both Pointsman's and Mexico's claims. Pointsman is a villain, willing to kill Slothrop for the sake of an experiment. Mexico, in contrast, is a wholly sympathetic character, deeply and unselfishly in love, and determined to resist war's cruelty: "They are in love. Fuck the war" (p. 42). While the reader is thus encouraged rhetorically to support Mexico's antirational campaign, the actual events of the novel lend credence to Pointsman's perspective. Slothrop was indeed conditioned to respond sexually to Imipolex G; there is in fact an empirical explanation of his liaison with the V-2. A single event, by means of peculiarly appropriate characterization, is thus made to assert both causal and casual cosmologies, producing the power of paradox.

Pynchon polarizes the characters of *Gravity's Rainbow* into antithetical pairs. Black Enzian, for example, corresponds to white Gottfried: for good or evil, the Rocket launches them both. Bianca Erdmann and Ilse Pokler, fathered respectively by a movie actor and a movie spectator, are "the same child" born on either side of the screen (p. 577). Suspended like an arch between the paradoxes, Slothrop serves both the Schwarzkommando and "the White Visitation," balanced between "Them" and "the Counterforce." "Everything in the Creation," as Slothrop's Puritan ancestor William put it, "has its equal and opposite counterpart" (p. 555). Containing "opposites together" (p. 563), the Rocket itself is dual in nature, "a good Rocket to take us to the stars, an evil Rocket for the World's suicide, the two perpetually in struggle" (p. 727).

The title of *Gravity's Rainbow* itself proclaims the novel's paradox, in that gravity and rainbows are antithetic phenomena. Gravity pulls mass, while the rainbow has no mass. The rainbow is visible but intangible, gravity tangible but invisible. Only in the title of Pynchon's novel does the rainbow "belong" to gravity; for, like its title, the whole novel yokes contraries, embraces contradictions, propounds paradox.

The genre of paradox, as *Gravity's Rainbow* exemplifies it, bears close links and striking resemblances to the genre of "Menippean satire," as defined and discussed by the Russian formalist critic Mikhail Bakhtin in his study *Problems of Dostoevsky's Poetics* (first published in 1929). For example:

> The menippea is characterized by extraordinary freedom of philosophical invention within the plot [. . . and by] the organic combination within it of free fantasy, symbolism, and—on occasion—the mystical-religious element, with extreme and (from our point of view) crude *underworld naturalism (truschebyi naturalizm)*. Truth's early adventures take place on highroads, in brothels, dens of thieves, taverns, market places, prisons, and at secret cults' erotic orgies, etc. The idea here has no fear of the underworld or of the filth of life.[1]

We recall, among other instances in *Gravity's Rainbow*, *Der Kinderofen*, where Blicero corrupts and despoils Katje and Gottfried. To resume Bakhtin's characterization of the genre:

> Boldness of invention and fantasy combines in the menippea with extraordinary philosophical universalism and extreme ideologism (*mirosozercatel' nost'*). The menippea is a genre of "ultimate questions."

> In the menippea syncresis (i.e. juxtaposition) of precisely such stripped-bare "ultimate positions in the world" is typical. [. . .] In all of them the *pro et contra* of the ultimate questions are laid bare.   (*Dostoevsky's Poetics*, pp. 94–95)

Pynchon's unflinching dramatizations, in *Gravity's Rainbow*, of the implications and ramifications of physical annihilation and of spiritual salvation clearly lie within the purview of such a genre at Bakhtin outlines. Furthermore:

> Characteristic of the menippea are scandalous scenes and scenes of eccentric behavior. [. . .] The "incongruous word"—incongruous either because of its cynical frankness, because it profanely exposes something which is holy, or because it crudely violates etiquette—is also quite characteristic of the menippea.   (*Dostoevsky's Poetics*, pp. 96–97)

Roger Mexico's and Seaman Bodine's joint "gross-out" of the dinner party of oil executives comes to mind as supportive evidence on this

1. Mikhail Bakhtin, *Problems of Dostoevsky's Poetics*, trans. R. William Rotsel (Ann Arbor: Ardis, 1973), pp. 93–94.

point. Bakhtin's reference to the "many sharp contrasts and oxymoronic combinations" aptly applies to the yoked contraries we have seen at work throughout the novel and in the title itself of *Gravity's Rainbow.*

> The menippea characteristically makes wide use of other genres: novellas, letters, oratory, symposia, etc.; the mixture of prose and verse diction is also characteristic. [. . .] The verse parts are almost always to a certain degree parodical.   (*Dostoevsky's Poetics,* p. 97)

Pynchon's distinctive use of devices and conventions from comic strips, films, spy thrillers, and especially his larding of the text with corny song lyrics are all included by this attribute of the genre. Finally, "the menippea's last characteristic—its topicality and publicistic quality," (*Dostoevsky's Poetics,* p. 97) may be seen in the performance given in *Gravity's Rainbow* by Mickey Rooney, Richard Nixon, and the Shell Oil Company.

Bakhtin concluded, proleptically, that "in modern literature the menippea has been the predominant conduit for the most pronounced and vivid forms of carnivalization" (p. 113). In parallel fashion, it may be concluded that Menippean satire has served as a major tributary nourishing the loose structure and wildly fantastic, ethically paradoxical texture of *Gravity's Rainbow* as well. For, to the extent that Pynchon's novel is "dialogical"—that is, its "polyphonic" implied author refrains from taking sides in the crucial debates enacted in his pages—*Gravity's Rainbow* may correctly be termed a Menippean satire. But in Bakhtin's analysis, however, the action of a Menippean satire focuses upon "the man of an idea—the wise man" (p. 94); and Tyrone Slothrop, the harried schlemihl who is mysteriously sublimated right out of the novel's crucible, fails utterly to live up to that description. While taking note of the affinities between *Gravity's Rainbow* and the genre of Menippean satire, then, we can better account for the particularities of Pynchon's novel by regarding its means and its end as generically paradoxical.

The self-consciousness of *Gravity's Rainbow* strengthens its paradoxical power. The novel both seems and seems not to be about the reader's "real" world, leaving the reader suspended between two attitudes towards the text itself: (1) the text is an accurate transcription of reality; and (2) the text is a piece of self-conscious artifice subject to no rules but its own. Like *Ulysses, Gravity's Rainbow* is both minutely mimetic and egregiously ludic; it amalgamates literary realism with surreal fantasy.

On the one hand, the world Pynchon depicts is obviously our own.

Our World War Two, with its bombs and its death camps. Our Jack Kennedy, Mickey Rooney, Malcolm X. But on the other, Pynchon's world is obviously made up. The narrator speaks directly to the reader:

> You will want cause and effect. All right. Thanatz was washed overboard in the same storm that . . .   (p. 663)

Pynchon's omniscient narrator (who does indeed seem to know everything) shows himself making up his story as he goes along. The names he gives people and places are often ludicrously fake: the Russian thief Nocolai Ripov, the German spa Bad Karma. The narrator frequently steps back a frame to suggest that his own narrative voice is but one more deceptive strategy among many:

> (the voice speaking here grows more ironic, closer to tears which are not all theatre as the list goes on . . .)   (p. 302)

The novel characteristically pretends to be a movie: "If there is music for this it's windy strings and reed sections [. . .]" (p. 398). And the narrator takes pleasure in directly challenging the reader:

> [. . .] They are not, after all, to be lovers in parachutes of sunlit voile, lapsing gently, hand in hand, down to anything meadowed or calm. Surprised? (p. 222)

In the very paragraphs from which these quotes are taken, however, the narrator proceeds to create illusions of reality that are masterful in their verisimilitude. This same paradoxical process is at work in the novel's opening pages, where, after being "taken in" by wonderfully evocative, detailed description, we learn to our surprise that we have been reading not of events but of a dream.

These two different ways of reading the text—as accurate transcription or as elaborate invention—provoke two antithetical responses. By dramatizing within the novel the relation between *Gravity's Rainbow* and its readers, Pynchon fortifies the central paradox of the causal/casual relation, not only among events in his book, but between his book and real life. If events within the novel are related *causally*, and if, as the references to historical figures and actual multinational corporations suggest, the world the novel depicts *is* the world the reader lives in, then the reader's appropriate response to the text is one of paranoia: "nothing less than the onset, the leading edge, of the discovery that *everything is connected,* everything in the Creation [. . .]" (p. 703). One need not be stoned or

paranoid to recognize, for example, that the giant German chemical car-
tel I.G. Farben, which gave the world aspirin and penicillin and the poi-
son for Hitler's gas chambers, was in historical fact preserved from
postwar dismantling by the multinational oil companies.[1] Shell Oil did
indeed "fight" for both sides during the war. "They," the oil cartels, that
is, *have* persisted through outward political upheaval and mass death.
Henry Kissinger did work for the family that founded Standard Oil.
"They" sponsor much of our public arts and televised entertainment, and
own the companies that publish many of our books. It's no joke.

If, however, events in the novel are related merely *casually*, and if,
as the self-conscious narration, the ludicrously artificial names, and the
preposterous plot suggest, the text itself is no more than canard or
self-indulgence, then the reader's appropriate response is that of "anti-
paranoia, where nothing is connected to anything" (p. 434). To make
sense of the novel we are expected to believe not only that a human being
named Tyrone Slothrop gets an erection for every German rocket fired at
London, but also that he finds a woman to share it with as frequently
and in as many places as the rockets fall. The novel's premises are absurd.
It's all a big joke. Joke or no joke, the novel offers us the choice: "Is the
baby smiling, or is it just gas? Which do you want it to be?" (p. 131).

All three of Pynchon's novels are fictions of "suspended meaning," in
Frank Kermode's phrase, as in each case the text withholds its logical
conclusions from character and reader alike.[2] In *The Crying of Lot 49,* the
heroine never learns the secret of the Trystero conspiracy, since the novel
ends just as Oedipa is *about* to hear Lot 49 "cried."[3] The mysterious
woman V., whom Stencil pursues in Pynchon's first novel, is gradually
replaced by prosthetic devices until finally she stops ticking and "comes
apart."[4] As V. falls apart before Stencil can learn her secret, so Slothrop
falls apart without finding his Rocket. In *V.,* the *object* of the search falls
apart; in *Gravity's Rainbow,* the *subject* disintegrates. (The two novels
thus juxtapose each other in more ways than the noted recurrence of
characters; the phallic V-2 Rocket responds to vaginal V.) And just as
disintegrated Slothrop never learns his Rocket's secret, so the reader of

1. See, for example, Joseph Borkin, *The Crime and Punishment of I. G. Farben* (New
York: The Free Press, 1978).

2. Kermode discusses the "radical equivocations" of *The Crying of Lot 49* in "Decoding
the Trystero," in *Approaches to Poetics,* ed. Seymour Chatman (New York: Columbia University Press, 1973), pp. 68–74, reprinted in *Pynchon Essays,* ed. Mendelson, pp. 162–66.

3. Thomas Pynchon, *The Crying of Lot 49* (Philadelphia: J. B. Lippincott, 1966; Bantam
pbk. ed., 1967), p. 138. References are to the latter edition.

4. Thomas Pynchon, *V.* (Philadelphia: J. B. Lippincott, 1963), p. 342.

Gravity's Rainbow never learns the secret of his "own" final rocket, the one about to explode over "our" heads on the novel's last page:

> And it is just here, just at this dark and silent frame, that the pointed tip of the Rocket, falling nearly a mile per second, absolutely and forever without sound, reaches its last unmeasurable gap above the roof of this old theatre, the last delta-t.   (p. 760)

Will the Rocket bring the flash of inspiration, or the annihilation of death? Pynchon's conclusions are suspended: there is no way to tell.

The prose style of *Gravity's Rainbow* is not single style but an impressive compendium of many styles which contribute considerable power to the paradox within the novel.

> Later, toward dusk, several enormous water bugs, a very dark reddish brown, emerge like elves from the wainscoting, and go lumbering toward the larder—pregnant mother bugs too, with baby translucent outrider bugs flowing along like a convoy escort. At night, in the very late silences between bombers, ack-ack fire and falling rockets, they can be heard, loud as mice, munching through Gwenhidwy's paper sacks, leaving streaks and footprints of shit the color of themselves behind. They don't seem to go in much for soft things, fruits, vegetables, and such, it's more the solid lentils and beans they're into, stuff they can gnaw at, paper and plaster barriers, hard interfaces to be pierced, for they are agents of unification, you see. Christmas bugs. They were deep in the straw of the manger at Bethlehem, they stumbled, climbed, fell glistening red among a golden lattice of straw that must have seemed to extend miles up and downward—an edible tenement-world, now and then gnawed through to disrupt some mysterious sheaf of vectors that would send neighbor bugs tumbling ass-over-antennas down past you as you held on with all legs in that constant tremble of golden stalks. A tranquil world: the temperature and humidity staying nearly steady, the day's cycle damped to only a soft easy sway of light, gold to antique-gold to shadows, and back again. The crying of the infant reached you, perhaps, as bursts of energy from the invisible distance, nearly unsensed, often ignored. Your savior, you see. . . .   (pp. 173–74)

The suppleness of this prose is admirable. It creates paradox by embracing within individual sentences a diction that is base, obscene, and suggestive of disorder and decay, and a diction that is lofty, spiritual, and evocative of transcendent harmonies. In the paragraph just cited, the style serves to amplify the paradoxical quality of the thought: impressions both of trivial decay and of holy redemption are rendered with great vividness. Does the mentino of insect excrement heighten the passage's religious values or, on the contrary, is the reference to "your savior" ironic? Again, the reader is suspended between antitheses of great seriousness. The inobtrusive shifts in tense and the recurrent mention of "you" succeed in bringing the reader vividly into the presence of both holiness and filth. Like Nabokov, Pynchon is a practitioner of phrasal tmesis, and a twister of old clichés into new meanings. His "hyperdense metaphors," as Joseph Slade puts it,[1] and the extraordinarily energetic packing of ideas into his sentences make *Gravity's Rainbow* into a virtuoso performance that is beyond the endurance of many readers. While there remains much to be said about Pynchon's style, as about much else in the novel, its significance to this discussion is clear. Pynchon's paradoxically self-conscious style reminds the reader that we are reading a fiction even as we are being taken in by it. As Joseph Slade describes it, "Having begun a sentence of great fragility, Pynchon will cheerfully clamber out upon it to hammer in the last word, and allow the reader to see him do it."[2]

Unlike narrative tragedies or comedies, the genre of paradox requires not a specific sequence of events, but rather the steady elaboration and reiteration of the paradoxical effect. *Gravity's Rainbow* is therefore very loose in form and has, perhaps unfortunately, no necessary beginning, middle, or end. There is always room for more discussions of ideas, scientific principles, historical facts, philosophic controversies, ancient myths, surreal dreams, and drug-induced fantasies that have apparently little or nothing to do with the novel's central action, but which all contain the means to sustain or intensify the paradoxical effect. In almost any nonparadoxical work, for example, the seemingly whimsical digression on Katje's ancestor Frans Van der Groov, exterminator of dodoes in the seventeenth century (pp. 108–111), would be considered an intrusive violation of the work's esthetic unity. The unity of *Gravity's Rainbow*, however, derives from the concatenation, in no necessary order other than that of intelligibility and interest, of precisely such events and discussions as these; for the story of Frans Van der Groov is narrated so as to underscore a paradoxical twinning of destruction and devotion:

> To some, it made sense. They saw the stumbling birds ill-made to the point of Satanic intervention, so ugly as to embody argument against a Godly creation. Was Mauritius some first poison trickle through the sheltering dikes of the Earth? Christians must stem it here, or perish in a second Flood, loosed

1. Joseph W. Slade, *Thomas Pynchon* (New York: Warner Paperback Library, 1974), p. 17. Slade's was the first book-length study of Pynchon's work.
2. Slade, *Thomas Pynchon*, p. 247.

this time not by God but by the Enemy. The act of ramming home the charges into their musketry became for these men a devotional act, one whose symbolism they understood.

But if they were chosen to come to Mauritius, why had they also been chosen to fail, and leave? Is that a choosing, or is it a passing-over? Are they Elect, or are they Preterite, and doomed as dodoes?   (p. 110)

Discussions of all scientific paradoxes such as the Heisenberg uncertainty principle *belong* in *Gravity's Rainbow*, although their effectiveness varies with their relevance to what is happening in the plot. The novel's power is intensified, for example, by repeated references to science's inability to reconcile Euclidean and non-Euclidean geometry, classical and Einsteinian physics, and wave and particle theories of light:

"We seem up against a dilemma built into Nature, much like the Heisenberg situation. There is nearly complete parallelism between analgesia and addiction. The more pain it takes away, the more we desire it. It appears we can't have one property without the other, any more than a particle physicist can specify position without suffering an uncertainty as to the particle's velocity—"   (p. 348)

The narrative techniques of *Gravity's Rainbow*, its structure, characterization, style, and themes are thus all to a certain extent metaphors for the central causal/casual, order-or-chaos paradox. Pynchon has elsewhere been called "an author in search of a metaphor, a fictional scheme to ask and answer the question of what prevails in the physical and in the spiritual universe."[1] But I would add that the pursuit of metaphor is itself paradoxical, as Oedipa Maas learns in *The Crying of Lot 49*:

The act of metaphor then was a thrust at truth and a lie, depending on where you were: inside, safe, or outside, lost. Oedipa did not know where she was.   (*The Crying of Lot 49*, p. 95)

Metaphor, as Pynchon reminds us, is a potentially self-conscious trope: it both asserts an identity and denies it. A is like B but it is really A. Like each of the metaphors of which it is composed, Pynchon's entire novel claims to represent the world as it is, and denies that such representation is possible. *Gravity's Rainbow* is itself both "a thrust at truth and a lie."

Pynchon's novels are thus metaphors for our own reading experience of them. As Edward Mendelson has noted, "To read the encyclopedic *Gravity's Rainbow* is, necessarily, to read *among* the various probable in-

1. Alan J. Friedman and Manfred Puetz, "Science as Metaphor: Thomas Pynchon and *Gravity's Rainbow*," *Contemporary Literature*, 15:3 (Summer 1974), 345.

terpretations of the book."[1] In order to find out what happens, that is, we must re-enact Slothrop's effort to read the "holy Text" of the Rocket (p. 520). Hero and reader are launched on the same quest to distinguish signal from noise, to find a message in the mess. As Frank Kermode observed of the heroine of *The Crying of Lot 49*, "What Oedipa is doing is very like reading a book."[2]

Paranoia is Pynchon's most comprehensive metaphor for both the act of reading and the act of writing, for in this "Puritan reflex of seeking other orders behind the visible" (p. 188), the paradoxical relations between the self and the world are most clearly juxtaposed.[3] Seen from the outside, paranoia is a form of solipsism, in which the victim imagines existence to be an orderly pattern focused upon himself. This is the threat to her sanity that confronts Oedipa Maas in *The Crying of Lot 49*: "*Shall I project a world?*" (p. 59). It is also the solipsistic madness of Slothrop "finding in every bone and cabbage leaf paraphrases of himself" (*Gravity's Rainbow*, p. 625).[4]

Seen from the inside, however, paranoia is a form of artistic or exegetical creativity. Every artist is paranoid to the extent that he or she imposes pattern on his experience. And every reader is paranoid to the extent that he or she extracts a "meaning" from a text which, like *Gravity's Rainbow*, both invites and forbids interpretation. As William James observed on behalf of pragmatism, "The actual universe is a thing wide open, but rationalism makes systems, and systems must be closed."[5] The "motive to metaphor," as Northrop Frye calls the esthetic impulse,[6] is thus a paranoid reflex. *Gravity's Rainbow* dramatizes both our need for fictions and the invalidity of our fictions. "The knife cuts through the apple like a knife cutting an apple" (p. 758): the novel is a metaphor for the limitations of metaphor.

1. Edward Mendelson, "Gravity's Encyclopedia," in *Mindful Pleasures: Essays on Thomas Pynchon*, ed. George Levine and David Leverenz (Boston: Little, Brown, 1976), p. 188.

2. Kermode, "Decoding the Trystero," p. 163.

3. Joseph Slade has commented upon "the similarity between paranoia and art and understanding," in *Thomas Pynchon*, p. 177.

4. Frank McConnell has noted that, "Like many contemporary novelists, Pynchon performs an elaborate, graceful arabesque around the abyss of self-consciousness and inauthenticity, a trapeze act whose continually averted disaster is the fall into solipsism, into a terminal inauthenticity." Frank D. McConnell, *Four Postwar American Novelists: Bellow, Mailer, Barth, and Pynchon* (Chicago: University of Chicago Press, 1977), p. 177.

5. William James, *Pragmatism: A New Name for Some Old Ways of Thinking* (New York: Longmans, Green, 1907; Pocket Books ed., 1963), p. 27.

6. Northrop Frye, *The Educated Imagination* (Bloomington: Indiana University Press, 1964).

Paranoids also see plots wherever they look, just as storytellers do. Even the universe may be made to yield a story, and its title, according to Pynchon, is Entropy. Entropy refers to the inescapable loss of energy in every transaction; it is an irreversible law of nature codified in the Second Law of Thermodynamics which, theoretically extrapolated, predicts an eventual heat-death for the universe. As Pynchon described it in an early story called, simply, "Entropy," "the entropy of an isolated system always continually increased [. . .] from differentiation to sameness, from ordered individuality to a kind of chaos."[1] Entropy most clearly describes the behavior of heated gases but may also be applied, metaphorically, to the breakdown of biological and political organisms, to the "Energy Crisis," and to the theory of information (as the parlor game of "telephone" neatly illustrates). Because of its irreversibility, entropy is intimately related to time; as Hans Meyerhoff has noted, "Time may be said to move in the direction of an increase in entropy."[2]

In its cosmic extension, entropy implies that the universe, for all its apparent chaos, in fact conforms to a "plot" of steady decline. "Pynchon's entropic vision," as Scott Sanders has noted, "is paranoia grown cosmic."[3] So it is natural for Pynchon to choose entropy as a metaphor for the plots that may or may not surround us. As a phenomenon, entropy is pervasive: its use as a metaphor implicates our world even further into that of Pynchon's fiction. And as a "plot," entropy is persuasive; it implies that every other system is optimistic and false. "In plain words," as Henry Adams puts it, "Chaos was the law of nature; Order was the dream of man."[4] Entropy is thus so central a theme to the paradoxical, self-conscious *Gravity's Rainbow* because it is a system that impugns all systems.

Pynchon's novel *enacts* entropy in the eventual falling apart of its hero, Slothrop's decline "from ordered individuality to a kind of chaos." The novel itself knows and acknowledges, in a sense, that it must come to an end, even if that end comes, as it does, in midsentence: "Now every-

1. Thomas Pynchon, "Entropy," *Kenyon Review,* 22:2 (Spring 1960), 282, 283–84; reprinted in his *Slow Learner: Early Stories* (Boston: Little, Brown, 1984), 87, 88.

2. Hans Meyerhoff, *Time in Literature* (Berkeley: University of California Press, 1955), pp. 64–65 cited by Alvin Greenberg, "The Novel of Disintegration: Paradoxical Impossibility in Contemporary Fiction," *Wisconsin's Studies in Contemporary Literature,* 7:1 (Winter-Spring 1966), 104.

3. Scott Sanders, "Pynchon's Paranoid History," in *Mindful Pleasures,* ed. Levine and Leverenz, p. 148.

4. *The Education of Henry Adams* (Boston: Massachusetts Historical Society, 1918; Houghton Mifflin pbk. ed., 1961), p. 451.

body—" (p. 760). The incomplete last line shows the novel resisting its own termination, engaging in yet another struggle of opposites between entropy and energy. Entropy seems to have won the day in finally bringing the novel to its end, but the victory is only apparent. For the novel is *not,* as the success of entropy requires, a closed system, but rather it continually absorbs new quantities of energy from both writer and reader, as it is written and each time it is read. The novel demands rereading, with an insistence that denies it is really used up when one has read the last page. In the last line, a rocket is about to explode over "our" heads. The novel's first line describes the sound of a rocket rushing in, *after* the supersonic missile has already exploded: "A screaming comes across the sky" (p. 3). So the novel's conclusion leads us back to its beginning: its ends are joined. The annular structure of *Gravity's Rainbow* refutes the entropic curtailment of its own narrative energy.

Pynchon's metaphors, like those of the Symbolist poets, have no specific referents. They thus invite readings of almost infinite subtlety, an irresistible temptation to some critics. Slothrop's disintegration, for example, can be read as a metaphor for any number of things. I have concentrated on his falling apart as a metaphor for entropy and as a source of paradoxical power. In Joseph Slade's reading, it is a metaphor for the helplessness of innocence before the immensity of power: "He literally fragments, cut to pieces by energy grids, the victim of his innocence, which is no defense against the complexities of the systems that reform after the war."[1] William Plater cleverly reads Slothrop's disintegration as a metaphor for the Heisenberg uncertainty principle: "Slothrop even begins to disperse and spread throughout the Zone as his psychoanalytical observers learn more about the sexual energy he appears to derive from the Rocket."[2] And according to Edward Mendelson, "Slothrop's disintegration [. . .] summarizes the historical fate of literary modernism."[3]

This is not to say, however, that Pynchon's texts mean whatever one wants them to, and that there is no such thing as a wrong reading. David Richter, for example, in an otherwise interesting study, extracts a "thesis" from *V.,* and then blithely admits that "I am unable to understand" why

---

1. Slade, *Thomas Pynchon,* p. 202.

2. Plater continues: "There is no doubt that Pynchon consciously uses the Heisenberg uncertainty principle as a metaphor in all his major works; whether he does so with an accuracy that would please a physicist is another matter." William M. Plater, *The Grim Phoenix: Reconstructing Thomas Pynchon* (Bloomington: Indiana University Press, 1978), p. 102.

3. Mendelson, "Gravity's Encyclopedia," p. 166.

the novel's last two chapters are so ambiguous.[1] Ignoring the possibility that *V.,* like *Gravity's Rainbow,* may be generically paradoxical, Richter wedges the novel into the category of "apologue," and then blames the poor fit on *Pynchon's* "failure of completeness." This we may call an erroneous reading.

By opposing each assertion to its own negation, *Gravity's Rainbow* resists the critic's effort to extract a single paraphrasable meaning. As Edward Mendelson has written of Pynchon's novel, "self-conscious narrative can admit serious meanings only through indirection."[2] Good is good and evil is evil, this much is always clear, but the novel never gives either side the upper hand: "Just as there are, in the World, machineries committed to injustice as an enterprise, so too there seem to be provisions active for balancing things out once in a while" (p. 580). The concentration camp Dora is here, and so is a Christmas Eve service in Kent: both are allowed to speak for themselves. The characters live, in a sense, beyond moral distinctions, for even the "good guys" do evil. Before joining "the Counterforce," for example, Katje turns three Jewish families over to the Gestapo in return for a Nazi promotion:

> Don't forget the real business of the War is buying and selling. [...] So, Jews are negotiable. Every bit as negotiable as cigarettes, cunt, or Hershey bars.   (p. 105)

Pynchon's horror is in the language, where it belongs.

Thus, despite its deliberate posturing as allegory, Pynchon's fiction is *not* an ethical statement in disguise. The most unambiguous affirmation in his work, in fact, is the advice of a laid-back musician in *V.* to "Keep cool, but care" (p. 366); and even this, as David Richter notes, is "mighty slim pickings as affirmations of life go."[3] Keenly aware, as we have seen, of its own ambiguous stance as a fiction, *Gravity's Rainbow* allows itself no such direct moralization. What it offers instead is a sense of *possibility:* that perhaps there is a choice to be made, but perhaps not; that perhaps our lives are our own, but perhaps not; that perhaps fiction may divulge the truth about the human condition, but perhaps not.

To some readers, this sense of certainties suspended is unbearable. Frederick J. Hoffman, for example, complains that one of the "principal faults" of Pynchon's fiction is that "it makes fun of the reasons why it

1. Richter, "Failure of Completeness," p. 129.
2. Mendelson, "Gravity's Encyclopedia," p. 181.
3. Richter, "Failure of Completeness," p. 117.

makes fun of everything else."[1] To others, however, including myself, Pynchon's balance of vividly evoked sympathy, humor and passion with an acute recognition of the fiction's own contingency is as enchanting as it is disturbing. If there are some in whom *le goût du paradoxe* is lacking, there are others for whom, as Kierkegaard put it, "Either/Or is the key of heaven."[2] This is not to reduce the evaluation of *Gravity's Rainbow* to a matter of taste, but rather to suggest why, as we noted at the outset, many people cannot read it.

To be certain about any clear message in *Gravity's Rainbow* is thus in some sense to distort the text. And yet, as E.D. Hirsch reminds us, "knowledge of ambiguity is not necessarily ambiguous knowledge."[3] We may reasonably hope to understand, for example, what general rules Pynchon followed in composing *Gravity's Rainbow*. The genre of paradox seems to me a more useful category for interpreting the novel than "encyclopedic narrative," since the latter label implies only that Pynchon threw everything in.[4] The requirements of paradox account for more. The novel is immensely funny, as paradoxes often are, and as no encyclopedia ever is. Puns, as we have noted, are paradoxical, and entire episodes of *Gravity's Rainbow* are contrived for the sake of one.[5] Nor is any encyclopedia self-conscious; but without its self-consciousness *Gravity's Rainbow* would be less paradoxical, and not itself. We have also been able to learn from paradox why the novel is preoccupied with paranoia, with entropy, and with its own relation to the reader's life. Not everything is lost to equivocation, then, for by displaying its own art, *Gravity's Rainbow* obliges us to affirm its value.

1. Cited in *Contemporary Authors* (Detroit: Gale Research Co., 1968), Vol. 17–20, p. 594.

2. Søren Kierkegaard, in the *Instant*, 14, 106, cited by Walter Lowrie, "Introduction" to his translation of *Either/Or* (Princeton: Princeton University Press, 1971), II, xv.

3. E.D. Hirsch, Jr., *Validity in Interpretation* (New Haven: Yale University Press, 1967), p. ix.

4. The term is the basis for Edward Mendelson's discussion in "Gravity's Encyclopedia." Cf. the Editor of *PMLA*: "surely it appears likely that, after Pynchon, nothing need ever be excluded from the novelist's repertoire." William D. Schaefer, "Editor's Column," *PMLA*, 92:5 (Oct. 1977), 867.

5. My favorites include Bloody Chiclitz's elaborate story culminating in, "For De Mille, young fur-henchmen can't be rowing!" (p. 599), and the numerous changes that Slothrop rings on the text, "You never did the Kenosha Kid" (pp. 60–61, 71). I am indebted for the former example to Edward Mendelson, "Gravity's Encyclopedia," p. 194.

Chapter VIII

A Trestle of *LETTERS*[1]

JOHN BARTH'S reputation seems to weigh less heavily in the scale of literary history than do those of Joyce, Nabokov, Gaddis, and Pynchon. Yet his fictions have been more explicit about their place in that history; his self-consciousness, that is, has been more self-conscious than theirs. And Barth is the most explicit of the five in his endeavors to explain, within fiction, where self-conscious fiction is headed. The value of his major novel, and not only as an exemplar, is considerable.

The issue of morality was raised when his novel, *LETTERS,* was first published in 1979. At a symposium of the Modern Language Association at the end of that year,[2] Benjamin DeMott launched a vigorous attack on what he portrayed as the increasing toleration of incest in our society. DeMott's invective was implicitly directed at *LETTERS,* since John Barth was present as one of the panel's featured speakers. I will briefly consider the question raised by DeMott's polemic: *is* the generous presence of seemingly unpunished incest in *LETTERS* immoral?

First of all, to correct that "seemingly": DeMott and other reviewers, misled by the novel's crafty concealment of its own climax, are mistaken in believing that the incest goes unpunished. In fact, the explosive finale in which the multiple plot-lines of *LETTERS* culminate is not even dramatized in the novel, but is only *about* to take place at the end of the novel's latest (but not its last) letter. The climax may thus be said to be hidden between two of the novel's eighty-eight epistles. Here is what actually happens.

Marshyhope State University College is about to dedicate "the Morgan Memorial Tower, variously and popularly known as the Schott Tower, the Shit Tower, and the Tower of Truth."[3] But a young student

---

1. This chapter appeared in slightly altered form in *fiction international,* 12 (1980), 259–68.

2. "The Self in Writing: A Forum arranged by Norman N. Holland and Murray M. Schwartz, Center for Psychological Study of the Arts, State University of New York, Buffalo, and sponsored by the Division on Literary Criticism and Prose Fiction," at the 94th Annual Convention of the Modern Language Association of America, San Francisco, California, 28 December 1979.

3. John Barth, *LETTERS* (New York: G.P. Putnam's Sons, 1979), p. 734.

revolutionary (the year is 1969) has planted dynamite charges around the tower's base, and is resolved to blow it up at the precise instant of sunrise. In the tower (as can only be gleaned from small details scattered across several letters) lurk three characters, each there for reasons unknown to the others. Jerome Bray, an evil maniac who, during the course of the novel, has drugged and raped five women and murdered, among others, a filmmaker and a poet, has mounted the doomed tower, "his business finished," in order to "ascend" to his mythical grandmother. Ambrose Mensch, apparently unaware of the dynamite, has pursued Bray into the tower so as to bring him to justice for the rape of Ambrose's angelic, mad, fourteen-year-old niece. Finally, sixty-nine-year-old Todd Andrews has barricaded himself in the belfry, fully cognizant of the terrorist's plans, determined to rectify the suicide attempt he botched in Barth's earlier novel *The Floating Opera*. This time, Andrews has been driven to despair and self-disgust by his own sexual abuse of his probable daughter Jeannine and by his concomitant cruelty to his ex-secretary and lover Polly Lake.

The "codicil to the last will and testament of Todd Andrews," which Andrews drafts in the belfry and sets his initials to an instant before sunrise at 6:54 on 26 September 1969, is the last-dated epistle in *LETTERS*, although the novel's principle of organization requires that eight other letters ostensibly written before Andrews's sign-off appear *after* it in the book. Ambrose, in a letter to "the Author," has warned us that

> the narrative, like an icebreaker, like spawning salmon, incoming tide, or wandering hero, springs forward, falls back, gathers strength, springs farther forward, falls less far back, and at length arrives—but does not remain at—its high-water mark. . . .   (p. 767)

Thus, although the novel, like Ambrose's own fiction, recedes from its climax without actually dramatizing it, the explosion about to topple the Shit Tower/Tower of Truth and kill at least three characters does indeed mark, as "the Author" belatedly announces thirty-four pages after the fact, "the end" (p. 772). (A similarly undramatized climax, we should recall, concludes Pynchon's *Gravity's Rainbow*, where a falling rocket-bomb is *about* to explode over our heads in the novel's final line, but does not do so within the book's pages.) Along with a self-conscious writer and a homicidal rapist, whose depredations seem not to offend Barth's "moral" critic, the father whose incest does incense DeMott is thus just as certainly if surreptitiously punished for his sins.

So much for answering the limited accusation that Barth's novel is immoral because it contains generous scenes of unpunished incest: it does not. But surely there is a deeper issue here, and one more deeply troubling: the notion that works of art are to be condemned as immoral if they contain representations of vice unpunished or virtue unrewarded, or fail to hold up a model of moral behavior worthy of emulation. "Any [. . .] more or less artistic medium," John Gardner asserted in his book *On Moral Fiction* (1978),

> is good (as opposed to pernicious or vacuous) only when it has a clear positive moral effect, presenting valid models for imitation, eternal verities worth keeping in mind, and a benevolent vision of the possible [. . .].

> Moral art in its highest form holds up models of virtue [. . .].[1]

Now clearly it is natural and right for us to consider our reading of fiction as an integral, rather than an isolated, part of our lives, and it is neither philistine nor naive of us, when reading the best literature, to hope to learn something of "how to be." But just as clearly, what is objectionable in Gardner's proscriptive and prosaic call for "valid models for imitation" is that it ignores, overlooks, or deprecates those of fiction's inestimable resources—irony, obliquity, and above all metaphor—that "by indirections find directions out."

Confronted by Barth's novel, DeMott, as if he were intercepting letters passed between his own mother Gertrude and his uncle Claudius, condemns as wicked the posting of such incestuous sheets. This is the same sort of excessively literal mentality that leads Barth's character, Jerome Bray, in his efforts to "get the bugs out" of an experimental computer, to program the machine to delete all references to insects of any sort. Barth is no more recommending, in *LETTERS,* that fathers sleep with their daughters, than Nabokov, in *Lolita,* endorses the seduction of twelve-year-olds, or in *Ada* advocates that brothers and sisters should become lovers like Van and Ada. "Valid models for imitation" have nothing to do with it, for fiction is not, despite Gardner's efforts to portray it as such, a form of blunt weapon. The image of a father committing incest with his grown child, for example, is appropriate to *LETTERS* in specifically metaphorical, thematic terms, because the novel is not only centrally concerned with, but is itself the result of, an author's endeavor to beget new fictional life upon his imagination's previous offspring.

1. John Gardner, *On Moral Fiction* (New York: Basic Books, 1978), pp. 18, 82.

For, in order to cast his seventh work of fiction, Barth has gone back to his previous efforts and drawn one character from each book, and has thereby endeavored to make of *LETTERS* not only a sequel to each of them but also a critique that extends as it interweaves all of their themes. (Barth's efforts in this direction are paralleled by those of two *new* characters, one of whom, Lady Amherst, is reading her way through all of Barth's previous books as this one progresses, while another, Reg Prinz, is busy making a movie based upon Barth's prior opus that claims to "anticipate" Barth's current work-in-progress, requiring *LETTERS,* in effect, to try to keep up with the film that is being made of it in its own pages.) From *The Floating Opera* (1956) comes Todd Andrews: from *The End of the Road* (1958), Jacob Horner; descendants of Ebenezer Cooke, hero of *The Sot-Weed Factor* (1960) abound in *LETTERS,* and from "Grand Tutor Harold Bray" of *Giles Goat-Boy* (1966) Jerome Bray traces his descent; Ambrose Mensch, now grown into an avant-garde writer, is taken from three of the stories in *Lost in the Funhouse* (1968); and from the three novellas called *Chimera* (1972) comes the dramatized version of "the Author" who in the new novel is credited with writing letters to the other six characters as well as to the reader.

The recurrence of characters across a number of discrete fictional texts creates a strange and paradoxical effect. On the one hand, characters seem more like real people when they cannot be contained between the covers of a single book. This is the principal effect in Balzac, where, for example, the identities of Vautrin and Lucien de Rubempré acquire an almost palpable independence from the individual novels in which they figure, by dint of their repeated appearance throughout the *Comédie humaine*. In *Ulysses,* too, when Stephen Dedalus reminds us that he is "A child Conmee saved from pandies" (p. 156), he is asserting that he is the same Stephen as that of *A Portrait of the Artist as a Young Man,* and therefore somehow less of a fictional property and more of a human being living a continuous existence.

On the other hand, however, the recycling of characters from previous fictions ineluctably reminds us that they are, after all, fictional. The apparent ease with which Barth transplants his characters from one book to another underscores the fact that these figments can be at home nowhere but *in* books—an effect paradoxically opposed to the enhancement of plausibility just described. Recurrence earns characters a bonus of "apparent reality," but at the same time it brands them as bogus. The resultant tension—peculiar to art that displays its own art—invites us to believe in a self-evident fiction.

This paradoxical twinning of narrative illusion and disillusion is nowhere more evident in *LETTERS* than in the dramatized presence of "the Author." According to the novel's subtitle, "the Author" is to be regarded as one of the "seven fictitious drolls & dreamers" whose correspondence comprises the text. "The Author" as he appears in the book is therefore not to be confused with the actual John Barth, presently living in Baltimore and occasionally to be seen (dramatizing himself in other ways) at conventions of the Modern Language Association, although the novel invites that confusion on every page. By reducing the representation of "John Barth" inside the novel to a level of fictional reality and *vraisemblance* equal to that of the other characters, the Barth who wrote *LETTERS* thereby seems to boost the implied reality of those characters to equivalence with his own. By blurring the line between Fiction and Fact, he bolsters the believability of what happens in his pages.

And yet—here is that paradox—each time "the Author" appears, supposedly (but not actually) *in propria persona,* it is infallibly brought to our attention that all the creatures in the book are "his" creation, and that the dramatized "Author" himself is a fictional creation of the actual John Barth. One of the novel's letters itself refers to "the 'Author' character in *LETTERS*" (p. 48), suggesting the image of a concentric series of masks stacked one behind another. It is not the same nor so simple a matter as the author's enhancing his characters' plausibility as real people by treating them as equals, for Barth's fictional "Author" overtly addresses them as "Characters from the Author's Earlier Fictions" (p. 190). The correspondents of *LETTERS* are thus rendered both more and less human by the same paradoxical gesture. When "the Author" writes to Ambrose, "never mind that in a sense this 'dialogue' is a monologue: that we capital-*A* Authors are ultimately, ineluctably, and forever talking to ourselves [. . .]" (p. 655), we acknowledge the statement's truth at the same time that we take its advice to put it out of our minds. Like other self-depicting fictions, *LETTERS* requires a revision of Coleridge's view, by inviting us to suspend our disbelief wittingly as well as willingly.

So that when Barth shows us Todd Andrews coupling with the grown woman whom he, Andrews, engendered in Barth's first novel, what we are to see, besides a true-to-character confirmation of both Andrews' inability to resist seduction and Jeannine's immunity to taboo, is one of a dozen or more metaphors by which *LETTERS* dramatizes the conceptual principles of its own composition. This is the sense in which the novel is most clearly "postmodern": it is both "about" the lives of its characters and the ways in which those lives intertwine with each other and with History; *and* it is about the very question of what it means to be "about" something. Like Joyce, Nabokov, Gaddis, and Pynchon, Barth uses fiction to probe and divulge fiction's own presuppositions. The stories of the characters' lives, as they are rendered in *LETTERS,* manage both to be engaging, engrossing, suspenseful, funny, and rewarding on their own, *and* to function as fully realized parables of their own problematic ontology. As befits the tradition in which he is working, Barth's goals are ambitious, and his achievement of them in *LETTERS* is extremely impressive.

Ambrose Mensch mentions to "the Author" of *LETTERS* that its "theme seems to me to want to be not 'revolution'—what do you and I know about such things?—but (per our telephone talk) *reenactment*" (p. 562). Without wishing to define the notion of "theme" too narrowly, we can agree with this reading. Germaine Pitt (Lady Amherst), although she is the "new" character, nonetheless reenacts the letter writing of her namesake and forebear Germaine de Staël; Todd Andrews draws diagrams to document what *LETTERS* dramatizes, "his life's recycling"; Jacob Horner spends the novel trying to "rewrite History"; A.B. Cook IV and VI rehearse the "action-historiography" of their forebears in vain hopes of avoiding those forebears' fates; Jerome Bray's quest is the computer-generation of *NUMBERS,* a digital rehash of that other J.B.'s *LETTERS;* Ambrose Mensch is careful to repeat each of his previous affairs within his present involvement with Germaine; while, like the filmmaker Reg Prinz, "the Author" (and *his* author) recycles Barth's previous characters and fictions. There is no immediate way of knowing which, in I.A. Richards' terminology, is vehicle, and which tenor; no way of knowing, that is, whether Barth has written a multileveled novel about reenactment because he sees reenactment as central to the lives we lead outside of books, or whether he has invented fictional images of reenactment in order to dramatize the conceptually prior strategy of his novel. In any case, the motto of Marshyhope State University College, "*Praeteritas futuras fecundant*"—the past fertilizes the future—may be taken as the motto of the novel as a whole. It accounts not only for the curious importance to the plot of preserved excrement (for "the past manures the future," too), but also for the efforts of all the characters to give direction to their futures by reenacting their pasts. The motto applies as well to the analogous attempts by fictional fathers and actual authors to enrich the future by embracing in the present what they have engendered in the past.

*   *   *

In fashioning his novel from the stuff of previous fictions, Barth might be charged with turning his back on the "real" world; with framing a fashionably hermetic response to Flaubert's familiar call for "a novel about nothing." It is *here*, rather than on the spurious issues of sexual metaphor or the lack of models of virtue, that the claims of morality upon fiction must be taken most seriously. For to deny that one's words engage the values of the world—to assert, as the title of Barth's novel seems to do, that one's book *signifies* no more than what, on the most material level it *is*, a more or less artful arrangement of letters printed on paper—this is surely to deprive fiction of the *spiritual* value which, from our greatest writers, we know to be among its most honored resources and justifications. Our readings, as a Biblical epistle urges, should be "Not of the letter, but of the spirit; for the letter killeth, but the spirit giveth life" (2 Corinthians 3:6). The morally serious question to be asked of John Barth's novel, therefore, is to what extent does its self-referential inversion prevent it from fulfilling fiction's ultimate responsibility to address the concerns of living men and women?

For a start, certainly, *LETTERS* must be recognized as prodigiously self-depictive. If the initial (alphabetic) letters of each of the novel's eighty-eight epistles are strung together, they form a coherent phrase: AN OLD-TIME EPISTOLARY NOVEL BY SEVEN FICTITIOUS DROLLS & DREAMERS EACH OF WHICH BELIEVES HIMSELF ACTUAL. The novel is thus a huge (772-page) acrostic that spells out its own self-descriptive subtitle. Furthermore, if the dates to which the novel ascribes its letters are x'ed-out on a calendar for 1969, the x'es will spell out a word: *LETTERS*. Not only, then, is the novel, *inter alia*, an acrostic of its own self-description, but it also mimics the physical shape of the word that is its title. *LETTERS* begins, in the first words of its first letter, "At the end," and ends at "the end," that is to say, back where it started; so that the form of the whole book is that of the closed ring or Ouroboros, familiar from *Finnegans Wake* or Nabokov's story

"The Circle" as the structure that proclaims an artwork's autonomy, purity, and inviolability from the messy claims of the chaotic world outside. Clearly, "art" is at the center of Barth's strategy as it is of his name. The book's whole intricate baroque patterning, in fact, produced (as in *Ulysses*) by the characters' unwitting conformity to the author's scheme, suggests that its concern is less with the world than with the playing of its own neat games.[1] And when every page reminds us of "the Author" responsible for the novel we are reading—and reminds us that it *is* a novel, and that we *are* reading—it becomes impossible seriously to believe that any of the narrated occurrences *did* ever occur or *might* ever occur in the world in which we live.

LETTERS thus denies its literal validity to transcribe the World; all it claims to do, literally, is to transcribe the Word—or its letters, rather, as alphabetic units, as epistles, and as the domain of literature (*belles-lettres*) in general. However: Barth's novel retains its claim to moral seriousness by offering, in place of the literal validity it disowns, a *metaphoric* validity to render the World. This metaphoric validity is strongly felt by every reader of the novel; and it is obviously nonsense to maintain that Barth, for whatever esthetic purposes, has excluded felt life from his book, when clearly the claims of the "real" world to enter this fiction are heeded with such encyclopedic generosity. Whether it be sequential, as in A.B. Cook's vivid reports of key battles in the War of 1812, or sliced up and restacked according to Jacob Horner's "Anniversary View," there is (as in *Ulysses* and *Gravity's Rainbow*) an enormous amount of History inside this fiction. The wedding of a seemingly chaotic welter of fictional matter to a highly organized, ornate structure is a ceremony that Dante, Joyce, and Gaddis, among others, have previously invited us to attend, although we still have not understood all its mysteries. It is the Grecian urn filled with an ideal gas. It is the heroic imposition of order upon chaos, the resistance against entropy, the analogue of whirling, bouncing atoms of carbon and hydrogen assuming the stunningly shapely forms of life. We may learn from *LETTERS,* if we choose to, a prodigious amount about the world outside books: not only about American history, but also how to sail a skipjack, how to crack a code, what it's like to love at seventy, how it feels to lose a brother to cancer. Of all of Barth's work, surely

---

1. For example: Lady Amherst lives at "24 L Street," an anagram for "LetterS" plus the number of letters she is credited with writing; Jerome Bray, who calls his mother's mother "Granama," is thus descended from an anagram of "anagram."

LETTERS is imbued with the most convincing and genuine of human feelings: love of parents for their children, of sons for their fathers, of siblings for each other. Nor are the darker sides laughed away.

The novel thus *does* achieve what one of its characters calls "the transcension of paralyzing self-consciousness to productive self-awareness" (p. 652).[1] It succeeds in "transcending" its self-consciousness by renouncing its claims to "truth" on a literal plane, while restating those claims on a metaphoric plane that is perhaps ultimately more tenable. We recall William H. Gass's Wilde-ly perverse warning that "The appeal to literature as a source of truth is pernicious. Truth suffers, but more than that, literature suffers."[2] Barth, however, acknowledges the relation between fiction and fact to be considerably more complex. As the narrator of one of the stories in *Lost in the Funhouse* puts it,

> inasmuch as the old analogy between Author and God, novel and world can no longer be employed unless deliberately as a false analogy, certain things follow: 1) fiction must acknowledge its fictitiousness and metaphoric invalidity or 2) choose to ignore the question or deny its relevance or 3) establish some other, acceptable relation between itself, its author, its reader. ("Life-Story," p. 125)

In *LETTERS,* Barth has established that "other, acceptable relation." The epistolary form, as recovered by Barth from the literary past, achieves "a détente with the realistic tradition" (p. 52), by ostensibly refining the author out of existence to the point of allowing the characters to speak exclusively in their own voices, while at the same time permitting those apparently authentic voices to acknowledge the ventriloquist who produces them. Hence the characters' stories are plausible as fictions and yet do not overstate the author's claim to have a handle on reality. All that the implied author of *LETTERS* claims, as far as realism goes, is that "This is what such a character would write were he or she to indite a letter about the situation in which I have chosen to place him or her." That is, "epistolarism" weds authentically moving stories to a conspicuously inauthentic text.

1. This "transcension" is best dramatized in the growth of the character who introduced himself in *The End of the Road,* "In a sense, I am Jacob Horner," and who starts out in *LETTERS* by writing to himself, "In a sense, you remain Jacob Horner." By the end of *LETTERS,* however, he has "remobilized" himself, and is able to conclude affirmatively (no longer "in a sense"), "I am, sir,/Jacob Horner" (p. 745).

2. "William H. Gass" (an interview by Carole Spearim McCauley), in *The New Fiction: Interviews with Innovative American Writers,* ed. Joe David Bellamy (Urbana: University of Illinois Press, 1974), p. 34.

This yoking of seemingly opposite tendencies is analogous to that paradoxical rendition of character as simultaneously "real" and "fictional." The novel embodies an invisible but dramatic struggle between the characters' seeming independence from authorial constraint (no, they *won't* cooperate with him; yes, they *will* lead their own lives) and their equally apparent subordination to the (geometric, alphabetic, chronologic) demands of the novel's organizing principles. Lady Amherst, for example, resists "the Author"'s expressed wish to allegorize her—"I am *not* Literature! I am *not* the Great Tradition! I am *not* the aging Muse of the Realistic Novel! I am not / Yours," (p. 57)—and yet in her last letter to "the Author" she acknowledges herself to be "Your / Germaine" (p. 692). Her efforts recall Molly Bloom's plea to the author of *Ulysses,* "O Jamesy let me up out of this." Like Nabokov's Van and Ada, Barth's marionettes steal our hearts even as they deny the existence of the strings that we all can see. In fact we feel for and pity these self-conscious characters more, not less, for their being visibly trapped inside the fiction. Their situation, moreover, as subversively acknowledged fictional characters, is ultimately not subversive after all, in that Barth makes their situation into a metaphor for our own contingent relation to life itself. The characters allude to their Author much as, were we in their shoes, we should call upon our own. Thinks Todd Mensch of the daughter he has abused and lost track of, "Jeannine, Jeannine: what has our Author done with you? And if your little cruise with me furthered His plot, can you forgive me? We've little time" (p. 735).

The error of self-proclaimed moralists such as Gardner and DeMott is that they wrongly assume that fiction must be *either* mimetic *or* reflexive. When confronted by a work that is clearly concerned with the autonomous nature of language, they condemn it for immorally neglecting the serious concerns of real life. But, as we have seen, the wonderful and inadequately appreciated fact is that self-depicting fiction may be *both* ethically effective and esthetically reflexive. Ambrose Mensch describes the calendrical organization of the novel in which he appears as

> a form that spells itself while spelling out much more and (one hopes) spellbinding along the way, as language is always also but seldom simply about itself. (p. 767)

LETTERS thus offers a TRESTLE (in the sense of a bridge) between "postmodern" sophistication and the "old-fashioned" springs of narrative; between the World as the writer's only legitimate subject and the Word as his or her only available medium; between the word as exploratory tool and the word as reflexive toy; a TRESTLE between History and Fiction, between believable characters who stand on their own and an acknowledged "Author" who just as clearly pulls their strings; a TRESTLE between tradition and experiment, as between earnest and game. This farrago of ambition and obsessions, this macédoine of Modernist Formalism and "Historical Fiction" is, like *Ulysses,* an inquiry into History that endeavors to roll all time and space into one neat, compact ball. An atomization of language conjoined to a conflation of the entire tradition of the Novel in English, a narrative in which character and fate cooperate with alphabetical priority and postmodernist generative devices in establishing the novel's texture and form, *LETTERS* takes a bold step forward with eyes fixed firmly behind. The past fecundates the future, in our lettered lives as in these lively letters.

Chapter IX

The Criticism of Self-Consciousness

I N this chapter I should like to look briefly at some recent *practical* criticism of the authors I have been discussing and then, in greater detail, at some recent *theoretical* criticism pertaining to the self-conscious novel.

* * *

In *Nabokov: The Critical Heritage,* Norman Page has handily compiled more than seventy of the most discerning reviews and articles devoted to Nabokov's novels during the author's lifetime.[1] Page reproduces a translation of Vladislav Khodasevich's landmark essay in the Paris émigré journal *Vozrozdenie,* entitled—after Nabokov's early *nom de plume*—"On Sirin." Writing well before Humbert Humbert's false claim that "poets never kill," Khodasevich observed that

> The life of the artist and the life of a device in the consciousness of the artist—this is Sirin's theme, revealing itself to some degree or other in almost every one of his writings, beginning with *The Defense.* However, the artist (and more concretely speaking, the writer) is never shown by him directly, but always behind a mask: a chessplayer, a businessman, etc.[2]

With similar insight if somewhat less enthusiasm, Jean-Paul Sartre, reviewing a French translation of *Despair* for the journal *Europe,* noted that

> In the history of the novel, we must distinguish between the period in which authors were devising the tools and that in which they were reflecting on the tools that had been devised. Mr. Nabokov is an author of the second period; he deliberately sets himself the task of reflection; he never writes without *watching himself* in the act of writing, just as others listen to themselves speaking, and he is almost exclusively interested in the subtle workings of his own reflective consciousness. . . .[3]

1. Norman Page, ed., *Nabokov: The Critical Heritage* (London: Routledge & Kegan Paul, 1982).
2. Vladislav Khadasevich, "On Sirin," in *The Critical Heritage,* ed. Page, pp. 63–64.
3. Jean-Paul Sartre, Review of *La Méprise* [*Despair*], by Vladimir Nabokov, *Europe,* 15 June 1939, 240–49; trans. in *The Critical Heritage,* ed. Page, p. 65.

In these now classic essays by Khodasevich and Sartre, dating from 1937 and 1939 respectively, we find a clue to the qualitative decline of more recent Nabokov criticism. The terrain was claimed early and firmly by some first-rate critical minds, critics who recognized in "Sirin" a perfect target for their "New" or formalist approaches. Sartre, comparing Nabokov to "other émigrés who are *rootless*," concluded that "They do not concern themselves with any society, not even in order to revolt against it, because they do not belong to any society. [Hermann] Carlovitch is consequently reduced to committing perfect crimes, and Mr. Nabokov to writing in the English language on subjects of no significance" (p. 66).

The existentialist's complaint that the esthete is insufficiently *engagé* points to one of the unexpected charms of *The Critical Heritage:* many of the entries predate the hagiographic period of Nabokov criticism. In 1942, a reviewer for the *New York Times* could still dare to say (of *The Real Life of Sebastian Knight*) that "Mr. Nabokov's English style is interesting in a Walt Disney sort of way."[1] After *Lolita*'s success and the reception of *Pale Fire* as "one of the very great works of art of this century"[2] such spirited attacks on the sage of Montreux became practically taboo. As the historical parade of opinion marches across Page's pages, one witnesses a definite slackening of critical posture, a distinct shift in reaction from occasional snipe to dependable stroke. Critics continue to perform the exegetical spadework that the novels and stories demand, but the evaluative consensus becomes increasingly benign.

Page, in his introduction, deftly dramatizes the peculiar ontogeny of Nabokov's reputation. The *oeuvre* available to readers of English began to appear at roughly the middle of Nabokov's career. It grew outward in both directions at once—a feat achieved by the alternate publication of new work written in English and translations of "old" work written in Russian. For instance, after the arrival of *Ada* in 1969, Nabokov brought out *Mary*, the translation of his first Russian novel originally published as *Mashenka* forty-five years before. As Page puts it, "Under the rubric of 'new novels,' reviewers were liable to find themselves discussing books written, perhaps, before they were born, and doing so with prior knowledge of books by the same author written much later but published ear-

1. P.M.J. in *New York Times Book Review,* 11 January 1942, p. 14; *The Critical Heritage,* ed. Page, p. 67.
2. Mary McCarthy, review of *Pale Fire, The New Republic,* 4 June 1962, p. 27.

lier" (p. 4) Peering at early works through the lattice of later ones, critics were often led to play such bizarre games as spot-the-nymphet while reading *Invitation to a Beheading*. Looking back at the results, one is occasionally reminded of Pierre Menard.

Nabokov's Fifth Arc: Nabokov and Others on His Life's Work, edited by J.E. Rivers and Charles Nicol, takes up where Norman Page's anthology leaves off: "To the four arcs of Nabokov's life—the Russian, the European, the American, and the neo-European—a fifth arc is now being added: [. . .] the arc of literary history."[1] The twenty-one essays, most of them written for inclusion in this volume, tend to be somewhat elementary in nature. As the editors acknowledge at the outset, "the book is aimed at a wide audience. The general reader, we hope, will be able to use the book as an introduction to Nabokov." Thus the opening biographical sketch of Nabokov by Alfred Appel, Jr., composed while the novelist was at work on *Transparent Things*, offers no surprises to the reader of Field's cranky biography. The portrait is graced, however, by some lovely parenthetical details: "('Ah, a duel!' Nabokov had exclaimed, when [Robert M.] Adams appeared at the [Cornell English] departmental office one morning with his newly broken arm in a sling)."[2]

By far the most valuable entries in *Nabokov's Fifth Arc* are two contributions by Nabokov himself, both previously unavailable here. The author appended a "Postscript to the Russian Edition" of *Lolita* when he translated "my best English book" into Russian in 1967; now we have a translation of that Postscript (back) into English. It is delightful and informative. We learn, for instance, that Nabokov put the name of Vivian Darkbloom into *Lolita* at a time when he intended to publish the scandalous novel anonymously: "The anagram of my name and surname in the name and surname of one of my characters is a memorial of that hidden authorship." Thus, as the translator, Earl D. Sampson, rightly notes, "the anagrammatical characters [. . .] were not just the result of linguistic playfulness but also a means of insuring that Sirin's novels would be identified with Vladimir Nabokov."[3]

The other bit of authentic Nabokoviana that Rivers and Nicol offer us

1. J.E. Rivers and Charles Nicol, eds., *Nabokov's Fifth Arc: Nabokov and Others on His Life's Work* (Austin: University of Texas Press, 1982), p. xii.

2. Alfred Appel, Jr., "Nabokov: A Portrait," in *Fifth Arc*, ed. Rivers and Nicol, p. 14.

3. Earl D. Sampson, "Translator's Note" to "Postscript to the Russian Edition of *Lolita*," by Vladimir Nabokov, in *Fifth Arc*, ed. Rivers and Nicol, p. 189.

are the "Notes to *Ada* by Vivian Darkbloom" that Nabokov included in the British Penguin edition of *Ada* published in 1970, an edition never available in the United States and now out of print in England. These are fifteen pages of matter-of-fact annotations, mainly for readers lacking either Russian or French: "p. 8. *lieu de naissance:* birthplace." Occasionally, familiar hobbyhorses trot into view: "p. 11. Raspberries; ribbon: allusions to ludicrous blunders in Lowell's version of Mandelshtam's poems (in the *N.Y. Review,* 23 December 1965)." And there are even a few trapdoors of wit set to spring open underfoot: "p. 303. *topinambour:* tuber of the girasole; pun on 'pun' (*'calembour'*)."[1]

Just as "distance lends charm to the view," so do those who write from a chronological distance, the tracers of that fifth arc, enjoy certain perceptual advantages. Critics are now free to apply critical methods that the subject himself despised, and to do so without fear of his withering reprisals. Thus Phyllis A. Roth treats us to a psychoanalytic inquiry into Nabokov's *"need* to control," highlighting "the wrong-man-murdered theme."[2] An even better use of critical distance is made by Margaret Byrd Boegeman, who effectively disproves Nabokov's insistence that Kafka's *The Trial* had no influence on his *Invitation to a Beheading.* Boegeman temperately infers that "Nabokov seems to have borrowed a great deal from Kafka but not Kafka's themes or teleology," and proceeds to a sensitive demonstration of the pivotal role played by the *Invitation* in Nabokov's crucial switch from Russian to English.[3]

Controversy, too, may lend its charm, and in this volume the most provocative instance is James M. Rambeau's attack on a fellow contributor, Alfred Appel. Rambeau writes of Appel's *Annotated Lolita,* "This edition, wrapped as it is around the text of *Lolita,* does a disservice by creating the illusion that the mysteries and difficulties of the text are herein solved."[4] My own objection to *The Annotated Lolita* has been that Appel identifies "Mrs. Richard F. Schiller" right at the start, so that the emotional time bomb that Nabokov carefully concealed is abruptly dug

1. Vladimir Nabokov, "Notes to *Ada* by Vivian Darkbloom," in *Fifth Arc,* ed. Rivers and Nicol, p. 253.

2. Phyllis A. Roth, "Toward the Man Behind the Mystification," in *Fifth Arc,* ed. Rivers and Nicol, p 56.

3. Margaret Byrd Boegeman, *"Invitation to a Beheading* and the Many Shades of Kafka," in *Fifth Arc,* ed. Rivers and Nicol, p. 111.

4. James M. Rambeau, "Nabokov's Critical Strategy," in *Fifth Arc,* ed. Rivers and Nicol, p. 23.

up and deprived of its explosive power. But Rambeau's charge that Appel confuses explication and explanation goes further. Rambeau rebukes Field, Alvarez, Appel and others for following Nabokov into the mirror-lined halls of self-consciousness; self-conscious critics are, he says, "the victims of Nabokov's strategies":

> That critical skills are indispensable we have no doubt; but criticism is not an art and should not be displayed in artful terms [. . .]. The qualities of muteness, of being overheard, are what literary critics must deal with, must articulate, must explain; they will not do these difficult chores well if they are, in some sense, in competition with their subjects in creating works of art.[1]

Critics are wrong to play Nabokovian games, Rambeau argues, because such sport distracts us from "what, finally, makes Nabokov worth reading. Beyond all the games, the ultimately sterile parodies, the splendid verbal jokes and puns, Nabokov creates for us characters who touch us."[2]

Rambeau is here sounding the reactionary note that is increasingly audible in current Nabokov criticism: the call of those who would reclaim Nabokov for the mainstream, and champion him as a paragon of all of the novel's most traditional values. Martin Amis began the present backlash in a piece in Peter Quennell's collection *Vladimir Nabokov: A Tribute* (1979),[3] and there is further evidence of it elsewhere in *Nabokov's Fifth Arc*, in an essay by William C. Carroll:

> For all its baroque modernity, its arch allusiveness, its fashionably shifting relationships between author, narrator, reader, and character, *Despair* succeeds largely because of its old-fashioned virtue: the creation of a concretely realized world of intriguing interest.[4]

There is no doubt that to focus *exclusively* on Nabokov's games is to lose sight of the great emotional appeal of his fiction; but surely it is going too far in the other direction to forbid critics, as Rambeau would, from acknowledging the contingency of their own enterprise:

> We need to be reminded of these human concerns, and Nabokov's critics can only discuss them when they lose the self-consciousness induced by Nabokov's complex and sophisticated literary games. And it is only possible to

1. Rambeau, "Critical Strategy," p. 25.
2. Ibid., p. 33.
3. Martin Amis, "The Sublime and the Ridiculous: Nabokov's Black Farces," in Peter Quennell, ed., *Vladimir Nabokov: A Tribute* (London: Weidenfeld & Nicolson, 1979; New York: Morrow, 1980), pp. 73–87.
4. William C. Carroll, "The Cartesian Nightmare of *Despair*," in *Fifth Arc*, ed. Rivers and Nicol, p. 82.

lose that self-consciousness by recognizing how small a part those games finally play in Nabokov's genuine appeal to his readers.[1]

Nabokov criticism will sink to mere cacophony if critics go on insisting that the novelist must be *either* a great teller of human stories *or* a player of self-conscious, hermetic games. John Ray, Jr.'s preface to *Lolita* makes the excessively ethical claim; the afterword, "On a Book Entitled *Lolita*," makes the equally exaggerated esthetic claim; and the truth, like the text of *Lolita* itself, lies between the two, incorporating elements of both.

Perhaps critics *have* been wrong, as Rambeau argues, to focus exclusively on the games and the reflexivity; but the error is understandable, since the invitations to spot the "pun on 'pun'" are so abundant. Without his games, Nabokov's fiction would be a golf course without holes: beautiful perhaps, but deprived of its function. What is truly distinctive about the novels and stories, as we have seen, is *neither* that they touch us and move us with their mimicry of human emotion, *nor* that they demand recognition as self-contained games, but that they manage to do *both* these things at the same time. That Russian Postscript to *Lolita* is emblematic: Vivian Darkbloom's name is both a neat game and a reminder that Nabokov was reluctant to offend his colleagues at Cornell. In order to avoid mere decadence and entropy, Nabokov criticism must rank fidelity above facility by keeping both the mimetic and ludic functions of the fiction in view.

*　　*　　*

Although John Kuehl and Steven Moore, the editors of *In Recognition of William Gaddis*[2] don't acknowledge it in their introduction, one of the surprises of this collection of fourteen essays is how much disagreement there is about Gaddis. There is disagreement, for instance, on the extent to which he has been influenced by James Joyce. Kuehl and Moore themselves, with surprising negativity, refer to Bernard Benstock's early appreciation of *The Recognitions* as "an inaccurate demonstration of the novel's nonexistent debt to Joyce's *Ulysses*" (p. 13). Less shrilly, John Seelye's essay takes a similar swipe at "a mistaken comparison with Joyce."[3] In this

---

1. Rambeau, "Critical Strategy," p. 33.
2. John Kuehl and Steven Moore, eds., *In Recognition of William Gaddis* (Syracuse, N.Y.: Syracuse University Press, 1984).
3. John Seelye, "Dryad in a Dead Oak Tree: The Incognito in *The Recognitions*," in *In Recognition,* ed. Kuehl and Moore, p. 71.

same volume, though, Frederick R. Karl demonstrates rather persuasively that "The Faulknerian presence (and behind that, Joycean) is, in fact, everywhere, in phrasing, in interrupted speech that suggests great unspoken depths, and in broad verbal wit."[1]

Behind the unacknowledged disputes, however—and there are others simmering beneath the placid surface of this collection—there does seem to be a consensus on many things pertaining to the outstanding "unknown" novelist of the 1950s and 1970s. There seems to be relative agreement, for instance, that the principal structural tension of *The Recognitions*—that "perfectly ordered chaos," as we have seen it dubbing itself—comes from the balanced opposition of art's perfect order and that power of disorder which forever fatally threatens to spatter every pattern into perfect chaos. We have seen *The Recognitions* lugubriously dramatizing entropy's inroads as amputated body parts are stolen and shuffled around the city, paintings are cut into strips of canvas, and lofty cathedrals crumple into fallen blocks of stone. The critics assembled by Kuehl and Moore seem to agree that the central tension between the order of art and the chaos of temporal life, which characterizes *The Recognitions*, is transposed in Gaddis's second novel *JR* into a conflict between paper and money, between signal and noise: the paper that may bear the meaning of a novel, the notes of a composition, or the contours of human design, versus the money to which the system ascribes value but which in fact drives all order back toward chaos again.

And if Gaddis's literary antecedents are in dispute, there seems nevertheless to be general agreement on who his descendants are, or who, at least, are prominent among his filiations: Barthelme, Barth, Nabokov, and Pynchon. Especially Pynchon. Several of these essayists point from Gaddis to Pynchon, with Frederick Karl again making the most interesting and valuable discriminations, and tracing intriguing parallels between Gaddis's progress from *The Recognitions* to *JR* and that of Thomas Pynchon from *V.* to *Gravity's Rainbow.*

But disputes among these critics have the effect of scattering the impression of coherence the editors claim to have sought. (The introduction boasts without irony that it "dispels several rumors and sets the record straight" [p. x].) While some of these critics find in *JR* a confirmation of the principles embraced in *The Recognitions,* others find

1. Frederick R. Karl, "Gaddis: A Tribune of the Fifties," in *In Recognition,* ed. Kuehl and Moore, p. 188.

in Gaddis's second novel a repudiation of the encyclopedic ambitions of the first. This is a collection whose editorial intention is clearly hagiographic—"the creator of these two remarkable novels will inevitably join Herman Melville as a major force in the history of American letters;"[1] *The Recognitions* is successively enshrined as "one of the most finely wrought books in American letters"[2], "one of the great underread novels of our times"[3], and "perhaps the novel of the fifties"[4],—and yet even in such a hagiography, there are essays of a religious cast that find Gaddis's influence pernicious, even "a book for burning":

> To recognize this shocking metaphor [eating, loins] is to realize that *The Recognitions* is a black book indeed, is to understand the alchemical beast lurking beneath the ecclesiastical colors of the jacket [. . .]: a book for burning, it burns with a flame of infinite intricacy, deep within which can be discerned, dimly at first, and then more clearly, a savage smile betraying "the white teeth of violation."[5]

In short, this collection offers us the appearance of perfect order, whereas in fact it parades before us a perfect chaos. If the narrator of *JR* absents himself so as to let the multifarious voices speak their disparate monologues, so too do the editors of this so-called "collection," which confronts us therefore with a paradox not unlike that experienced by the reader of Gaddis's fiction.

Where lies the truth? For Gaddis it is clear that despite the conflict of voices there is always a strong and frequently acerbic moral consciousness at work behind the narrative. In *The Recognitions,* this moral consciousness endeavors to know and to show where the value of art truly lies—not in the detritus of the brief, fatuous, mundane, or corrupt life, but in the redemptive, enduring, all-justifying power of the generous deed of art left behind. In *JR* and in *Carpenter's Gothic,*[6] this same intense, unflinching if often comic moral consciousness strives to locate and to laud the source of genuine human value in the midst of all *this*— this fumbling, sniffling, greedily acquisitive striving. Moral value *always* burns beneath a bushel of catastrophes in Gaddis.

1. Kuehl and Moore, "Preface" to *In Recognition,* p. ix.
2. Christopher Knight, "Flemish Art and Wyatt's Quest for Redemption in William Gaddis's *The Recognitions,*" in *In Recognition,* ed. Kuehl and Moore, p. 68.
3. Susan Strehle, "Disclosing Time: William Gaddis' *JR,*" in *In Recognition,* ed. Kuehl and Moore, p. 132.
4. Frederick R. Karl, "A Tribune," p. 174.
5. John Seelye, "Dryad," p. 80.
6. William Gaddis, *Carpenter's Gothic* (New York: Viking Penguin, 1985).

It is a bit of a pity that the editors of essays on an author who has embraced the motto "Love, and do what you will" show themselves to be so intolerant in the way they treat critics who either got to Gaddis before they did or disagree with them on certain readings. (They typically dismiss one critic's "jaundiced, misleading view based on her evident inability to comprehend" [p. 15].) But again, as a satirist, Gaddis fills his fiction with views that contradict his own. And so as a novelist, he has attracted to himself critics who frequently contradict their author's principles in their nonetheless successful effort to celebrate William Gaddis.

*   *   *

The three theoretical studies I wish to discuss are Gerald Graff, *Literature Against Itself: Literary Ideas in Modern Society*[1]; Linda Hutcheon, *Narcissistic Narrative: The Metafictional Paradox*[2]; and Alan Wilde, *Horizons of Assent: Modernism, Postmodernism, and the Ironic Imagination*.[3]

*   *   *

In his first chapter, entitled "Culture, Criticism, and Unreality," Gerald Graff writes:

> This is a book about our ways of talking about literature—how they got started, why they have taken the turn they have taken recently, where they go wrong, what we can do about setting them right. [. . .] It is also a book about the social context of literature and criticism—how both literature and our ways of talking about it have been conditioned by social pressures and how they in turn influence social life. [. . .] In this sense, literary thinking is inseparable from moral and social thinking.   (p. 1)

Graff feels strongly the need to reassert the mimetic or truth-bearing value of literature, on the grounds that anti-mimetic theorists (especially J. Hillis Miller) have trivialized literature and led humanists to ineffectualize themselves. "This book, then, seeks to understand why it is that

1. Gerald Graff, *Literature Against Itself: Literary Ideas in Modern Society* (Chicago: University of Chicago Press, 1979).
2. Linda Hutcheon, *Narcissistic Narrative: The Metafictional Paradox* (Waterloo, Ontario: Wilfred Laurier University Press, 1980; revised, New York: Methuen, 1984).
3. Alan Wilde, *Horizons of Assent: Modernism, Postmodernism, and the Ironic Imagination* (Baltimore: The Johns Hopkins University Press, 1981; pbk. rpt. Philadelphia: University of Pennsylvania Press, 1987).

we as literary intellectuals have defined our enterprise in ways that implicitly trivialize it" (p. 28).

In a chapter entitled "The Myth of the Postmodern Breakthrough," Graff argues that postmodernist nihilist epistemology is not a break with modernist esthetics, as often claimed, but an extension from it. There is thus a strong tinge of Platonism to Graff's approach, as he tends to be a lumper rather than a splitter, and writes out of a nostalgia for Truth. He implies that a dead end confronts "the denial of the propositional nature of literature" (p. 48), and laments critics' "inability to define the cognitive function of art in any but the most equivocal terms" (p. 51).

Aristotle, befitting Graff's University of Chicago Press imprint, reasserts himself, perhaps, in Graff's distinguishing "The Two Postmodernisms." The good kind is nostalgic for lost certainties, as in Graff's readings of Borges and Nabokov:

> Borges's kind of postmodern writing, even in presenting solipsistic distortion as the only possible perspective, nevertheless presents this distortion *as* distortion—that is, it implicitly affirms a concept of the normal, if only as a concept which has been tragically lost.   (p. 56)

> At its best, the contemporary wave of self-reflexive fiction is not quite so totally self-reflexive as it is taken to be, since its very reflexivity implies a "realistic" comment on the historical crisis which brought it about.   (p. 57)

Graff thus stretches the perimeter of mimesis until self-conscious novelists are corralled in. But in (by implication) bad self-consciousness—"the more celebratory forms of postmodernism"—"there is scarcely any memory of an objective order of values in the past and no regret over its disappearance in the present" (p. 57). One danger of Graff's approach, here, is that it seems to reduce the crux of merit to a question of tone: good fiction laments its loss of authority, while bad fiction exults in it.

In his most alarmed-sounding chapter, "How Not to Save the Humanities," Graff admonishes that

> The literary way of talking about fictions pretends that no such unrefusable facts exist. This way of talking has endowed not only literature but all communication and discourse with an unaccountability that would be terrifying if its implications were taken seriously. No problem seems more pressing in the humanities right now than the radical unaccountability that infects its talk. (p. 204)

Seeing literature settling "all the more deeply into its familiar role as our vehicle and exemplar of socially sanctioned narcissism," Graff urges:

> A corrective is needed. As important as it was for critics to learn that literature and language are systems of humanly created conventions and not simple mirrors or photographic copies, it is now at least as important that they rescue some sense in which those conventions are accountable to something beyond themselves.　(p. 205)

Graff wants to restore literature's accountability to Truth, and shows how fiction, criticism, and cultural analysis have leap-frogged each other towards the pit of indeterminate, nonreferential inconsequentiality. His program is necessarily unbalanced, since it bills itself as "a corrective." Poking convincing holes in the anti-mimeticists' more extreme claims, he admirably manages to avoid sounding corny in his nostalgia for referential certainty. And surely Graff is right to warn of a logical dead end, as long as we remember that his "correction" is monocular on a subject that is dual in nature.

*　　*　　*

Linda Hutcheon's *Narcissistic Narrative* was first published by Canada's Wilfred Laurier University Press in 1980; the more widely available Methuen reprint (1984) comes with a new preface that takes some distance from the positions of the original edition. She acknowledges that the study began as a dissertation written for, among others, the reader-response critics Tzvetan Todorov and Wolfgang Iser; but now, in the "Preface to the Paperback Edition" (1984), Hutcheon states that "my focus is [. . .] to describe the 'poetics' of postmodernism."

Hutcheon offers a neat scheme of periods and their emphasis:

Romantic	—	author	
Realism	—	world	
Modernism	—	text	
Postmodernism	—	reader	(p. xiii)

She seems untroubled by Gerald Graff's epistemological alarm:

> Metafiction teaches, as does contemporary theory, that discourse is language as *énonciation,* involving, that is, the contextualized production and reception of meaning.　(p. xv)

> [. . .] *Narcissistic Narrative* [. . .] is a reflection of the impact in the '70s of all the varieties of reader-response criticism. Today, however, [. . .] the balance of power has to be restored.　(p. xv)

I would still see metafiction's "vital" link between art and life (by which we define the novel as mimetic) as existing, as I argue throughout this book, on the level of imaginative process. But today, I would wish to situate that process and its products much more firmly within a consideration of discourse.   (p. xvii)

Hutcheon thus would describe her method as a "blend of formalist and hermeneutic perspectives" (p. xvii).

For Hutcheon, the term "Narcissistic [. . .] is not intended as derogatory but rather as descriptive and suggestive" (p. 1). She conducts a dialogue with Graff's *Literature Against Itself*, arguing that self-conscious texts do not drive a wedge between language and truth, but in fact *do* tell the truth (albeit about driving that wedge).

Unlike Gerald Graff, I would not argue that in metafiction the life-art connection has been either severed completely or resolutely denied. Instead, I would say that this "vital" link is reforged, on a new level—on that of the imaginative process (of story-telling), instead of on that of the product (the story told). And it is the new role of the reader that is the vehicle of this change.
(p. 3)

[. . .] The realism of the nineteenth century [. . .] is based almost entirely on what will be called a mimesis of product [. . .]. Modern metafiction is largely what shall be referred to here as a mimesis of process [. . .]   (p. 5)

Here we go again with another Procrustean stretching of mimesis to make the self-conscious novel fit. By this reasoning, abstract expressionism might be called a figurative or even realistic mode of painting. E.H. Gombrich, we recall, addressed this issue persuasively in "Meditations on a Hobby Horse or the Roots of Artistic Form." He argued that the child's hobby horse does not "represent" our idea of a horse, and that mimesis loses its value as a term if one claims that abstract or playful forms mimic reality-on-some-deeper-level.[1] It is true, though, as we saw in *Tristram Shandy,* that the reader's experience of the text may supply a more or less overt plot line. This remains but one, however, among an array of rhetorical strategies designed to supplant and repudiate mimesis, not to bolster our belief in the "story."

Our rightful role as critics of self-conscious fiction, I would suggest, is to mediate between the extreme claims of these two schools. Both the

1. E.H. Gombrich, "Meditations on a Hobby Horse or the Roots of Artistic Form," in *Aspects of Form,* ed. Lancelot Law Whyte (London: Lund Humphries, 1951), reprinted in *Aesthetics Today,* ed. Morris Philipson (New York: Meridian Books, 1961), pp. 114–28.

mimeticists and the ludicists have the power, in all logic, to co-opt the opposing position. Seemingly ludic fiction-players, as Graff argues, may be said to be mimicking their cultural moment ("reflexivity implies a 'realistic' comment on the historical crisis which brought it about" [p. 57]). Or, as Hutcheon prefers, they may have "expanded [. . .] the meaning of novelistic mimesis to include process as well as product" (p. 25). And from the extreme ludic perspective, we recall William Gass's formulation in which even the presumption to represent reality is itself a game of make-believe:

> The appeal to literature as a source of truth is pernicious. Truth suffers; but more than that, literature suffers.

The fact that either camp can co-opt the other ought to suggest to us that a fixed duality, a conceptual oxymoron, in fact a Pynchonesque excluded middle is what we are dealing with. Thus we witness an alternation of critics between the two inviting poles, when what we need is a way to keep both poles suspended in the paradoxical picture.

* * *

Irony is the mineral that Alan Wilde mines in his obliquely-titled study, *Horizons of Assent*—and particularly irony's ironclad "or."

Wilde seeks "to provide a way of understanding irony as a mode of consciousness, a perceptual response to a world without unity or cohesion [. . .]" (p. 2), declaring that "my position is [. . .] phenomenological" (p. 3). Definitely a splitter, Wilde distinguishes three kinds of irony, keyed to the concepts of pre-modern, modern, and post-modern. First, linked to pre-modern, we had

> *mediate irony*, which [. . .] imagines a world lapsed from a recoverable (and in the twentieth century, generally a primitivist) norm.   (p. 9)

Then there came

> *disjunctive irony* (the characteristic form of modernism) [which] strives, however reluctantly, toward a condition of paradox.   (p. 10)

And finally Wilde gives us

> *suspensive irony* (which I connect with postmodernism), with its yet more radical vision of the multiplicity, randomness, contingency, and even absurdity,

[which] abandons the quest for paradise altogether—the world in all its disorder is simply (or not so simply) accepted.   (p. 10)

He thus returns to the question of tone raised by Gerald Graff, but Wilde shares Linda Hutcheon's rather than Graff's evaluative tone. He also introduces, in a footnote, a further term,

the *anironic:* the complementary vision that accompanies irony in each of its forms and that includes, most notably, the "assent" of my title.   (p. 10n)

Mediate, disjunctive, and suspensive ironies are exemplified respectively in Wilde's study by E.M. Forster—whose career Wilde reads as a progression across all three, Ivy Compton-Burnett—for modernist disjunctive irony, and Donald Barthelme—as the post-modern exemplar.

In short, the characteristic movement of ironic art in this century describes a double and seemingly contradictory progression, which, on the one hand, recognizes the increasing disintegration of an already disjunct world and, on the other, not only submits but (again in some cases) assents to it, or to its inherent possibilities.   (pp. 15–16)

We recognize from his language—"double and seemingly contradictory"—and from the "on-the-one-hand" trope, that Wilde is on the right double-railed track, that he does seek to mediate the monocular views. Self-conscious novels, it seems, would make ambidextrous readers and critics of us all.

Particularly as a champion of Donald Barthelme, Alan Wilde seems thus to be hailing precisely the version of postmodernism that Gerald Graff views with alarm: the literature that views the fragmentation complacently, that exults, that fails to grieve.

Irony [. . .] strives [. . .] to achieve the simultaneous acceptance and creation of a world that is both indeterminate and, at the same time, available to consciousness.   (p. 16)

[. . .] in the indeterminacy of man's horizon the beginnings of new adjustments of consciousness effloresce.   (p. 16)

Neither reductive nor, on the other hand, hopeful of reestablishing in art or in life an aesthetic of total order, endorsing modest pleasures in a world accepted as making no ultimate sense, it [suspensive irony] is a vision that lacks the heroism of the modernist enterprise but that, for a later and more disillusioned age, recovers its humanity.   (p. 165)

Wilde concludes about Barthelme,

The ludic strain of his work persists, not as a denial of meaning, of referentiality, but as an assertion of the artist's privilege to create meaning.
(pp. 187–88)

*   *   *

The movement of these three critical works, from the 1970s into the 1980s, signifies neatly. Graff: something is wrong here, we're headed for implosion. Hutcheon: No, don't worry, it's self-contained, and besides, it's fun to watch. And Wilde: No-no, this fiction *is* connected, and it's right to suggest that something's wrong, because we can all agree on that. *Ironically.*

Logical consistency is what Graff is worried about; if we took the principles of self-conscious fiction seriously, all our discourse would lose its license to bear truth, to be of consequence. Hutcheon's subject is ludic inversion, the self-conscious novel's transformation of the reader into its own playing field, its own reality. Wilde's true subject is irony, which he accordingly sees less as a solvent than as a solution.

The recent history of the criticism of self-consciousness, then, resembles the way we climb a ladder. One foot to the left of our center of gravity, the next foot to the right of it, and so on and up we go. A pedestrian image, perhaps, for the Hegelian helices of thesis-antithesis-synthesis. I see Graff and Hutcheon viewing a duality monocularly. Each of them has ceased to suspend judgment on what literature is. *Particle and wave:* as we need both models adequately to account for the behavior of light, so we need two, not one model, for our literary illuminations. In ludic mimesis, particles of reality are caught waving at the camera.

Chapter X

Reflexive Commentary in the Form of a Conclusion

Varieties of Self-Depiction

THIS inquiry has attempted to show that although self-depicting fictions share a common repertoire of devices and techniques, the results of their reflexivity are considerably diverse. The self-depiction of *Ulysses,* for example, by asserting the ubiquity of its authorial presence, contributes to that novel's celebration of art's power to redeem. The self-consciousness of Nabokov's novels and stories insulates his fictional world from the world outside, enabling his manifest shams to stir his readers' emotions. In the hands of a satirist such as Gaddis, self-depiction places the novel at the nexus of the "imitations" and "forgeries" that it itself derides. For a paradoxer like Pynchon, self-consciousness undercuts his novel's assertions, thereby preserving the fundamental ambiguity he pursues. And for Barth, self-depiction builds an artful bridge between "postmodern" sophistication and the "old-fashioned" springs of narrative.

The ways of handling self-depiction vary accordingly. For Joyce, a regular drama of reliability takes place as *Ulysses* progresses from narrator to narrator. The novel begins without self-consciousness in the "scrupulous meanness" and staunch objectivity of the 'Telemachia' episodes. Ambushed by the alien headlines of 'Aeolus' and travestied into a phylogeny of style in 'The Oxen of the Sun,' the text's reliability explodes in the phantasmagoria of 'Circe,' and ultimately staggers to a precarious equilibrium in Molly's objectively rendered subjective monologue. While Joyce thus *modulates* his novel's self-consciousness, Pynchon and Barth *moderate* the self-consciousness of their novels by keeping the mimetic and anti-mimetic elements of *Gravity's Rainbow* and *LETTERS,* respectively, in constant balance throughout. The self-depiction of Nabokov's fiction is essentially ludic, a reminder that art is a game of intricate enchantment and deception. His nesting narrators appeal to us even as they set the fictional world off from our own. Gaddis's satires, it was shown, are only slightly self-conscious, so as not to deflect the thrust of his attack, yet self-conscious enough to implicate his own endeavor. For Pynchon, self-consciousness is an inescapable limitation of perception; like gravity returning the launched rocket back to earth, self-consciousness deflects the characters' efforts to break out of themselves. The self-consciousness of *Gravity's Rainbow* suggests the possible futility of its own ambitious gesture.

Joyce and Nabokov use a variety of "unreliable" narrators; in order to understand the text properly, the reader must recognize the difference between the values of the narrators and those of the implied author. In *Ulysses,* Joyce changes narrative masks sequentially, while in *Ada,* Nabokov wears his narrative masks one inside another all at once. Gaddis and Pynchon, however, rely more conventionally upon a single omniscient narrator who is much closer to the implied author than is the case in Joyce or Nabokov. In Gaddis's second novel, *JR,* in fact, narration is almost completely supplanted by dialogue, and ceases almost entirely to be a source of the self-conscious or any other effect. If a historical development is to be discerned in the works of these authors, then, it is a movement *away* from narration as a medium to be played with and shaped into abstract or expressive designs, and *towards* a re-engagement with experience related with less self-consciousness from a single, committed point of view.

This same movement—away from a pre-occupation with self-consciousness, towards an accommodation with it—may be seen most clearly in several works of fiction written in the second half of the 1970s. In John Irving's *The World According to Garp* (1978), for example, many of the familiar reflexive devices may be readily recognized: the writer writing about the writer writing, the consequent reminders to the readers that he or she is reading, the *mises-en-abyme* of fictions-within-fictions that are printed in a variety of typefaces, and so on.[1] But Irving, clearly aiming at a more general, less sophisticatedly literate readership, carefully avoids shedding any doubt upon the veridicity of his own narrative. He vigorously maintains the illusion that Garp, his mother Jenny Fields, his wife Helen and the other characters are genuine human beings who have actually existed. He never hints that he, John Irving, has invented these

---

1. John Irving, *The World According to Garp* (New York: E. P. Dutton, 1978).

characters and their story, nor does he draw attention to his own telling of it. Thus *The World According to Garp* treats *thematically* the paradoxical relations of fiction and fact in the life of its central character, but in its narration, structure, characterization, and style, Irving's novel ignores the bearing of those paradoxical relations upon its own authenticity. *The World According to Garp* wins a wide audience by subsuming some of the thematic devices of self-consciousness to a generally conventional narrative full of vivid sex and violence.

Jeremy Leven's *Creator* (1980) may similarly be seen as pressing the resources of self-consciousness into the service of a fiction that flirts with, without confronting directly, its own ontological status. Among his various generative activities—sexual, biological, spiritual, esthetic—the hero of *Creator,* Dr. Harry Wolper, is engaged in the writing of a novel whose hero's main struggle is with his own author. The echoes of Pirandello, of Flann O'Brien, of Gide himself are all distinct, though unacknowledged. A transparently phony preface claims that *Creator* consists of "Doctor Henry Wolper's Notebooks on Parthenogenesis," and the novel culminates with Wolper's death. But his supposedly fictional creation Boris lives on, only to claim credit for having invented the novel's principal narrator:

> (December) 25th And so it came to pass that, after years of torment, I finally rid myself of Harry Wolper. For the truth of it is, as I'm sure you've long ago come to realize, there never was a Harry Wolper. There never was a great Biologist and Author who propelled me through one unlikely adventure after another, but, rather, it was I who concocted the preposterous Dr. Wolper, and now, as I had long ago promised, I had no choice but to kill him off.[1]

Leven's final flourish resembles Nabokov's strategy at the conclusion of *The Real Life of Sebastian Knight,* where the biographer and his subject struggle elegantly for the right to claim authorship of the text in which they appear. With an important difference, however: Nabokov's novel ends with a sly reminder of his own ultimate inventive presence behind his two fictional antagonists: "I am Sebastian, or Sebastian is I, or perhaps we both are someone whom neither of us knows." Leven's *Creator,* on the other hand, like Irving's *Garp,* stops short of reminding the reader of the performing author pulling the strings of his invented characters. There is, in Leven's and Irving's novels, no disclosure of that "somebody

1. Jeremy Leven, *Creator* (New York: Coward, McCann and Geoghegan, 1980), p. 489.

else" at work fabricating the fiction, and thus no distracting disruption of the fundamental fictional illusion. Again, the writers-writing-about-writers-writing and the fictions-within-fictions have been "lifted" from the self-conscious tradition, but the overt artifice formerly insisted upon is now, more moderately, merely included inobtrusively. The art still displays art, but no longer its own.

In Philip Roth's *Zuckerman Unbound* (1981) we find still further evidence of this contemporary movement away from a pre-occupation with self-consciousness, towards an accommodation with it. *Zuckerman Unbound* is a writerly novel about a very Roth-like writer whose main complaint is that readers confuse him with his fictional creations. Nathan Zuckerman has been thrust into celebrity by the great commercial success of his novel *Carnovsky*, a first-person narrative about a Jewish masturbator described by Roth in terms that make it indistinguishable from Roth's own *Portnoy's Complaint* (1969). As with the recycled characters of Barth's *LETTERS*, Zuckerman comes from a recent engagement as the protagonist of Roth's previous novel, *The Ghost Writer*; and the epigraph to *Zuckerman Unbound* is similarly attributed not to an actual person but to E. I. Lonoff, a character from that earlier fiction. Roth thus promotes the very confusion between fact and fiction that his hero condemns. A friend of Zuckerman's ex-wife, for instance, complains about

"The things you wrote about her in that book."

"About Laura? You don't mean Carnovsky's girlfriend, do you?"

"Don't hide behind that 'Carnovsky' business. Please don't compound it with that."

"I must say, Rosemary, I'm shocked to find that a woman who taught English in the New York school system for over thirty years cannot distinguish between the illusionist and the illusion. Maybe you're confusing the dictating ventriloquist with the demonic dummy."[1]

Roth's "dummy," however, so clearly impersonates its ventriloquist that the novel both seems to be self-conscious, yet denies that it is. The novel's title itself propounds the paradox, for while Zuckerman, a fictional character, is literally bound into the signatures of the book, it is Roth who, as its author, remains unbound. Like *JR* and *Carpenter's Gothic, Creator,* and *The World According to Garp,* Roth's subsequent fiction typifies the latter-day trend among self-conscious novels toward a

1. Philip Roth, *Zuckerman Unbound* (New York: Farrar, Straus and Giroux, 1981), pp. 167–68.

new balance among the elements of self-depiction: the characters, accorded more respect, assume more narrational responsibility, while the implied author is less disruptive and insistent in asserting his own, ultimately responsible presence. Thus, while the most recent self-conscious novels continue to acknowledge imitation's limitations, the emphasis is shifting from the limitations back to the imitations.

Honest Dishonesty: Fiction's Claim to Truth

Beckett once wrote of Joyce, "His writing is not *about* something; *it is that something itself.*"[1] This remains an unresolved question in our discussion: *Can* writing *not* be about something? It is commonly thought that *words* stand for *things:* is this not so?

Not necessarily, says the self-conscious novel. The world and the book may have but little to do with each other. Nabokov once described the impression he wished his fiction to leave upon the reader in these words:

> I think that what I would welcome at the close of a book of mine is a sensation of its world receding in the distance and stopping somewhere there, suspended afar like a picture in a picture: *The Artist's Studio* by Van Bock.[2]

Tautologically, perhaps, but truly, creative writing *creates*. In a critical defense of the self-conscious novel (although he does not use the term), William H. Gass makes a claim similar to Nabokov's for the isolation of fiction from the world that surrounds it:

> On the other side of a novel lies the void. Think, for instance, of a striding statue; imagine the purposeful inclination of the torso, the alert and penetrating gaze of the head and its eyes, the outstretched arm and pointing finger; everything would appear to direct us toward some goal in front of it. Yet our eye travels only to the finger's end, and not beyond. Though pointing, the finger bids us stay instead, and we journey slowly back along the tension of the arm. In our hearts we know what actually surrounds the statue. The same surrounds every other work of art: empty space and silence.[3]

1. Samuel Beckett, "Dante . . . Bruno . Vico . . Joyce," in Samuel Beckett et al., *Our Exagmination Round his Factification for Incamination of Work in Progress* (Paris: Shakespeare and Co., 1929), p. 14.

2. Interview with Alfred Appel, Jr., reprinted in Vladimir Nabokov, *Strong Opinions* (New York: McGraw-Hill, 1973), pp. 72–73. As Appel points out, "Van Bock" is no painter, but a partial anagram of the novelist's own name.

3. William H. Gass, "The Concept of Character in Fiction," in *Fiction and the Figures of Life* (New York: Knopf, 1970), p. 49.

Creations, be they statues, minuets, or novels, do not reflect but add to what already is. Only mirrors mirror.

No wonder what is lately called "textuality" remains a mystery always ready to be probed. Language is inherently paradoxical, serving simultaneously as symbol and sign, both meaning and a sound. The paradox lurks not only in puns and anagrams, but also in such a fundamental creative resource as metaphor. The recent renaissance of critical interest in metaphor reflects in part a pursuit, down to its elementary particles, of that same paradoxical ligament between *logos* and *res* that is playfully stretched if not snapped by the self-conscious novel.[1]

But the ambiguous relation between language and reality has not prevented authors from communicating with readers. Shakespeare, for example, was as fully aware as any Wittgenstein or Borges of the problematic reality of literature: all Hamlet has to read is "Words, words, words." Beckett, it is often noted, dramatizes the solipsistic futility of writing, and yet he writes, and is understood. For more self-conscious novelists, then, as for Pynchon, not everything is lost to equivocation. Reflexivity may *seem* to threaten fiction's power of affirmation, but we have seen that it qualifies without cancelling out. For all the self-conscious playfulness that we have seen in *Ulysses,* for example, the novel remains a triumphant endorsement of paternal sympathy and love.

By artfully displaying its own art, the self-conscious novel need not entirely cut itself off from the world. Rather, it acknowledges that its relation to the world is imaginary, or metaphorical, or problematic at best. The novel's claim to truth is indeed a sort of *honest dishonesty.* By qualifying its own relation to life in a way that shows respect for its readers' sophistication, the self-conscious novel remains playful while sustaining literature's serious claim to ethical responsibility.

Beyond Self-Consciousness?

Edward Mendelson, in his preface to an anthology of essays on Pynchon, claims that *Gravity's Rainbow* takes fiction *beyond* "the unmourned dead end" to which "hermetic self-referentiality [. . .] has already brought literary Modernism":

> Pynchon is one of a few, as yet a very few, major writers for whom self-consciousness is a central problem only in their early work, a problem they eventually manage to put aside.

1. For example, "Special Issue on Metaphor," *Critical Inquiry,* 5:1 (Autumn 1978).

Pynchon's challenge to confront the motives of criticism, his insistence that readers consider the *effects* of interpretation in the world of ethics, is precisely the challenge that criticism must face if it is to escape at last from the centripetal, reflexive momentum of romantic and Modernist writing and of the literary theory that such writing has engendered.[1]

Similarly, William Plater notes that

Like many other contemporary novelists, Pynchon will not permit his readers the luxury of suspended belief—he reminds us that we are reading a text. But Pynchon is not content with forcing mere self-awareness on the reader; he insists on inflicting the awareness of all that is the case.[2]

Mendelson's swift burial of Modernism and Plater's echoes of Wittgenstein imply that self-consciousness is something "mere," a dead end from which fiction is already withdrawing to turn elsewhere. Certainly it is hard not to see *Finnegans Wake,* for example, as one of the most glorious dead ends in literature, which we are fortunate to have as a warning of where certain artificial principles lead. Not even the combined knowledge and intelligence of several readers trying together in the same room to make sense of Joyce's final novel—which is how the *Wake* is often read—can always provide an understanding of the book that feels satisfactory.

But if, as Ellmann puts it, we are still learning to be Joyce's contemporaries,[3] if fiction of the past fifty years can still be called "Afterjoyce," and if we have yet to learn to read *Finnegans Wake,* how can Joyce's endeavor be called a dead end? Inexhaustibility of *anything* sounds chimerical these days, but there is some justice to Robert Alter's claim for the self-conscious novel as "the inexhaustible genre."[4] Alter appropriately quotes Borges:

Literature is not exhaustible for the simple and sufficient reason that no single book is. A book is not an isolated entity; it is a relationship, an axis of innumerable relationships.[5]

From Joyce's mock-heroic epic to Gaddis's reflections of a central vacancy and on to Pynchon's atomized protagonist, I have noted that

1. Edward Mendelson, "Introduction" to *Pynchon: A Collection of Critical Essays,* ed. Edward Mendelson (Englewood Cliffs, N.J.: Prentice-Hall, 1978), pp. 2, 15.

2. William M. Plater, *The Grim Phoenix: Reconstructing Thomas Pynchon* (Bloomington: Indiana University Press, 1978), pp. 15–16.

3. Richard Ellmann, *James Joyce* (New York: Oxford University Press, 1959), p. 1.

4. This is the title of the final chapter of Robert Alter's *Partial Magic: The Novel as a Self-Conscious Genre* (Berkeley: University of California Press, 1975), pp. 218–45.

5. Cited by Alter, *Partial Magic,* p. 128.

character, or at least the concept of heroism, is under attack in the self-conscious novel. Yet it is in *character* and its treatment that the novel form currently seems to see its ramp up and out of the ever-deepening epistemological pit of reflexivity. *How can I know anything if all I can know is myself? By imagining I'm also someone else.* Thus character empties the crucible of doubt—but it has not been an easy struggle.

The integrity of character has taken its worst beating in the most extreme forms of self-consciousness, either in the Nabokovian mirror world where "my characters are my galley slaves," or in the alphabetical architecture of Walter Abish, where hapless humans are wiped out of the story on an authorial whim:

> Downcast, feeling dejected after first frustrating African experience, Ferdinand flies back. Flies first class Eastern. Enjoys fried frogs for dinner. Fabulous dinner. Fabulous frogs, author decides. But erases Ferdinand.[1]

In recent fiction, though, writers seem to be moving away from a preoccupation with self-consciousness towards an accommodation with it, and the reassertion of character is the vehicle of that stabilizing movement. The epistolary form of *LETTERS,* as was noted, pointed fiction in this direction. Two other recent writers are worth looking at for this tendency: Raymond Carver and Primo Levi.

Carver's oft-noted minimalism springs in part from a deep suspicion of language that recalls, in many ways, Hemingway's injunction, "You'll lose it if you talk about it." The line was spoken, of course, by a character in a novel. If you can't talk about it, you *can* talk about not talking about it—which is what Jake and Brett do in *The Sun Also Rises.* Talk about not talking about: the title of one of Carver's collections, *What We Talk About When We Talk About Love,* not only displays the nearly monosyllabic redundancy characteristic of his style, but also carries the implication that either we mean something we don't say, or we say something we don't mean.[2]

Inarticulateness leads Carver's characters to alcohol, to divorce, to solitude, to mutual incomprehension. Yet, slicing away his own language, Carver is always careful to remind us of the artifice of language in which his stories are contained.

---

1. Walter Abish, *Alphabetical Africa* (New York: New Directions, 1974), first F chapter, pp. 12–13.

2. Raymond Carver, *What We Talk About When We Talk About Love* (New York: Knopf, 1981; Vintage, 1982).

Are you still with me? Are you getting the picture?
  I am, she says.
  That's good, he says.[1]

The tale is not only framed by such reminders of the storytelling environment, but the frame recurs during the story, as if to break the narrative into panels:

Tell the story, she says.   (p. 128)

And at the end:

He gets up from his chair and refills their glasses.
  That's it, he says. End of story. I admit it's not much of a story.
  I was interested, she says.
  He shrugs and carries his drink over to the window. It's dark now but still snowing.
  Things change, he says. I don't know how they do. But they do without your realizing it or wanting them to.
  Yes, that's true, only—But she does not finish what she started.   (p. 134)

The characters, unnervingly, have no names, but for them, "getting the picture" is "good." When they fail to, the results are pathetic. Connecting is good. The self-consciousness is part of the frame, is in fact what the frame is made of. And within that frame the characters are compelling, seem real, disturb us.

The Italian chemist and memoirist Primo Levi pushes still further along this line in pursuit of greater self-conscious stability. In his fiction-containing memoir *The Periodic Table*,[2] Levi shows an intense awareness of imitation's limitations, and specifically the inadequacy of language before life:

Today I know that it is a hopeless task to try to dress a man in words, make him live again on the printed page, especially a man like Sandro.   (pp. 48–49)

Sandro himself, though, embodies the paradox, since his own language, un- or pre-rhetorical, does have access to Truth:

He did not belong to that species of person who do things in order to talk about them (like me); he did not like high-sounding words, indeed words. It

---

1. Carver, "Everything Stuck to Him," in *What We Talk About*, p. 128.
2. Primo Levi, *The Periodic Table*, translated from the Italian by Raymond Rosenthal (New York: Schocken, 1984).

appeared that in speaking, as in mountain climbing, he had never received lessons; he spoke as no one speaks, saying only the core of things.   (p. 44)

Where Abish atomized language, reducing it to its arbitrary alphabetical elements and devoting chapters to each letter, Levi atomizes nature. By naming each chapter for a chemical element, the Italian writer significantly treats as his raw material not the artifice of semiology but the edifice of matter itself. And he finds in the Periodic Table, that array of scientific certainty, "the bridge, the missing link, between the world of words and the world of things" (pp. 41–42).

Epistemological skepticism, be it radical or merely passive, is ruled out by Levi:

> We are here for this—to make mistakes and to correct ourselves, to stand the blows and hand them out. We must never feel disarmed: nature is immense and complex, but it is not impermeable to the intelligence; we must circle around it, pierce and probe it, look for the opening or make it.   (p. 75)

Out of the crucible of doubt, Primo Levi's positivism makes the world safe for fiction again. In the last chapter, "Carbon," Levi tells a number of instructive and imaginary histories of individual carbon atoms:

> It is possible to demonstrate that this completely arbitrary story is nevertheless true. I could tell innumerable other stories, and they would all be true: all literally true, in the nature of the transitions, in their order and data. The number of atoms is so great that one could always be found whose story coincides with any capriciously invented story.   (p. 232)

In his concluding carbon copy of reality, Levi traces the metamorphoses of a single carbon atom down through history to a synapse in his own brain, as he is engaged in writing the final sentence of *The Periodic Table:*

> This cell belongs to a brain, and it is my brain, the brain of the *me* who is writing; and the cell in question, and within it the atom in question, is in charge of my writing, in a gigantic minuscule game which nobody has yet described. It is that which at this instant, issuing out of a labyrinthine tangle of yeses and nos, makes my hand run along a certain path on the paper, mark it with these volutes that are signs: a double snap, up and down, between two levels of energy, guides this hand of mine to impress on the paper this dot, here, this one.   (pp. 232–33)

If Modernism represented a concern for the medium, often foregrounded as translucent or opaque before the subject itself, then perhaps Postmodernism suggests a mediation that has been prepared for and enacted by self-consciousness. We are, I think, seeing a return to character, to humanism, to story, but a return *accompanied* by a heightened awareness of the medium and its contingencies. "Wised-up storytelling" might describe the result.

The self-conscious novel teaches us to read the word F*ICTI*ON itself as a model of how we read. "IT"—reality—is inside fiction, but it is preceded by "F," the fictional frame, the fundamental acknowledgment of falsity. "IT" is interrupted by "C," see, to suggest that fiction shows us reality from inside as well as from without. And that final "ION" indicates that fiction is charged, as if electrically, and requires contact with our minds in order to spark its jolt.

Literary criticism, as the title of *this* chapter suggests, has lately followed its subject into the ways of self-consciousness. Fredric Jameson, for example, invites critics to practice "metacommentary":

> In matters of art, and particularly of artistic perception, in other words, it is wrong to want to *decide,* to want to *resolve* a difficulty: what is wanted is a kind of mental procedure which suddenly shifts gears, which throws everything in an inextricable tangle one floor higher, and turns the very problem itself (the obscurity of this sentence) into its own solution (the varieties of Obscurity) by widening its frame in such a way that it now takes in its own mental processes as well as the object of those processes. In the earlier, naive state, we struggle with the object in question: in this heightened and self-conscious one, we observe our own struggles and patiently set about characterizing them.[1]

Although, in *The Self-Conscious Novel,* I have tried to remain aware of my own assumptions and to acknowledge the inadequacy of all definitions of works of the spirit, I have nonetheless eschewed such a self-conscious cast to my own discussion. For I wish to be unequivocal in my contention that fiction which artfully displays its own art remains valuable and of abiding interest. Like all art, whether or not it acknowledges its origins, the perverse and paradoxical self-conscious novel offers a variety of new insights with each fresh perspective taken upon it. And that, no doubt, is another reason why the critic's work is never done.

1. Fredric Jameson, "Metacommentary," *PMLA,* 86:1 (Jan. 1971), 9.

Bibliography

Abish, Walter. *Alphabetical Africa*. New York: New Directions, 1974.

Abrams, M. H. *A Glossary of Literary Terms*. New York: Holt, Rinehart and Winston, 1957.

Adams, Robert Martin. *Afterjoyce: Studies in Fiction After* Ulysses. New York: Oxford University Press, 1977.

——. *James Joyce: Common Sense and Beyond*. New York: Random House, 1966.

——. Review of *Fable's End: Completeness and Closure in Rhetorical Fiction*, by David H. Richter. *Modern Philology*, 76 (August 1978), 106–08.

——. "Transparency and Opaqueness." *Novel*, 7:3 (Spring 1974), 197–209.

Aldridge, A. O. "Shifting Trends in Narrative Criticism." *Comparative Literature Studies*, 6 (Sept. 1969), 225–29.

Alter, Robert. "*Ada,* or the Perils of Paradise." In *Vladimir Nabokov: A Tribute*. Ed. Peter Quennell. New York: William Morrow, 1980, pp. 103–18.

——. Review of *Ada*, by Vladimir Nabokov. *Commentary*, (August 1969), 47–50. Rpt. in *Nabokov: The Critical Heritage*. Ed. Norman Page. London: Routledge and Kegan Paul, 1982, pp. 212–20.

——. *Partial Magic: The Novel as a Self-Conscious Genre*. Berkeley: University of California Press, 1975.

Amis, Kingsley. Review of *Lolita*, by Vladimir Nabokov. *Spectator*, 6 Nov. 1959, 635–36. Rpt. in *Nabokov: The Critical Heritage*. Ed. Norman Page. London: Routledge and Kegan Paul, 1982, pp. 102–107.

——. "The Sublime and the Ridiculous: Nabokov's Black Farces." In *Vladimir Nabokov: A Tribute*. Ed. Peter Quennell. New York: William Morrow, 1980, pp. 73–87.

Anderson, Quentin. Review of *Despair*, by Vladimir Nabokov. *New Republic*, 4 June 1966, 23–28. Rpt. in *Nabokov: The Critical Heritage*. Ed. Norman Page. London: Routledge and Kegan Paul, 1982, pp. 195–202.

Appel, Alfred, Jr. "Backgrounds of *Lolita*." In *Nabokov: Criticism, Reminiscences, Translations and Tributes*. Ed. Alfred Appel, Jr. and Charles Newman. New York: Simon and Schuster, 1970, pp. 17–40.

——. "Introduction" to *The Annotated Lolita*, by Vladimir Nabokov. New York: McGraw-Hill, 1970, pp. ix–lxxvi.

——. "Nabokov: A Portrait." In *Nabokov's Fifth Arc: Nabokov and Others on his Life's Work*. Ed. J. E. Rivers and Charles Nicol. Austin: University of Texas Press, 1982, pp. 3–21.

——. "Remembering Nabokov." In *Vladimir Nabokov: A Tribute*. Ed. Peter Quennell. New York: William Morrow, 1980, pp. 11–33.

Appel, Alfred, Jr. and Charles Newman, eds. *Nabokov: Criticism, Reminiscences, Translations and Tributes*. New York: Simon and Schuster, 1970.

Aristotle. *The Poetics*. Trans. S. H. Butcher. New York: Hill and Wang, 1961.

———. *The Rhetoric*. Trans. Lane Cooper. 1932; Englewood Cliffs, N.J.: Prentice-Hall, 1960.

Auerbach, Erich. *Mimesis: The Representation of Reality in Western Literature*. Trans. Willard R. Trask. Princeton, N.J.: Princeton University Press, 1953.

Bader, Julia. *Crystal Land: Artifice in Nabokov's English Novels*. Berkeley: University of California Press, 1972.

Bakhtin, Mikhail. *Problems of Dostoevsky's Poetics*. Trans. R. W. Rotsel. Ann Arbor: Ardis, 1973.

Bambrough, Renford. "Literature and Philosophy." In *Wisdom: Twelve Essays*. Ed. Renford Bambrough. Totowa, N.J.: Rowman and Littlefield, 1974, pp. 274–92.

Banning, Charles Leslie. "William Gaddis' *JR:* The Organization of Chaos and the Chaos of Organization." *Paunch,* 42–43 (Dec. 1975), 153–65.

Barfield, Owen. *The Rediscovery of Meaning and Other Essays*. Middletown, Conn.: Wesleyan University Press, 1977.

Barnes, Hazel E. "Modes of Aesthetic Consciousness in Fiction." *Bucknell Review,* 12 (March 1964), 82–93.

"Baroque." *The Reader's Encyclopedia*. Ed. William Rose Benet. 2nd ed. New York: Thomas Y. Crowell, 1965.

Barth, John. *Chimera*. New York: Random House, 1972.

———. *End of the Road*. New York: Doubleday, 1958.

———. *The Floating Opera*. 2nd ed. New York: Doubleday, 1967.

———. *The Friday Book: Essays and Other Nonfiction*. New York: G. P. Putnam's Sons, 1984.

———. "John Barth" [an interview]. Int. Joe David Bellamy. In *The New Fiction: Interviews with Innovative American Writers*. Ed. Joe David Bellamy. Urbana: University of Illinois Press, 1974, pp. 1–18.

———. "John Barth: An Interview." *Wisconsin Studies in Contemporary Literature,* 6 (Winter-Spring 1965), 3–14.

———. *LETTERS*. New York: G. P. Putnam's Sons, 1979.

———. "The Literature of Exhaustion." *The Atlantic,* August 1967. Rpt. in *Surfiction: Fiction Now . . . and Tomorrow*. Ed. Raymond Federman. Chicago: The Swallow Press, 1975, pp. 29–34.

———. "The Literature of Replenishment: Postmodernist Fiction." *The Atlantic,* January 1980, 65–71.

———. *Lost in the Funhouse*. New York: Doubleday, 1968.

———. *Sabbatical: A Romance*. New York: G. P. Putnam's Sons, 1982.

———. *The Sot-weed Factor*. 2nd ed. New York: Doubleday, 1967.

Barth, John and John Hawkes. "A Dialogue." In *Anything Can Happen: Interviews with Contemporary American Novelists*. Ed. Tom LeClair and Larry McCaffery. Urbana: University of Illinois Press, 1983, pp. 9–19.

Barthelme, Donald. "An Interview with Donald Barthelme." Int. Larry McCaffery. In *Anything Can Happen: Interviews with Contemporary American Novelists*. Ed. Tom LeClair and Larry McCaffery. Urbana: University of Illinois Press, 1983, pp. 32–44.

———. *Come Back, Dr. Caligari*. Boston: Little, Brown and Co., 1964.

——. *The Dead Father*. New York: Farrar, Straus and Giroux, 1975.

——. "Donald Barthelme" [an interview]. Int. Jerome Klinkowitz. In *The New Fiction: Interviews with Innovative American Writers*. Ed. Joe David Bellamy. Urbana: University of Illinois Press, 1974, pp. 45–54.

——. *Sixty Stories*. New York: G. P. Putnam's Sons, 1981.

——. *Snow White*. New York: Atheneum, 1967.

Barthes, Roland. *Le degré zéro de l'écriture*. Paris: Editions du Seuil, 1953.

Batchelor, John Calvin. "The Ghost of Richard Farina." *Soho Weekly News* (New York), 28 April 1977, 19–26.

——. "Thomas Pynchon is not Thomas Pynchon." *Soho Weekly News* (New York), 22 April 1976, pp. 19–26.

Bayley, John. "Under Cover of Decadence: Nabokov as Evangelist and Guide to the Russian Classics." In *Vladimir Nabokov: A Tribute*. Ed. Peter Quennell. New York: William Morrow, 1980, pp. 42–58.

Beckett, Samuel. *En attendant Godot*. Paris: Editions de Minuit, 1952.

——. "Dante . . . Bruno. Vico . . Joyce." In *Our Exagmination Round his Factification for Incamination of Work in Progress*. Ed. Samuel Beckett et al. Paris: Shakespeare and Co, 1929, pp. 1–22.

——. *Le dépeupleur*. Paris: Editions de Minuit, 1970.

——. *Molloy*. Paris: Editions de Minuit, 1951.

——. *Murphy*. 1938; rpt. New York: Grove Press, 1957.

——. *Premier Amour*. Paris: Editions de Minuit, 1970.

——. *Three Novels: Molloy, Malone Dies, The Unnamable*. New York: Grove Press, 1958.

——. *Waiting for Godot*. New York: Grove Press, 1954.

——. *Watt*. Paris: Olympia Press, 1953; rpt. New York: Grove Press, 1959.

Bellamy, Joe David, ed. *The New Fiction: Interviews with Innovative American Writers*. Urbana: University of Illinois Press, 1974.

Bellow, Saul. *Nobel Lecture*. Stockholm: The Nobel Foundation, 1976.

——. "A World Too Much with Us." *Critical Inquiry*, 2:1 (Autumn 1975), 1–9.

Benstock, Bernard. "On William Gaddis: In Recognition of James Joyce." *Wisconsin Studies in Contemporary Literature*, 6 (Summer 1965), 177–89.

Bergerson, Howard E. *Palindromes and Anagrams*. New York: Dover Publications, 1973.

Bienstock, Beverly Gray. "Focus Pocus: Film Imagery in *Bend Sinister*." In *Nabokov's Fifth Arc: Nabokov and Others on his Life's Work*. Ed. J. E. Rivers and Charles Nicol. Austin: University of Texas Press, 1982, pp. 125–38.

Black, Joel Dana. "The Paper Empires and Empirical Fictions of William Gaddis." In *In Recognition of William Gaddis*. Ed. John Kuehl and Steven Moore. Syracuse, N.Y.: Syracuse University Press, 1984, pp. 162–73.

Boegeman, Margaret Byrd. "*Invitation to a Beheading* and the Many Shades of Kafka." In *Nabokov's Fifth Arc: Nabokov and Others on his Life's Work*. Ed. J. E. Rivers and Charles Nicol. Austin: University of Texas Press, 1982, pp. 105–21.

Bollème, Geneviève, ed. *Gustave Flaubert: Extraits de la Correspondance; ou Préface à la Vie d'écrivain*. Paris: Editions du Seuil, 1963.

Booth, Wayne C. "Did Sterne Complete *Tristram Shandy?*" *Modern Philology,* 48 (1951), 172–83.

———. "Distance and Point-of-View: An Essay in Classification." *Essays in Criticism,* 11 (1961), 60–79 Rpt. in *The Theory of the Novel.* Ed. Philip Stevick. New York: The Free Press, 1967, pp. 87–107.

———. "In Defense of Authors." *Novel,* 11 (Fall 1977), 6–19.

———. "Is There Any Knowledge that a Man *Must* Have?" In *The Knowledge Most Worth Having.* Ed. Wayne C. Booth. Chicago: University of Chicago Press, 1967, pp. 1–28.

———. "Metaphor as Rhetoric: The Problem of Evaluation." *Critical Inquiry,* 5:1 (Autumn 1978), 49–72.

———. *The Rhetoric of Fiction.* Chicago: University of Chicago Press, 1961.

———. *A Rhetoric of Irony.* Chicago: University of Chicago Press, 1974.

———. "The Self-Conscious Narrator in Comic Fiction before *Tristram Shandy.*" *PMLA,* 67 (March 1952), 163–85.

———. "Ten Literal 'Theses.' " *Critical Inquiry,* 5:1 (Autumn 1978), 175–76.

———. "*Tristram Shandy* and its Precursors: The Self-Conscious Narrator." Ph.D. diss., University of Chicago, 1950.

———, ed. *The Knowledge Most Worth Having.* Chicago: University of Chicago Press, 1967.

Borges, Jorge Luis. *Ficciones.* Trans. Alastair Reid et al. New York: Grove Press, 1962.

———. *A Personal Anthology.* Ed. Anthony Kerrigan. New York: Grove Press, 1967.

Borkin, Joseph. *The Crime and Punishment of I. G. Farben.* New York: The Free Press, 1978.

Bradbury, Malcolm. "The House that Gaddis Built." *Washington Post Book World,* 7 July 1985, pp. 1, 11.

———. *The Modern American Novel.* New York: Oxford University Press, 1983.

Brecht, Bertolt. *Brecht on Theatre.* Ed. and trans. John Willett. New York: Hill and Wang, 1964.

Brenner, Conrad. "Introduction" to *The Real Life of Sebastian Knight,* by Vladimir Nabokov. New York: New Directions, 1959, pp. vii–xvi.

Brenton, André. *Manifestes du surréalisme.* Paris: Pauvert, 1953.

Brown, Rosellen. "An Interview with Rosellen Brown." Int. Tom LeClair. In *Anything Can Happen: Interviews with Contemporary American Novelists.* Ed. Tom LeClair and Larry McCaffery. Urbana: University of Illinois Press, 1983, pp. 45–62.

Budgen, Frank. *James Joyce and the Making of* Ulysses. 1934; rpt. Bloomington: Indiana University Press, 1960.

Buffon, Georges-Louis LeClerc, comte de. "Discours [...] prononcé à l'Académie française par M. de Buffon le jour de sa réception [...] le samedi 25 août 1753." In *Œuvres complètes de Buffon.* Paris: Delangle Frères, 1874, I, 1–15.

Burgess, Anthony. "To Vladimir Nabokov on his 70th birthday." In *Nabokov: Criticism, Reminiscences, Translations and Tributes.* Ed. Alfred Appel, Jr. and Charles Newman. New York: Simon and Schuster, 1970, p. 336.

Calvino, Italo. *If on a winter's night a traveler.* New York: Harcourt, Brace, Jovanovich, 1981.

———. "Myth in the Narrative." Trans. Erica Freiberg. In *Surfiction: Fiction Now . . . and Tomorrow.* Ed. Raymond Federman. Chicago: The Swallow Press, 1975, pp. 75–81.

Carroll, Lewis [Charles Lutwidge Dodgson]. *Alice's Adventures in Wonderland.* 1865; New York: Grosset and Dunlap, 1946.

Carver, Raymond. *What We Talk About When We Talk About Love.* New York: Knopf, 1981.

Chapman, John. "Clementines." *The Catholic Encyclopedia.* Ed. Charles G. Herbermann, et al. New York: Appleton, 1908.

Clement of Rome. *The Recognitions of Clement.* Trans. Thomas Smith. In *Ante-Nicene Christian Library: Translations of the Writings of the Fathers Down to A.D. 325.* Ed. Alexander Roberts and James Donaldson. Edinburgh: T. and T. Clark, 1867, III, 135–471.

Cohen, Alan M. "Joyce's Notes on the End of 'Oxen of the Sun.' " *James Joyce Quarterly,* 4 (Spring 1967), 194–201.

Colie, Rosalie L. "Literary Paradox." *Dictionary of the History of Ideas.* Ed. Philip P. Wiener. New York: Scribner's, 1973.

Colvin, Sidney. "Fine Arts." *Encyclopedia Britannica.* 11th ed.

Cone, Edward T. "One Hundred Metronomes." *The American Scholar,* 46:4 (Autumn 1977), 443–57.

Conrad, Joseph. *Heart of Darkness.* 1902; rpt. New York: Bantam, 1960.

Conrad, Peter. *Shandyism: The Character of Romantic Irony.* London: Basil Blackwell, 1978.

Coover, Robert. "An Interview with Robert Coover." Int. Larry McCaffery. In *Anything Can Happen: Interviews with Contemporary American Novelists.* Ed. Tom LeClair and Larry McCaffery. Urbana: University of Illinois Press, 1983, pp. 63–78.

Copeland, Roger. "When Films 'Quote' Films, They Create A New Mythology." *New York Times,* 25 Sept. 1977, Sec. 2, pp. 1, 24.

Cortázar, Julio. *Hopscotch.* Trans. Gregory Rabassa. New York: Random House, 1966; Avon, 1975.

"The Counterfeiters." Rev. of *The Recognitions,* by William Gaddis. *Time,* 14 March 1955, p. 112.

Cowart, David. "Pynchon's *The Crying of Lot 49* and the Paintings of Remedios Varo." *Critique,* 18:3 (1977), 5–17.

Crane, R. S. "The Concept of Plot and the Plot of *Tom Jones.*" In *Critics and Criticism: Ancient and Modern.* Ed. R. S. Crane. Chicago: University of Chicago Press, 1952, pp. 616–48.

———. *Critical and Historical Principles of Literary History.* With a foreword by Sheldon Sacks. Chicago: University of Chicago Press, 1971.

———. *The Languages of Criticism and the Structure of Poetry.* Toronto: University of Toronto Press, 1953.

———, ed. *Critics and Criticism: Ancient and Modern.* Chicago: University of Chicago Press, 1952.

Cuddon, J. A. *A Dictionary of Literary Terms.* New York: Doubleday, 1977.

Daiches, David. *"Dubliners."* In his *The Novel and the Modern World*. Chicago: University of Chicago Press, 1960, pp. 66–82. Rpt. in *Twentieth-Century Interpretations of* Dubliners. Ed. Peter K. Garrett. Englewood Cliffs, N.J.: Prentice-Hall, 1968, pp. 27–37.

Dante Alighieri. *The Divine Comedy*. Trans. Dorothy L. Sayers. 3 vols. Harmondsworth: Penguin Books, 1974.

de Man, Paul. "The Purloined Ribbon." *Glyph*, 1 (1977), 28–49.

Dembo, L. S., ed. *Nabokov: The Man and his Work*. Madison: University of Wisconsin Press, 1967.

De Mott, Benjamin. "Six Novels in Search of a Novelist." *The Atlantic*, November 1979, 89–92.

Derrida, Jacques. *Ulysse gramophone: deux mots pour Joyce*. Paris: Editions Galilée, 1987.

Dickstein, Morris. "The Autobiography Bug." *Harper's*, June 1980, 79–82.

———. *Gates of Eden: American Culture in the Sixties*. New York: Basic Books, 1977.

Durrell, Lawrence. *Clea*. New York: E. P. Dutton and Co., 1960.

Edwards, Thomas R. "A Novel of Correspondences." *The New York Times Book Review*, 30 Sept. 1979, pp. 1, 32–33.

Elias, Julias A. "Art and Play." *Dictionary of the History of Ideas*. Ed. Philip P. Wiener. New York: Scribner's, 1973.

Elkin, Stanley. "An Interview with Stanley Elkin." Int. Tom LeClair. In *Anything Can Happen: Interviews with Contemporary American Novelists*. Ed. Tom LeClair and Larry McCaffery. Urbana: University of Illinois Press, 1983, pp. 106–25.

Ellmann, Richard. *The Consciousness of Joyce*. New York: Oxford University Press, 1977.

———. "The Critic as Artist as Wilde." In *The Artist as Critic: Critical Writings of Oscar Wilde*. Ed. Richard Ellmann. New York: Random House, 1969, pp. ix–xxviii.

———. *Golden Codgers: Biographical Speculations*. New York: Oxford University Press, 1973.

———. "Introduction" to *My Brother's Keeper*, by Stanislaus Joyce. New York: The Viking Press, 1958; New York: McGraw-Hill, 1964, pp. i–xxi.

———. *James Joyce*. New York: Oxford University Press, 1959.

———. "Preface" to "The Corrected Text" of *Ulysses*, by James Joyce. New York: Random House, 1986.

———. *Ulysses on the Liffey*. New York: Oxford University Press, 1972.

———, ed. *The Artist as Critic: Critical Writings of Oscar Wilde*. New York: Random House, 1969.

Esslin, Martin. *The Theatre of the Absurd*. 2nd ed. New York: Doubleday, 1969.

Fahy, Joseph. "Thomas Pynchon's *V.* and Mythology." *Critique*, 18:3 (1977), 5–17.

Federman, Raymond. "An Interview with Raymond Federman." Int. Larry McCaffery. In *Anything Can Happen: Interviews with Contemporary American Novelists*. Ed. Tom LeClair and Larry McCaffery. Urbana: University of Illinois Press, 1983, pp. 126–51

————. "Surfiction—Four Propositions in Form of an Introduction." In *Surfiction: Fiction Now . . . and Tomorrow.* Ed. Raymond Federman. Chicago: The Swallow Press, 1975, pp. 5–15.

————. "Voicelessness." *Chicago Review,* 28:4 (Spring 1977), 109–14.

————, ed. *Surfiction: Fiction Now . . . and Tomorrow.* Chicago: The Swallow Press, 1975.

Field, Andrew. "The Artist as Failure in Nabokov's Early Prose." In *Nabokov: The Man and his Work.* Ed. L. S. Dembo. Madison: University of Wisconsin Press, 1967, pp. 57–65.

————. *Nabokov: His Life in Art.* Boston: Little, Brown and Co., 1967.

————. *Nabokov: His Life in Part.* New York: The Viking Press, 1977.

Flaubert, Gustave. *Correspondance 1850–1859.* In his *Oeuvres complètes.* Paris: Club de l'Honnête Homme, 1974, t. 13.

"Form." *Encyclopedia Britannica.* 11th ed.

Fowler, Douglas. *A Reader's Guide to* Gravity's Rainbow. Ann Arbor: Ardis, 1980.

Frank, Joseph. "The Dehumanization of Art." In his *The Widening Gyre: Crisis and Mastery in Modern Literature.* New Brunswick, N.J.: Rutgers University Press, 1963, pp. 163–78.

————. "Spatial Form: An Answer to Critics." *Critical Inquiry,* 4:2 (Winter 1977), 231–52.

————. "Spatial Form in Modern Literature" (1945). In his *The Widening Gyre: Crisis and Mastery in Modern Literature.* New Brunswick, N.J.: Rutgers University Press, 1963, pp. 3–62.

Frazer, Sir James George. *The Golden Bough: A Study in Magic and Religion.* Abridged ed. New York: Macmillan, 1922.

Friedman, Alan J. and Manfred Puetz. "Science as Metaphor: Thomas Pynchon and *Gravity's Rainbow.*" *Contemporary Literature,* 15:3 (Summer 1974), 345–59.

Friedman, Norman. "Point of View in Fiction: The Development of a Critical Concept." *PMLA,* 70 (1955). Rpt. in *The Theory of the Novel.* Ed. Philip Stevick. New York: The Free Press, 1967, pp. 108–37.

Fromberg, Susan. "Folding the Patterned Carpet: Form and Theme in the Novels of Vladimir Nabokov." Ph.D. diss. University of Chicago, 1966.

Frosch, Thomas R. "Parody and Authenticity in *Lolita.*" In *Nabokov's Fifth Arc: Nabokov and Others on his Life's Work.* Ed. J. E. Rivers and Charles Nicol. Austin: University of Texas Press, 1982, pp. 171–87.

Frye, Northrop. *Anatomy of Criticism: Four Essays.* Princeton: Princeton University Press, 1957; New York: Atheneum, 1967.

————. *The Educated Imagination.* Bloomington: Indiana University Press, 1964.

Fussell, Paul. "The Brigadier Remembers." In his *The Great War and Modern Memory.* New York: Oxford University Press, 1975, pp. 328–34. Rpt. in *Pynchon: A Collection of Critical Essays.* Ed. Edward Mendelson. Englewood Cliffs, N.J.: Prentice-Hall, 1978, pp. 213–19.

Gaddis, William. *Carpenter's Gothic.* New York: Viking Penguin, 1985.

————. *JR.* New York: Knopf, 1975.

————. *The Recognitions.* New York: Harcourt, Brace, 1955.

————. "Stop Player. Joke No. 4." *The Atlantic,* 188 (July 1951), 92–93.

Gardner, John. *On Moral Fiction.* New York: Basic Books, 1978.

Garrett, Peter K., ed. *Twentieth-Century Interpretations of* Dubliners. Englewood Cliffs, N.J.: Prentice-Hall, 1968.

Gass, William H. "A Conversation with William Gass." Int. Thomas LeClair. *Chicago Review,* 30:2 (Autumn 1978). Rpt. in *Anything Can Happen: Interviews with Contemporary American Novelists.* Ed. Tom LeClair and Larry McCaffery. Urbana: University of Illinois Press, 1983, pp. 152–75.

————. *Fiction and the Figures of Life.* New York: Knopf, 1970.

————. "William H. Gass" [an interview]. Int. Carole Spearim McCauley. In *The New Fiction: Interviews with Innovative American Writers.* Ed. Joe David Bellamy. Urbana: University of Illinois Press, 1974, pp. 32–44.

————. "Upright Among Staring Fish." In his *The World Within the Word.* New York: Knopf, 1978, pp. 203–07.

Gass, William H. and John Gardner. "A Debate." In *Anything Can Happen: Interviews with Contemporary American Novelists.* Ed. Tom LeClair and Larry McCaffery. Urbana: University of Illinois Press, 1983, pp. 20–31.

Ghiselin, Brewster. "The Unity of Joyce's *Dubliners.*" *Accent,* 16 (Spring 1956), 75–88; 16 (Summer 1956), 196–213. Rpt. in *Twentieth-Century Interpretations of Dubliners.* Ed. Peter K. Garrett. Englewood Cliffs, N.J.: Prentice-Hall, 1968, pp. 57–85.

Gide, André. *Les Faux-monnayeurs.* Paris: Gallimard, 1925.

————. *Journal des Faux-monnayeurs.* Paris: Eos, 1926. Rpt. in *Œuvres complètes d'André Gide.* Vol. 3. Paris: N.R.F., 1937, 1–82.

Gifford, Don, with Robert J. Seidman. *Notes for Joyce: An Annotation of James Joyce's* Ulysses. New York: E. P. Dutton and Co., 1974.

Gilbert, Stuart. *James Joyce's* Ulysses. 1931; New York: Random House, 1955.

Glines, David. "Four Prose Tone Poems." *Chicago Review,* 28:2 (Fall 1976), 19–23.

Gold, Herbert. "Vladimir Nabokov, 1899–1977." *New York Times Book Review,* 31 July 1977, p. 1 ff.

Goldberg, S. L. *The Classical Temper.* London: Chatto and Windus, 1961.

————. "The Development of the Art: *Chamber Music* to *Dubliners.*" In his *James Joyce.* New York: Barnes and Noble, 1962, pp. 36–46. Rpt. in *Twentieth-Century Interpretations of* Dubliners. Ed. Peter K. Garrett. Englewood Cliffs, N.J.: Prentice-Hall, 1968, pp. 86–92.

Gombrich, E. H. "Meditations on a Hobby Horse or the Roots of Artistic Form." In *Aspects of Form.* Ed. Lancelot Law Whyte. London: Lund Humphries, 1951. Rpt. in *Aesthetics Today.* Ed. Morris Philipson. New York: Meridian Books, 1961, pp. 114–28.

Gosse, Edmund. "Euphuism." *Encyclopedia Britannica.* 11th ed.

Grady, Jack. "Suspended Animation." *Chicago Review,* 28:2 (Fall 1976), 24–28.

Graff, Gerald. "Fear and Trembling at Yale." *The American Scholar,* 46:4 (Autumn 1977), 467–78.

————. *Literature Against Itself: Literary Ideas in Modern Society.* Chicago: University of Chicago Press, 1979.

Graham, John. "*Ut Pictura Poesis.*" *Dictionary of the History of Ideas.* Ed. Philip P. Wiener. New York: Scribner's, 1973.

Greenberg, Alvin. "The Novel of Disintegration: Paradoxical Impossibility in Contemporary Fiction." *Wisconsin Studies in Contemporary Literature,* 7:1 (Winter–Spring 1966), 103–24.

"Grim Masquerade." Review of *The Recognitions,* by William Gaddis. *Newsweek,* 14 March 1955, 106–07.

Hanley, Miles L., ed. *Word-Index to James Joyce's* Ulysses. Madison: University of Wisconsin Press, 1937.

Hausdorff, Donald. "Thomas Pynchon's Multiple Absurdities." *Wisconsin Studies in Contemporary Literature,* 7:3 (Autumn 1966), 258–69.

Hawkes, John. "John Hawkes" [an interview]. Int. Robert Scholes. In *The New Fiction: Interviews with Innovative American Writers.* Ed. Joe David Bellamy. Urbana: University of Illinois Press, 1974, pp. 97–112.

Heidegger, Martin. "The Origin of the Work of Art." In his *Poetry, Language, Thought.* Trans. Albert Hofstadter. New York: Harper and Row, 1971, pp. 15–87.

Heller, Amanda. Review of *JR,* by William Gaddis. The *Atlantic,* Nov. 1975, 118.

Hendin, Josephine. "Experimental Fiction." In *Harvard Guide to Contemporary American Writing.* Ed. Daniel Hoffman. Cambridge, MA: The Belknap Press, 1979, pp. 240–86.

Henkle, Roger B. "Pynchon's Tapestries on the Western Wall." *Modern Fiction Studies,* 17:2 (Summer 1971), 207–20.

Herring, Phillip F., ed. *Joyce's* Ulysses *Notesheets in the British Museum.* Charlottesville: University Press of Virginia, 1972.

Hicks, Granville. "Phonies Everywhere." Rev. of *The Recognitions,* by William Gaddis. *New York Times Book Review,* 13 March 1955, p. 6.

Hoffman, Daniel, ed. *Harvard Guide to Contemporary American Writing.* Cambridge, MA: The Belknap Press, 1979.

Huizinga, J. *Homo Ludens: A Study of the Play-Element in Culture.* Boston: Beacon Press, 1955.

Hunt, John W. "Comic Escape and Anti-Vision: The Novels of Joseph Heller and Thomas Pynchon." In *Adversity and Grace: Studies in Recent American Literature.* Ed. Nathan A. Scott, Jr. Chicago: University of Chicago Press, 1968, pp. 87–112.

Hutcheon, Linda. *Narcissistic Narrative: The Metafictional Paradox.* Waterloo, Ontario: Wilfred Laurier University Press, 1980; rpt. New York: Methuen, 1984.

Huysmans, Joris-Karl. *A Rebours.* 1884; Paris: U.G.E., 1975.

Irving, John. *The World According to Garp.* New York: E. P. Dutton, 1978.

James, William. *Pragmatism: A New Name for Some Old Ways of Thinking.* New York: Longmans, Green, 1907; New York: Pocket Books, 1963.

Jameson, Fredric. "Metacommentary." *PMLA,* 86:1 (Jan. 1971), 9–17.

Janic, Allan, and Stephen Toulmin. *Wittgenstein's Vienna.* New York: Simon and Schuster, 1973.

Jenkins, Iredell. "Art for Art's Sake." *Dictionary of the History of Ideas.* Ed. Philip P. Wiener. New York: Scribner's, 1973.

Josipovici, Gabriel. "A Modern Master." Rev. of *Francois Rabelais: A Study,* by Donald M. Frame. *New York Review of Books,* 24:6 (13 Oct. 1977), 34–37.

————. *The World and the Book: A Study of Modern Fiction.* London: Macmillan, 1971.

Joyce, James. *Collected Poems.* New York: The Viking Press, 1957.

————. *The Critical Writings of James Joyce.* Ed. Ellsworth Mason and Richard Ellmann. New York: The Viking Press, 1964.

————. *Dubliners.* New York: B. W. Huebsch, 1916; New York: The Viking Press, 1961.

————. *Finnegans Wake.* New York: The Viking Press, 1939.

————. *A Portrait of the Artist as a Young Man.* New York: B. W. Huebsch, 1916; New York: The Viking Press, 1964.

————. *Selected Letters.* Ed. Richard Ellmann. New York: The Viking Press, 1975.

————. *Stephen Hero.* New York: New Directions, 1944.

————. *Ulysses.* Paris: Shakespeare and Co., 1922; New York: Random House, 1986.

Karl, Frederick R. *American Fictions 1940–1980.* New York: Harper and Row, 1983.

————. "Gaddis: A Tribune of the Fifties." In *In Recognition of William Gaddis.* Ed. John Kuehl and Steven Moore. Syracuse, N.Y.: Syracuse University Press, 1984, pp. 174–98.

Karlinsky, Simon. "Illusion, Reality and Parody in Nabokov's Plays." In *Nabokov: The Man and his Work.* Ed. L. S. Dembo. Madison: University of Wisconsin Press, 1967, pp. 183–94.

————. "Russian Transparencies." *Saturday Review of the Arts,* 1 (Jan. 1973), 44–45.

————, ed. *The Nabokov–Wilson Letters 1940–1971.* New York: Harper and Row, 1979.

Karlinsky, Simon and Alfred Appel, Jr., eds. *The Bitter Air of Exile: Russian Writers in the West 1922–1972.* Berkeley: University of California Press, 1977.

Kellman, Steven G. *The Self-Begetting Novel.* New York: Columbia University Press, 1980.

Kenner, Hugh. "The Computerized *Ulysses.*" *Harper's,* April 1980, 89–95.

————. *Dublin's Joyce.* Bloomington: Indiana University Press, 1956.

————. *A Homemade World: The American Modernist Writers.* New York: William Morrow and Co., 1975.

————. *Joyce's Voices.* Berkeley: University of California Press, 1978.

Kermode, Frank. "Decoding the Trystero." In *Approaches to Poetics.* Ed. Seymour Chatman. New York: Columbia University Press, 1973, pp. 68–74. Rpt. in *Pynchon: A Collection of Critical Essays.* Ed. Edward Mendelson. Englewood Cliffs, N.J.: Prentice-Hall, 1978, pp. 162–66.

————. *The Sense of an Ending: Studies in the Theory of Fiction.* New York: Oxford University Press, 1967.

Kern, Edith. "Beckett as *Homo Ludens.*" *Journal of Modern Literature,* 6 (Feb. 1977), 47–60.

Kern, Sharon, ed. *Movies about Movies/Chicago '77.* Film festival catalog. Chicago: Art Institute of Chicago, 1977.

Khodasevich, Vladislav. "On Sirin." Trans. Michael H. Walker. In *Nabokov: Criticism, Reminiscences, Translations and Tributes.* Ed. Alfred Appel, Jr. and Charles Newman. New York: Simon and Schuster, 1970, pp. 96–101.

Kiely, Robert. *Beyond Egotism: The Fiction of James Joyce, Virginia Woolf, and D. H. Lawrence.* Cambridge, MA: Harvard University Press, 1980.

Kierkegaard, Søren. *Either/Or.* 2 vols. Trans. David F. Swenson, Lillian Marvin Swenson, and Walter Lowrie. Ed. Howard A. Johnson. Princeton: Princeton University Press, 1944.

Klemtner, Susan Strehle. " 'For a Very Small Audience': The Fiction of William Gaddis." *Critique,* 19:3 (1978), 61–73.

Klinkowitz, Jerome. *Literary Disruptions: The Making of a Post-Contemporary American Fiction.* 2nd ed. Urbana: University of Illinois Press, 1980.

———. *The Self-Apparent Word: Fiction as Language/Language as Fiction.* Carbondale: Southern Illinois University Press, 1984.

Knight, Christopher. "Flemish Art and Wyatt's Quest for Redemption in William Gaddis' *The Recognitions.*" In *In Recognition of William Gaddis.* Ed. John Kuel and Steven Moore. Syracuse: Syracuse University Press, 1984, pp. 58–69.

Koenig, Peter William. "Recognizing Gaddis' *Recognitions.*" *Contemporary Literature,* 16 (Winter 1975), 61–72.

Kostelanetz, Richard. "New Fiction in America." In *Surfiction: Fiction Now . . . and Tomorrow.* Ed. Raymond Federman. Chicago: The Swallow Press, 1975, pp. 85–100.

Krafft, John M. " 'And How Far-Fallen': Puritan Themes in *Gravity's Rainbow.*" *Critique,* 18:3 (1977), 55–73.

Kuehl, John and Steven Moore, eds. *In Recognition of William Gaddis.* Syracuse, N.Y.: Syracuse University Press, 1984.

Langer, Susanne K. *Philosophy in a New Key: A Study in the Symbolism of Reason, Rite, and Art.* 3rd ed. Cambridge, MA: Harvard University Press, 1957.

Lasch, Christopher. *The Culture of Narcissism: American Life in an Age of Diminishing Expectations.* New York: W. W. Norton, 1979.

Leeman, Fred, Joost Elffers, and Michael Schuyt. *Anamorphoses: Games of Perception and Illusion in Art.* New York: Harry N. Abrams, 1976.

Leven, Jeremy. *Creator.* New York: Coward, McCann and Geoghegan, 1980.

Levi, Primo. *The Periodic Table.* Trans. Raymond Rosenthal. New York: Schocken, 1984.

Levin, David Michael. "The Novelhood of the Novel: The Limits of Representation and the Modernist Discovery of Presence." *Chicago Review,* 28:4 (Spring 1977), 87–108.

Levin, Harry. "Editor's Introduction" to *The Portable James Joyce.* Ed. Harry Levin. New York: The Viking Press, 1947, pp. 1–16.

———. "From *Gusle* to Tape Recorder." *Comparative Literature Studies,* 6 (Sept. 1969), 262–73.

———. "James Joyce." *Atlantic Monthly,* Dec. 1946, 125–29.

———. *Memories of the Moderns.* New York: New Directions, 1980.

Levine, George. "V-2." *Partisan Review,* 40 (1973), 517–29. Rpt. in *Pynchon: A Collection of Critical Essays.* Ed. Edward Mendelson. Englewood Cliffs, N.J.: Prentice-Hall, 1978, pp. 178–91.

Levine, George and David Leverenz. "Mindful Pleasures." In *Mindful Pleasures:*

Essays on Thomas Pynchon. Ed. George Levine and David Leverenz. Boston: Little, Brown and Co., 1976, pp. 3–11.

———, eds. *Mindful Pleasures: Essays on Thomas Pynchon*. Boston: Little, Brown and Co, 1976.

Lewis, Wyndham. *Rude Assignment: A Narrative of My Career Up-to-date*. London: Hutchinson and Co., 1950.

———. *Time and Western Man*. London: Chatto and Windus, 1927.

Litz, A. Walton. *The Art of James Joyce*. London: Oxford University Press, 1961.

———. "Literary Criticism." In *Harvard Guide to Contemporary American Writing*. Ed. Daniel Hoffman. Cambridge, MA: The Belknap Press, 1979, pp. 51–83.

Lokrantz, Jessie Thomas. *The Underside of the Weave: Some Stylistic Devices Used by Vladimir Nabokov*. Ph.D. diss. Uppsala University, 1973. *Studia Anglistica Upsaliensa* No. 11. Uppsala: Acta Universitatis Upsaliensis, 1973.

Lubin, Peter. "Kickshaws and Motley." In *Nabokov: Criticism, Reminiscences, Translations and Tributes*. Ed. Alfred Appel, Jr. and Charles Newman. New York: Simon and Schuster, 1970, pp. 187–208.

Lyly, John. *Euphues: The Anatomy of Wit* and *Euphues and his England*. London, 1579–80; London: Constable, 1904.

Madden, David. "David Madden on William Gaddis' *The Recognitions*." In *Rediscoveries: Informal Essays in Which Well-Known Novelists Rediscover Neglected Works of Fiction by One of Their Favorite Authors*. Ed. David Madden. New York: Crown, 1971, pp. 291–304.

Magalaner, Marvin, and Richard M. Kain. *Joyce: The Man, the Work, the Reputation*. New York: New York University Press, 1956; New York: Collier Books, 1962.

Marks, M. "A Lot of It Going Around: Prose Sestina #2." *The North American Review,* Summer 1975, 32–39.

———. "Index to Volume 29." *Chicago Review,* 29:4 (Spring 1978), 125–31.

Mason, Bobbie Ann. *Nabokov's Garden: A Guide to* Ada. Ann Arbor: Ardis, 1974.

Mason, Ellsworth. "The 'Oxen of the Sun.' " *The Analyst,* 10 (March 1956), 10.

Matanle, Stephen. "Love and Strife in William Gaddis' *JR*." In *In Recognition of William Gaddis*. Ed. John Kuehl and Steven Moore. Syracuse: Syracuse University Press, 1984, pp. 106–18.

Mathews, Harry. *The Sinking of the Odradek Stadium and Other Novels*. New York: Harper and Row, 1975.

Matthews, J. H. "Poetic Principles of Surrealism." *Chicago Review,* 14 (Summer–Autumn 1962), 27–45.

———. *Surrealism and the Novel*. Ann Arbor: University of Michigan Press, 1966.

McConnell, Frank D. *Four Postwar American Novelists: Bellow, Mailer, Barth, and Pynchon*. Chicago: University of Chicago Press, 1977.

McElroy, Joseph. "The N Factor." *Saturday Review of the Arts,* 1 (Jan. 1973), 34–35.

McKeon, Richard. "Literary Criticism and the Concept of Imitation in Antiquity." In *Critics and Criticism: Ancient and Modern*. Ed. R. S. Crane. Chicago: University of Chicago Press, 1952, pp. 147–75.

Meltzer, Françoise. "Preliminary Excavations of Robbe-Grillet's Phantom City." *Chicago Review,* 28:1 (Summer 1976), 41–50.

Mendelson, Edward. "Gravity's Encyclopedia." In *Mindful Pleasures: Essays on Thomas Pynchon.* Ed. George Levine and David Leverenz. Boston: Little, Brown and Co., 1976, pp. 161–95.

————. "Introduction." In *Pynchon: A Collection of Critical Essays.* Ed. Edward Mendelson. Englewood Cliffs, N.J.: Prentice-Hall, 1978, pp. 1–15.

————. "Pynchon's Gravity." *The Yale Review,* 62:4 (June 1973), 624–31.

————. "The Sacred, the Profane, and *The Crying of Lot 49.*" In *Pynchon: A Collection of Critical Essays.* Ed. Edward Mendelson. Englewood Cliffs, N.J.: Prentice-Hall, 1978, pp. 112–46.

————, ed. *Pynchon: A Collection of Critical Essays.* Englewood Cliffs, N.J.: Prentice-Hall, 1978.

Morgan, Speer. "*Gravity's Rainbow:* What's the Big Idea?" *Modern Fiction Studies,* 23:2 (Summer 1977), 199–216.

Morrison, Philip. Rev. of *Gravity's Rainbow. Scientific American,* 229 (Oct. 1973), 131. Rpt. in *Pynchon: A Collection of Critical Essays.* Ed. Edward Mendelson. Englewood Cliffs, N.J.: Prentice-Hall, 1978, pp. 191–92.

Morrissette, Bruce. "Games and Game Structures in Robbe-Grillet." *Yale French Studies,* 41 (1968), 159–67.

————. "Un Héritage d'André Gide: La Duplication intérieure." *Comparative Literature Studies,* 8 (June 1971), 125–42.

————. "Post-Modern Generative Fiction: Novel and Film." *Critical Inquiry,* 2:2 (Winter 1975), 253–62.

————. "Problèmes du roman cinématographique." *Cahiers de l'association internationale des études françaises,* 20 (Mai 1968), 275–89.

————. "Robbe-Grillet No. 1, 2, . . . , X." In *Nouveau Roman: hier, aujourd'hui.* Ed. Jean Ricardou and Françoise van Rossum-Guyon. Paris: U.G.E., 1972, II, pp. 119–33.

————. *Les Romans de Robbe-Grillet.* 2nd ed. Paris: Editions de Minuit, 1974.

Murray, Peter and Linda. *A Dictionary of Art and Artists.* Baltimore: Penguin Books, 1959.

Nabokov, Dmitri. "A Few Things That Must Be Said on Behalf of Vladimir Nabokov." In *Nabokov's Fifth Arc: Nabokov and Others on his Life's Work.* Ed. J. E. Rivers and Charles Nicol. Austin: University of Texas, 1982, pp. 35–42.

————. "On Revisiting Father's Room." In *Vladimir Nabokov: A Tribute.* Ed. Peter Quennell. New York: William Morrow and Co., 1980, pp. 126–36.

Nabokov, Vladimir. *Ada.* New York: McGraw-Hill, 1969.

————. *Bend Sinister.* New York: Henry Holt, 1947; New York: McGraw-Hill, 1974.

————. *The Defense.* Trans. Michael Scammel. New York: G. P. Putnam's Sons, 1964; rpt. New York: Capricorn, 1970.

————. *Despair.* New York: G. P. Putnam's Sons, 1966; New York: Capricorn, 1970.

————. *Details of a Sunset and Other Stories.* New York: McGraw-Hill, 1976.

————. *The Eye.* New York: Phaedra, 1965.

————. *The Gift.* New York: G. P. Putnam's Sons, 1963; rpt. New York: Capricorn, 1970.

————. *Glory.* New York: McGraw-Hill, 1971.

————. *Invitation to a Beheading*. New York: G. P. Putnam's Sons, 1957; rpt. New York: Capricorn, 1965.

————. *King, Queen, Knave*. New York: McGraw-Hill, 1968.

————. *Laughter in the Dark*. New York: New Directions, 1938; New York: Berkley Medallion, 1958.

————. *Lectures on Don Quixote*. Ed. Fredson Bowers. New York: Harcourt Brace Jovanovich, 1983.

————. *Lectures on Literature*. Ed. Fredson Bowers. New York: Harcourt Brace Jovanovich, 1980.

————. *Lectures on Russian Literature*. Ed. Fredson Bowers. New York: Harcourt Brace Jovanovich, 1981.

————. *Lolita*. Paris: The Olympia Press, 1955; rpt. New York: G. P. Putnam's Sons, 1958.

————. *Lolita: A Screenplay*. New York: McGraw-Hill, 1974.

————. *Look at the Harlequins!* New York: McGraw-Hill, 1974.

————. *Mary*. Trans. Michael Glenny. New York: McGraw-Hill, 1970.

————. *Nabokov's Dozen*. New York: Doubleday, 1958.

————. "Notes to *Ada* by Vivian Darkbloom." Ed. J. E. Rivers and William Walker. In *Nabokov's Fifth Arc: Nabokov and Others on his Life's Work*. Ed. J. E. Rivers and Charles Nicol. Austin: University of Texas, 1982, pp. 242–59.

————. *Pale Fire*. New York: G. P. Putnam's Sons, 1962.

————. *Pnin*. New York: Doubleday, 1957.

————. *Poems and Problems*. New York: McGraw-Hill, 1970.

————. "Postscript to the Russian Edition of *Lolita*." Trans. Earl D. Sampson. In *Nabokov's Fifth Arc: Nabokov and Others on his Life's Work*. Ed. J. E. Rivers and Charles Nicol. Austin: University of Texas Press, 1982, pp. 188–94.

————. *The Real Life of Sebastian Knight*. Norwalk, Conn.: New Directions, 1941.

————. *A Russian Beauty and Other Stories*. New York: McGraw-Hill, 1973.

————. *Speak, Memory: An Autobiography*. Rev. ed. New York: G. P. Putnam's Sons, 1966.

————. *Strong Opinions*. New York: McGraw-Hill, 1973.

————. *Transparent Things*. New York: McGraw-Hill, 1972.

————. *Tyrants Destroyed and Other Stories*. New York: McGraw-Hill, 1975.

Nietzsche, Friedrich. *Beyond Good and Evil: Prelude to a Philosophy of the Future*. Trans. Walter Kaufmann. New York: Random House, 1966.

Nohrnberg, James. "Pynchon's Paraclete." In *Pynchon: A Collection of Critical Essays*. Ed. Edward Mendelson. Englewood Cliffs, N.J.: Prentice-Hall, 1978, pp. 147–61.

Nolte, Fred O. *Art and Reality*. Lancaster, Pa.: The Lancaster Press, 1942.

Oates, Joyce Carol. "Further Confessions." *Chicago Review*, 28:4 (Spring 1977), 61–77.

————. "Jocoserious Joyce." *Critical Inquiry*, 2 (Summer 1976), 677–88.

————. "Joyce Carol Oates" [an interview]. Int. Joe David Bellamy. In *The New Fiction: Interviews with Innovative American Writers*. Ed. Joe David Bellamy. Urbana: University of Illinois Press, 1974, pp. 19–31.

————. "A Personal View of Nabokov." *Saturday Review of the Arts,* 1 (Jan. 1973), 36–37.

O'Brien, Flann [Brian Nolan]. *At Swim-Two-Birds.* 1939; New York: Plume, 1976.

O'Connor, Frank [Michael O'Donovan]. "Work in Progress." In his *The Lonely Voice: A Study of the Short Story.* New York: World Publishing Co., 1963, pp. 113–27. Rpt. in *Twentieth-Century Interpretations of* Dubliners. Ed. Peter K. Garrett. Englewood Cliffs, N.J.: Prentice-Hall, 1968, pp. 18–26.

Olderman, Raymond M. *Beyond the Waste Land: A Study of the American Novel in the Nineteen-Sixties.* New Haven, Conn.: Yale University Press, 1972.

Olson, Elder. "The Argument of Longinus' *On the Sublime.*" In *Critics and Criticism: Ancient and Modern.* Ed. R. S. Crane. Chicago: University of Chicago Press, 1952, pp. 232–59.

————. *On Value Judgments in the Arts and Other Essays.* Chicago: University of Chicago Press, 1976.

Ortega y Gasset, José. "The Dehumanization of Art." In his *The Dehumanization of Art and Other Essays on Art, Culture, and Literature.* Trans. Helene Weyl. Princeton, N.J.: Princeton University Press, 1948, pp. 3–56.

OULIPO. *La littérature potentielle: créations, re-créations, recréations.* Paris: Gallimard, 1973.

Ovid. *Metamorphoses.* Trans. Mary M. Innes. Harmondsworth: Penguin Books, 1955.

Ozier, Lance W. "Antipointsman/Antimexico: Some Mathematical Imagery in *Gravity's Rainbow.*" *Critique,* 16:2 (1974), 73–90.

Page, Norman. Introduction to *Nabokov: The Critical Heritage.* Ed. Norman Page. London: Routledge & Kegan Paul, 1982, pp. 1–42.

————, ed. *Nabokov: The Critical Heritage.* London: Routledge & Kegan Paul, 1982.

Pater, Walter. *Appreciations.* London: Macmillan, 1910.

————. *Marius the Epicurean.* 1885; rpt. London: J. M. Dent, 1934.

————. *The Renaissance: Studies in Art and Poetry.* 3rd ed. London: Macmillan, 1888.

————. *Selected Writings of Walter Pater.* Ed. Harold Bloom. New York: Signet, 1974.

Pearce, Richard. "Enter the Frame." In *Surfiction: Fiction Now . . . and Tomorrow.* Ed. Raymond Federman. Chicago: The Swallow Press, 1975, pp. 47–57.

Philipson, Morris, ed. *Aesthetics Today.* New York: Meridian Books, 1961.

Plater, William M. *The Grim Phoenix: Reconstructing Thomas Pynchon.* Bloomington: Indiana University Press, 1978.

Plato. *The Republic.* Trans. Francis MacDonald Cornford. New York: Oxford University Press, 1945.

Poirier, Richard. "The Importance of Thomas Pynchon." *Twentieth Century Literature,* 21:2 (May 1975), 151–62. Rpt. in *Mindful Pleasures: Essays on Thomas Pynchon.* Ed. George Levine and David Leverenz. Boston: Little, Brown and Co., 1976, pp. 15–29.

————. "Rocket Power." *Saturday Review of the Arts,* 1 (3 March 1973), 59–64. Rpt. in *Pynchon: A Collection of Critical Essays.* Ed. Edward Mendelson. Englewood Cliffs, N.J.: Prentice-Hall, 1978, pp. 167–78.

Proffer, Carl R. "*Ada* as Wonderland: A Glossary of Allusions to Russian Literature." In *A Book of Things about Vladimir Nabokov.* Ed. Carl R. Proffer. Ann Arbor: Ardis, 1974, pp. 249–79.

———. *Keys to Lolita.* Bloomington: Indiana University Press, 1968.

———, ed. *A Book of Things about Vladimir Nabokov.* Ann Arbor: Ardis, 1974.

Proust, Marcel. *A la Recherche du temps perdu.* 3 vols. Paris: Bibliothèque de la Pléiade, 1954.

Pynchon, Thomas. *The Crying of Lot 49.* Philadelphia: J. B. Lippincott, 1966; rpt. New York: Bantam, 1967.

———. *Gravity's Rainbow.* New York: The Viking Press, 1973.

———. "Mortality and Mercy in Vienna." *Epoch,* 9:4 (Spring 1959), 195–213.

———. *Slow Learner: Early Stories.* Boston: Little, Brown and Co, 1984.

———. *V.* Philadelphia: J. B. Lippincott, 1963.

"Pynchon, Thomas." *Contemporary Authors.* Detroit: Gale Research Co., 1968.

Quennell, Peter. "Introduction" to *Vladimir Nabokov: Five Novels.* London: Collins, 1979, pp. i–v.

———, ed. *Vladimir Nabokov: A Tribute.* New York: William Morrow, 1980.

Rabinowitz, Peter J. "The Comedy of Terrors: Vladimir Nabokov as a Philosophical Novelist." Ph.D. diss. University of Chicago, 1972.

Rabkin, Eric S. "Spatial Form and Plot." *Critical Inquiry,* 4:2 (Winter 1977), 253–70.

Rambeau, James M. "Nabokov's Critical Strategy." In *Nabokov's Fifth Arc: Nabokov and Others on his Life's Work.* Ed. J. E. Rivers and Charles Nicol. Austin: University of Texas Press, 1982, pp. 22–34.

Rev. of *The Recognitions,* by William Gaddis. *The New Yorker,* 9 April 1955, 129.

Ricardou, Jean. *Le Nouveau Roman.* Paris: Editions du Seuil, 1973.

———. "Nouveau Roman, Tel Quel." Trans. Erica Freiberg. In *Surfiction: Fiction Now . . . and Tomorrow.* Ed. Raymond Federman. Chicago: The Swallow Press, 1975, pp. 101–33.

———. "Terrorisme, théorie." In *Robbe-Grillet: Analyse, Théorie.* Vol. 1. Ed. Jean Ricardou. Paris: U.G.E., 1976, 10–33.

———, ed. *Robbe-Grillet: Analyse, Théorie.* 2 vols. Paris: U.G.E., 1976.

Ricardou, Jean and Françoise van Rossum-Guyon, eds. *Nouveau Roman: hier, aujourd'hui.* 2 vols. Paris: U.G.E., 1972.

Richter, David H. *Fable's End: Completeness and Closure in Rhetorical Fiction.* Chicago: University of Chicago Press, 1974.

Rivers, J. E. and Charles Nicol, eds. *Nabokov's Fifth Arc: Nabokov and Others on his Life's Work.* Austin: University of Texas Press, 1982.

Robbe-Grillet, Alain. *L'année dernière à Marienbad.* Paris: Editions de Minuit, 1961.

———. *Dans le labyrinthe.* Paris: Editions de Minuit, 1959.

———. *Les gommes.* Paris: Editions de Minuit, 1953.

———. *La jalousie.* Paris: Editions de Minuit, 1957.

———. *La maison de rendez-vous.* Paris: Editions de Minuit, 1965.

———. *Pour un nouveau roman.* Paris: Editions de Minuit, 1963.

———. "Sur le choix des générateurs." In *Nouveau Roman: hier, aujourd'hui.* Ed. Jean Ricardou and Françoise van Rossum-Guyon. Paris: U.G.E., 1972, II, 157–62.

———. *Le voyeur.* Paris: Editions de Minuit, 1955.

Rosenbaum, Jonathan. "A Reply." *The New Review,* 3 (July 1976), 64. Rpt. in *Pynchon: A Collection of Critical Essays.* Ed. Edward Mendelson. Englewood Cliffs, N.J.: Prentice-Hall, 1978, pp. 67–68.

Roth, Philip. *The Anatomy Lesson.* New York: Farrar, Straus and Giroux, 1983.

———. *The Counterlife.* New York: Farrar, Straus and Giroux, 1987.

———. *The Ghost Writer.* New York: Farrar, Straus and Giroux, 1979.

———. *Reading Myself and Others.* New York: Farrar, Straus and Giroux, 1975.

———. "Writing American Fiction." *Commentary,* 31 (March 1961), 223–33.

———. *Zuckerman Bound.* New York: Farrar, Straus and Giroux, 1985.

———. *Zuckerman Unbound.* New York: Farrar, Straus and Giroux, 1981.

Roth, Phyllis A. "Toward the Man Behind the Mystification." In *Nabokov's Fifth Arc: Nabokov and Others on his Life's Work.* Ed. J. E. Rivers and Charles Nicol. Austin: University of Texas, 1982, pp. 43–62.

Roussel, Raymond. *Comment j'ai écrit certains de mes livres.* Paris: Pauvert, 1963.

Rubin, Louis D., Jr. *The Teller in the Tale.* Seattle: University of Washington Press, 1967.

Russell, Charles. "The Vault of Language: Self-Reflective Artifice in Contemporary American Fiction." *Modern Fiction Studies,* 20:3 (Autumn 1974), 349–59.

Sacks, Sheldon. *Fiction and the Shape of Belief.* Berkeley: University of California Press, 1964.

———. "Foreword" to *Critical and Historical Principles of Literary History,* by R. S. Crane. Chicago: University of Chicago Press, 1971, pp. v–xvii.

———. "Golden Birds and Dyings Generations." *Comparative Literature Studies,* 6:3 (Sept. 1969), 274–91.

———. "Novelists as Storytellers." *The Journal of Modern Philology,* 73:4, Pt. 2 (May 1976), S97–S109.

———. "The Psychological Implications of Generic Distinctions." *Genre,* 1 (April 1968), 106–115.

Salehar, Anna Maria. "Nabokov's *Gift:* An Apprenticeship in Creativity." In *A Book of Things about Vladimir Nabokov.* Ed. Carl R. Proffer. Ann Arbor: Ardis, 1974, pp. 70–83.

Salemi, Joseph S. "To Soar in Atonement: Art as Expiation in Gaddis's *The Recognitions.*" *Novel,* 10 (Winter 1977), 127–36.

Sanders, Scott. "Pynchon's Paranoid History." *Twentieth Century Literature,* 21:2 (May 1975), 177–92. Rpt. in *Mindful Pleasures: Essays on Thomas Pynchon.* Ed. George Levine and David Leverenz. Boston: Little, Brown and Co., 1976, pp. 139–59.

Sartre, Jean-Paul. "Préface" (1947) to *Portrait d'un inconnu,* by Nathalie Sarraute. Paris: Gallimard, 1956, pp. 5–14.

———. "Qu'est-ce que la littérature?" In his *Situations.* Paris: Gallimard, 1948, II, 55–330.

———. Review of *La Méprise* [*Despair*], by Vladimir Nabokov. *Europe,* 15 June 1939, 240–49. Rpt. and trans. in *Nabokov: The Critical Heritage.* Ed. Norman Page. London: Routledge & Kegan Paul, 1982, pp. 65–66.

Schaefer, William D. "Editor's Column." *PMLA,* 92:5 (Oct. 1977), 867–68.

Schapiro, Meyer. "Style." In *Anthropology Today.* Ed. A. L. Kroeber. Chicago:

University of Chicago Press, 1953. Rpt. in *Aesthetics Today*. Ed. Morris Philipson. New York: Meridian Books, 1961, pp. 81–113.

Schaub, Thomas H. *Pynchon: The Voice of Ambiguity*. Urbana: University of Illinois Press, 1981.

Schiffer, James. "What Is In Is Out Is In." *Chicago Review*, 28:3 (Winter 1977), 125–43.

Schmitz, Neil. "Robert Coover and the Hazards of Metafiction." *Novel*, 7:3 (Spring 1974), 210–19.

Scholes, Robert. *Fabulation and Metafiction*. Urbana: University of Illinois Press, 1979.

———. "Metafiction." *The Iowa Review*, 1:4 (Fall 1970), 100–15.

Scholes, Robert and Robert Kellogg. "The Problem of Reality: Illustration and Representation." In their *The Nature of Narrative*. New York: Oxford University Press, 1966. Rpt. in *The Theory of the Novel*. Ed. Philip Stevick. New York: The Free Press, 1967, pp. 371–84.

Schorer, Mark. "Technique as Discovery." *Hudson Review*, 1 (1948), 67–87. Rpt. in *The Theory of the Novel*. Ed. Philip Stevick. New York: The Free Press, 1967, pp. 65–84.

Schwarzbach, F. S. "A Matter of Gravity." *The New Review*, 3 (June 1976), 39–42. Rpt. in *Pynchon: A Collection of Critical Essays*. Ed. Edward Mendelson. Englewood Cliffs, N.J.: Prentice-Hall, 1978, pp. 56–67.

Seelye, John. "Dryad in a Dead Oak Tree: The Incognito in *The Recognitions*." In *In Recognition of William Gaddis*. Ed. John Kuehl and Steven Moore. Syracuse: Syracuse University Press, 1984, pp. 70–80.

Seidel, Michael. "The Satiric Plots of *Gravity's Rainbow*." In *Pynchon: A Collection of Critical Essays*. Ed. Edward Mendelson. Englewood Cliffs, N.J.: Prentice-Hall, 1978, pp. 193–212.

Shakespeare, William. *Hamlet, Prince of Denmark*. In *The Complete Works of William Shakespeare*. Ed. Peter Alexander. London: Collins, 1951, pp. 1028–72.

Shroder, Maurice Z. "The Novel as a Genre." *The Massachusetts Review*, 4 (1963), 291–308. Rpt. in *The Theory of the Novel*. Ed. Philip Stevick. New York: The Free Press, 1967, pp. 13–29.

Siegel, Mark Richard. "Creative Paranoia: Understanding the System of *Gravity's Rainbow*." *Critique*, 18:3 (1977), 39–54.

———. *Pynchon: Creative Paranoia in* Gravity's Rainbow. Port Washington, N.Y.: Kennikat Press, 1978.

Simmon, Scott. "A Character Index: *Gravity's Rainbow*." *Critique*, 16:2 (1974), 68–72.

———. "*Gravity's Rainbow* Described." *Critique*, 16:2 (1974), 54–67.

Sklar, Robert. "An Anarchist Miracle: The Novels of Thomas Pynchon." *The Nation*, 205 (25 Sept. 1967), 277–80. Rpt. in *Pynchon: A Collection of Critical Essays*. Ed. Edward Mendelson. Englewood Cliffs, N.J.: Prentice-Hall, 1978, pp. 87–96.

Slade, Joseph. " 'Entropy' and Other Calamities." In *Pynchon: A Collection of Critical Essays*. Ed. Edward Mendelson. Englewood Cliffs, N.J.: Prentice-Hall, 1978, pp. 69–86.

————. "Escaping Rationalization: Options for the Self in *Gravity's Rainbow.*" *Critique,* 18:3 (1977), 27–37.

————. *Thomas Pynchon.* Writers for the Seventies. New York: Warner Paperback Library, 1974.

Smith, Paul Jordan. *A Key to the* Ulysses *of James Joyce.* 1927; rpt. San Francisco: City Lights, 1970.

Sokolov, R. A. Review of *Ada,* by Vladimir Nabokov. *Newsweek,* 5 May 1969, p. 110.

Sollers, Philippe. "The Novel and the Experience of Limits." Trans. Christine Grahl. In *Surfiction: Fiction Now . . . and Tomorrow.* Ed. Raymond Federman. Chicago: The Swallow Press, 1975, pp. 59–74.

Sontag, Susan. "Against Interpretation." In her *Against Interpretation.* New York: Farrar, Straus and Giroux, 1966, pp. 1–14.

————. "Preface" to *Writing Degree Zero and Elements of Semiology,* by Roland Barthes. Boston: Beacon Press, 1967, pp. xi–xxv.

————. "Susan Sontag" [an interview]. Int. Joe David Bellamy. In *The New Fiction: Interviews with Innovative American Writers.* Ed. Joe David Bellamy. Urbana: University of Illinois Press, 1974, pp. 113–29.

Spencer, Sharon. *Space, Time and Structure in the Modern Novel.* New York: New York University Press, 1971.

Springer, Mary Doyle. *Forms of the Modern Novella.* Chicago: University of Chicago Press, 1975.

Stark, John. "William Gaddis: Just Recognition." *The Hollins Critic,* 14 (April 1977), 1–12.

Stathis, James J. "William Gaddis: *The Recognitions.*" *Critique,* 5 (Winter 1962–63), 91–94.

Stegner, Page. *Escape into Aesthetics: The Art of Vladimir Nabokov.* New York: The Dial Press, 1966.

Stein, Gertrude. *Narration.* With an introduction by Thornton Wilder. Chicago: University of Chicago Press, 1935.

Steiner, George. "Dead Letters." *The New Yorker,* 31 Dec. 1979, 60–62.

Stern, Richard. "Events, Happenings, Credibility, Fictions." In his *The Books in Fred Hampton's Apartment.* New York: E. P. Dutton and Co., 1973, pp. 92–101.

————. "Inside Narcissus." *The Yale Review,* 67 (March 1978), 404–17.

————. "An Interview with Richard Stern." Int. Larry Rima. *Chicago Review,* 28:3 (Winter 1977), 145–48.

————. "Proust and Joyce Underway: *Jean Santeuil* and *Stephen Hero.*" *Kenyon Review,* 18 (1956), 486–96.

Sterne, Laurence. *The Life and Opinions of Tristram Shandy, Gentleman.* London, 1759–67; rpt. New York: Modern Library, n.d.

Stevick, Philip. *The Chapter in Fiction: Theories of Narrative Division.* Syracuse: Syracuse University Press, 1970.

————. "Four Mannered Pieces." *Chicago Review,* 28:2 (Fall 1976), 80–83.

————, ed. *Anti-Story: An Anthology of Experimental Fiction.* New York: The Free Press, 1971.

————, ed. *The Theory of the Novel.* New York: The Free Press, 1967.

Stonehill, Brian. "Douglas Woolf's Ideal Fictions." *The Review of Contemporary Fiction,* 2:1 (Spring 1982), 96–100.

———. "Nabokov." *Contemporary Literary Criticism,* 11, 392–93.

———. "Nabokov: His Life *is* Art." *Chicago Review,* 29:2 (Autumn 1977), 72–82.

———. "On Harry Mathews." *Chicago Review,* 33:2 (1982), 107–111.

———. "Recent Nabokov Criticism." *Contemporary Literature,* 25:2 (Summer 1984), 235–41.

———. Review of *Quinx; or, The Ripper's Tale,* by Lawrence Durrell. *The Los Angeles Times Book Review,* 27 Oct. 1985, 3.

———. "Truth in fiction: to moralize or intellectualize?" *The Los Angeles Times Book Review,* 17 April 1983, pp. 1 ff.

———. "Vladimir Nabokov." *Contemporary Literature,* 24:1 (Spring 1983), 109–13.

———. "Vladimir Nabokov's *Lectures on Literature.*" *Chicago Review,* 32:2 (Autumn 1980), 115–16.

Strehle, Susan. "Disclosing Time: William Gaddis' *JR.*" In *In Recognition of William Gaddis.* Ed. John Kuehl and Steven Moore. Syracuse: Syracuse University Press, 1984, pp. 119–34.

Sukenick, Ronald. "The New Tradition in Fiction." In *Surfiction: Fiction Now . . . and Tomorrow.* Ed. Raymond Federman. Chicago: The Swallow Press, 1975, pp. 35–45.

Sully, James. "Aesthetics." *Encyclopedia Britannica.* 11th ed.

Sultan, Stanley. *The Argument of* Ulysses. [n. 1.]: Ohio State University Press, 1964.

Sypher, Wylie. *Rococo to Cubism in Art and Literature.* New York: Random House, 1960.

Tanner, Tony. *City of Words: American Fiction 1950–1970.* London: Jonathan Cape, 1971.

———. "Games American Writers Play: Ceremony, Complicity, Contestation and Carnival." *Salmagundi,* 35 (Fall 1976), 110–40.

———. "*V.* and V-2." *London Magazine,* 13 (February–March 1974), 80–88. Rpt. in *Pynchon: A Collection of Critical Essays.* Ed. Edward Mendelson. Englewood Cliffs, N.J.: Prentice-Hall, 1978, pp. 47–55.

Tave, Stuart M. *The Amiable Humorist.* Chicago: University of Chicago Press, 1960.

Tindall, W. Y. *James Joyce: His Way of Interpreting the Modern World.* New York: Scribner's, 1950.

Towers, Robert. "Return to Sender." *The New York Review of Books,* 20 Dec. 1979, 30–33.

Trachtenberg, Alan. "Intellectual Background." In *Harvard Guide to Contemporary American Writing.* Ed. Daniel Hoffman. Cambridge, MA: The Belknap Press, 1979, pp. 1–50.

Turk, H. C. "From *Inertia.*" *Chicago Review,* 28:2 (Fall 1976), 42–56.

Updike, John. *Bech: A Book.* New York: Knopf, 1970.

———. *Hugging the Shore: Essays and Criticism.* New York: Knopf, 1983.

———. Introduction to *Lectures on Literature,* by Vladimir Nabokov. Ed. Fredson Bowers. New York: Harcourt Brace Jovanovich, 1980, pp. xvii–xxvii.

————. Review of *The Defense*, by Vladimir Nabokov. *New Republic*, 26 Sept. 1964, 15–18. Rpt. in *Nabokov: The Critical Heritage*. Ed. Norman Page. London: Routledge & Kegan Paul, 1982, pp. 154–58.

Urmson, J. O. "Fiction." *American Philosophical Quarterly*, 12 (April 1976), 153–57.

Veeder, William. "Technique as Recovery: *Lolita* and *Mother Night*." In *Vonnegut in America*. Ed. Jerome Klinkowitz and Donald L. Lawler. New York: Delacorte Press, 1977, pp. 97–132.

Vesterman, William. "Pynchon's Poetry." *Twentieth Century Literature*, 21:2 (May 1975), 211–20. Rpt. in *Mindful Pleasures: Essays on Thomas Pynchon*. Ed. George Levine and David Leverenz. Boston: Little, Brown and Co., 1976, pp. 101–12.

Vidal, Gore. *Matters of Fact and Fiction: Essays 1973–1976*. New York: Random House, 1977.

Walkarput, Walter [Brian Stonehill]. "Nabokov: His Life *is* Art." *Chicago Review*, 29:2 (Autumn 1977), 72–82.

Waugh, Patricia. *Metafiction: The Theory and Practice of Self-Conscious Fiction*. New York: Methuen, 1984.

Weitz, Morris. "Truth in Literature." *Revue Internationale de Philosophie*, 9 (1955), 116–29.

Weston, Edward. *Edward Weston: Fifty Years*. Millerton, N.Y.: Aperture, 1973.

White, Edmund. "The Esthetics of Bliss." *Saturday Review of the Arts*, 1 (Jan. 1973), 33–34.

Wilde, Alan. *Horizons of Assent: Modernism, Postmodernism, and the Ironic Imagination*. Baltimore: The Johns Hopkins University Press, 1981. Paperback reprint Philadelphia: University of Pennsylvania Press, 1987.

Wilde, Oscar. *Intentions*. London, 1891; rpt. in *The Artist as Critic: Critical Writings of Oscar Wilde*. Ed. Richard Ellmann. New York: Random House, 1969, pp. 290–432.

————. "Phrases and Philosophies for the Use of the Young." *Chameleon*, 1:1 (Dec. 1894), 1–3. Rpt. in *The Artist as Critic: Critical Writings of Oscar Wilde*. Ed. Richard Ellmann. New York: Random House, 1969, pp. 433–34.

Wilson, Edmund. *Axel's Castle: A Study in the Imaginative Literature of 1870–1930*. New York: Scribner's, 1931.

Wittgenstein, Ludwig. *Philosophical Investigations*. 3rd ed. Trans. G.E.M. Anscombe. New York: Macmillan, 1968.

Wolfley, Lawrence C. "Repression's Rainbow: The Presence of Norman O. Brown in Pynchon's Big Novel." *PMLA*, 92 (Oct. 1977), 873–87.

Wood, Michael. "Joyce's Influenza." *New York Review of Books*, 24:16 (13 Oct. 1977), 10–13.

Worringer, Wilhelm. *Abstraction and Empathy: A Contribution to the Psychology of Style*. New York: International University Press, 1953.

Index